Sean Rossiter

THE UNIVERSAL AIRPLANES

OTTER & TWIN OTTER

Douglas & McIntyre
VANCOUVER/TORONTO

This book is respectfully dedicated to the late R. D. Hiscocks, aerodynamicist and lifetime advocate of Short Takeoff and Landing aviation.

Douglas & McIntyre Ltd.
1615 Venables Street
Vancouver, British Columbia
V5L 2H1

Canadian Cataloguing in Publication Data

Rossiter, Sean, 1946–
    Otter and Twin Otter

    ISBN 1-55054-637-6

    1. Otter (Transport planes). I. Title.
TL686.D4R672 1998   387.7'3343   C98-910645-4

Editing by Barbara Pulling
Jacket and text design by Peter Cocking
Jacket photographs courtesy de Havilland Inc
Airplane three-views by Rhonda Ganz
Printed and bound in Canada by Friesens
Printed on acid-free paper ∞

The publisher gratefully acknowledges the support of the Canada Council for the Arts and of the British Columbia Ministry of Tourism, Small Business and Culture. The publisher also acknowledges the financial support of the Government of Canada through the Book Publishing Industry Development Program.

Contents

Acknowledgements

The thing that interests me about an airplane is how it was visualized, how it came to be shaped the way it is and how it was developed into a better tool. The people who do this work fascinate me. They are the reason I write about aircraft.

I wrote a book about the de Havilland Beaver because no book had been written about the world's best bush plane. The same is very nearly true about the Otter and Twin Otter.

There is one excellent book about the Otter: Karl Hayes's *DHC-3 Otter*. It appeared in 1982 and is long out of print. Hayes dealt with every aspect of Otter operations up to then. I have made no attempt to be as encyclopedic here.

There is also a definitive and readable history of the company that designed and built the Otter and Twin Otter: Fred Hotson's *The de Havilland Canada Story*. My copy is the November 1983 edition. The book will be republished this year—the seventieth anniversary of the company—with, Fred says, 50 per cent more pictures.

It will be obvious to readers of this book how much I relied on these two sources, and easy to deduce how grateful I am to their authors.

There are godfathers of every book project, people who step forward with help as soon as they learn it is needed.

The first of these is Dr. John Blatherwick, the Medical Officer of Health for the Vancouver region, and the author of several works of aviation history focussing on specific types of civil aircraft. Dr. Blatherwick was MO of 418 (Edmonton) Squadron, an Otter unit. He supplied me not only with such books as Hayes's, as well as published production lists, but also with slides of nearly every Otter and Twin Otter built.

Peter M. Bowers is a world-renowned aviation historian who, aside from his landmark histories of such companies as Boeing and Curtiss, has brought his unique insights to the job of supplying photographs of Otters and Twin Otters with an unerring eye for the most important ones.

Harbour Air Seaplanes, who operate both Otters and Twin Otters, were, as always, unfailingly helpful. Bob Bator, recently retired as chief engineer, was a cheerful and accurate source. Calvin Reich arranged my familiarization flight in a Kenn Borek Air Twin Otter.

At de Havilland, of course, there have been several outstanding friends of this project: Colin Fisher and Anita Paalinen of Bombardier Regional Airliner Division public relations, who are becoming old friends; Bill Perry, editor of *Plane Facts*; George Lucas of the photography department, who showed initiative and dogged effort in finding old and unnumbered archival pictures; and Tom Bozanin, Program Manager, Out-of-Production Aircraft. John Garratt shared family material on his father, Philip C. Garratt, DHC managing director during the years covered by this book, and on the company in general.

It fell to Bob Fowler to spend innumerable hours with me in person and on the telephone, and to supply me with his personal photo archive. If Bob's career as a test pilot had taken place in the United States, he would long ago have been the subject of a best-selling biography. He was this book's finishing godfather, and I am deeply grateful. Bob, Mike Davy, former VP, Engineering, and former DHC president Russ Bannock kindly read the manuscript. The errors of fact and interpretation that remain within these covers are mine.

Neither this book nor its predecessor on the Beaver could have been researched without the hospitality and personal kindnesses of Judge J. F. Casey and Suzy Cohen, Palsy Aldana and Matt Cohen, and Franda Wargo and Steven Bock, all of Toronto.

I will not name all of the DHC engineers I spoke with here. I would rather take the space to say that little bits of their lives are scattered throughout these pages, and I am grateful to them for taking the time to explain their work to me. Two of them, Dick Batch, a former director of development engineering, and Bob Klein, a former chief of airworthiness, spent time explaining their specialties that was all out of proportion to their presence in this book.

Several people have been especially thoughtful in helping with this project and the earlier one that resulted in *The Immortal Beaver*. They include, among others, Gregg MacDougall and Peter Evans of Harbour Air Seaplanes, Vancouver; Greg (Bones) Hudson of Kenn Borek Air, Calgary; Gerry Bruder and Bill Whitney of Kenmore Air Harbor, Seattle; Dave Curtis of Viking Air, Victoria; Eric Munk of Holland, a longtime Beaver-Otter enthusiast; and Jack Schofield, editor of *West Coast Aviator* magazine. David Hiscocks told me much about his father, Dick.

The testimony of the engineers is the heart of this book and the source of whatever originality it offers. Their accomplishments are echoed every day when Pratt & Whitney engines are started and DHC airplanes, some of them 50 years old, go to work doing what they were designed to do, in every corner of the world.

PREFACE

The Ultimate Big Bush Planes

B y the time de Havilland Canada's DHC-6 Twin Otter was in widespread service during the late 1960s, the company had created its niche in the world aerospace market: it had designed and built airplanes that could lift payloads of up to nine tons from almost any relatively smooth surface three football fields long.[1]

With a record since the Second World War of having designed and produced six consecutive designs that sustained industrial programs, DHC made itself one of the most successful aircraft manufacturers in the world. DHC aircraft were unique in that each model, from the DHC-2 Beaver to the DHC-5 Buffalo (one of which recorded the weightlifting marvel noted above), comfortably surpassed its predecessor in payload while taking off from the same 1,000-foot dirt strip. (The DHC-6 Twin Otter, which followed the Buffalo in the DHC product sequence, has a maximum takeoff weight one-quarter that of the Buffalo and a correspondingly smaller payload.)

This emphasis on Short Takeoff and Landing (STOL) performance, while less celebrated in aviation lore than, for example, any company's string of successful

1

fighter aircraft, was at least equally valid as an aero engineering landmark. The ability to fly slowly with heavy loads, which underlies great STOL performance, is far more useful in everyday human endeavour. It contributes to safety aloft. All of DHC's aircraft are still in demand more than 50 years after the first DHC-2 Beaver emerged from the Experimental Shop at Downsview in 1947. They still do things people need to have done.

DHC's chief technical engineer from the DHC-2 Beaver to the Twin Otter of 1965 was R. D. (Dick) Hiscocks. Dick Hiscocks made the configurational and aerodynamic decisions that resulted in the flying qualities of most of DHC's postwar aircraft types. While he and his colleagues won almost every major aviation award available in Canada during that period, they remain virtually unknown outside the industry.

But by the time the Twin Otter became the kingpin of the nascent commuter airline industry during the late 1960s, some DHC engineers wondered what the point was of all the effort to perfect the science of STOL.[2] While the rigours of steep landing descents and abbreviated rollouts required a built-in ruggedness that makes DHC airplanes safer in marginal conditions, stronger airplanes are also heavier airplanes. That structural weight must be deducted from payload. The aerodynamic refinements demanded to achieve STOL performance can also reduce cruising speeds and increase fuel consumption.

The fact that Twin Otters were designed with the operational realities of Vietnam in mind, but were used by their original owners on long paved runways in Europe and North America, went a long way toward changing the direction of the company. Today de Havilland Aircraft of Canada Ltd. has become the Regional Aircraft Division of Bombardier Aerospace, building 70- to 100-seat commuter airliners. But there are many who would say that 1951 to 1966 or so—the Otter to Twin Otter era—were DHC's glory years.

This book is about those two types of airplanes. They made their first flights 15 years apart. The de Havilland Canada DHC-3 Otter took to the air in late 1951. The DHC-6 Twin Otter, although conceived as a straightforward twin-engine Otter replacement, took until 1965 to fly. During that period, de Havilland Canada went from being a builder of specialty bush planes to the verge of its present status as a manufacturing cornerstone of the world's fourth-largest aerospace company and the leading global supplier of regional airliners.

It is a great story. I have chosen to tell it in three parts, with the middle part first.

Part I, that middle part, is the fascinating account of how a now-forgotten experimental airplane, based on the Otter, developed from a standard production-line airplane into an exotic jet-powered STOL hot rod over the seven years from 1959 to 1966. Its sole purpose was to maximize the ability of fixed-wing aircraft to behave

Facing page: Royal Canadian Air Force Otter 3661, the seventh DHC-3 built and the first of 66 Otters to serve with the RCAF, balances on the edge of controlled flight in the gentle hands of George Neal in this dramatic air-to-air photo. Number 661 was passed on to the Indian Air Force in 1963. DHC 5877

like helicopters while exploiting the more familiar handling and flying qualities of airplanes. Otter 3682 (its Royal Canadian Air Force serial number) could stop in midair and execute a landing approach so steep that an important part of the program was to document the pilot's reactions to the scary descent.

There was a higher purpose to the Otter 3682 ultimate-STOL program than racking up high-angle glideslopes and impressive G numbers. DHC had envisaged an intercity network of airplanes ferrying passengers from downtown parking lots to inner-harbour docks, with DHC supplying the airplanes. The company pulled off a series of spectacular stunts with its ordinary production aircraft in war and peace to show how such a futuristic vision could work. But Otter 3682 was—we cannot know yet—either a dead end or the airplane of a future that has yet to arrive.

By the early 1960s, DHC had figured out how to get increasingly large payloads off the ground from a 1,000-foot stretch of dirt airstrip. This was a capability with obvious applications in both Asian wars the United States became involved in up to that time, and DHC sold close to 1,500 airplanes to the U.S. military (and many more to air arms worldwide) to supply and evacuate front-line troops and their equipment, often under fire. But the exploits of its military aircraft were byproducts of DHC's more peaceful quest for a civil aviation utopia that would bypass multiple

Philippine Air Lines Otters PI-C51 (68) and C-52 (70) photographed in May 1957 somewhere in the Philippine Islands. Number 68 was written off in 1964, but C-52, registered back in Canada as C-FCZP, survived a crash in the Northwest Territories and may still be active. DHC 5777

mile and a half–long runways and sprawling, ever-expanding exurban airport complexes. This is a worthy, if still unrealized, goal. The technology exists. Aircraft noise is now the main obstacle to fulfilling the inner-city STOLport dream (and DHC is working on that).

It so happens that Otter 3682, in its pursuit of the shortest takeoffs and landings possible without rotors, sums up DHC's quest for ultimate STOL performance during the 25 years that followed the Second World War. That experimental aircraft, an Otter that evolved to become a lot like a Twin Otter over the latter part of the 15 years between the two types' first flights, is also the book's narrative link.

Part II of this book is about the design, testing and service of the DHC-3 Otter, an airplane that is still unique today. It was designed to emulate the Beaver's STOL performance with twice the payload, an ambitious goal that cut into the margins of power the Beaver embodies. It cost lives to perfect. Next, DHC designed and built a military transport that would lift three times the Otter's payload from that same dirt strip. Although that airplane, the DHC-4 Caribou, is not one of the main subjects of this book, I have outlined the program to design and certify it, which stretched the company to its engineering and financial limits. The Caribou led to a five-ton-payload successor, the DHC-5 Buffalo that, sadly, was produced in numbers that totalled only 126.

So it was an older and perhaps wiser DHC that returned to the civil aircraft market with the airplane with which it had attempted, on three separate occasions, to replace the Otter. This is the DHC-6 Twin Otter, to which Part III is devoted. There is much that the engineers who designed and built the Twin Otter criticize about it. Like engineers everywhere, they would have preferred to start with a clean sheet of paper in designing the aircraft rather than be required to incorporate basic elements of its predecessor.

But what they achieved is the ultimate bush plane and the perfect airborne amphibian: a big but handy aircraft that is at home in some of the most remote corners of the world. Like the big jet airliners, it can land automatically, or be guided by crowfooted human eyes onto shadowy jungle lagoons. The Twin Otter has been given the ultimate compliment: a Chinese copy was certified for use in the First World 30 years after the original first took flight.

DHC didn't build enough Otters or Twin Otters. They are the last of their line. Re-engined Otters and Twin Otters being maintained to last indefinitely are the big bush planes of the past, the present and the foreseeable future. The challenge today is to keep 'em flying. It comes as little surprise that Mike Davy, one of the engineers who first designed them and felt he knew ways to make them even better then, is now deeply involved in making these airplanes last—theoretically—forever.

CHAPTER ONE

The X-Otter: 3682

B ob Fowler remembers best of all the look on the chief engineer's face as Fowler dropped the nose of Otter 3682 and turned the last minute or so of their flight into a midway ride. N. E. Rowe, in the right-hand seat, felt himself falling forward in his unlocked shoulder harness and braced himself against the top of the instrument panel to avoid hitting it. The airplane had almost stopped in the air and then, quite abruptly, started a very slow dive toward the runway.

Fowler had not intended for his boss, known to the respectful troops in Engineering at de Havilland Canada as "Nero," to experience quite such a thrill. Rowe wore glasses, and in that terrifying moment, Fowler remembers Rowe's eyes almost filling the frames of his spectacles.

The combined effects of several forces acting at once had dropped the nose a heartbeat faster than Fowler, DHC's experimental test pilot, would have liked. Holding the Otter on its downward trajectory were the jet engine, mounted just behind

7

them at the airplane's centre of gravity, directing its blast forward through thrust modulator valves; the Otter's big flaps dropping into the landing position; and the big radial engine out front turning its cut-down (but still very large) DC-3 propeller. These counteracting forces made the airplane feel as if it were at war with itself.

Fowler remembers the moment well, even though almost 40 years have elapsed since it took place. "The nose fell so much, and you had to increase drag with the jet so much, that the body just kept moving forward," he says, simplifying the physics of Rowe's predicament. He had neglected to warn Rowe to lock up his shoulder harness, and the DHC vice-president of engineering hung from his straps as the inertia reel played out.

Fowler, with his right hand on the twist-grip throttle-modulator that controlled the jet blast, his left hand on the control wheel, his eyes darting from the glide path indicator on the ground to his passenger, turned to the older man and calmly directed him, over the noise of two very loud engines, to pull his shoulder straps tight, and then throw his shoulders back to engage the inertia reel lock, which would hold him in his seat. It was Fowler's coolness in giving Rowe step-by-step instructions while manipulating the Otter's specialized controls that really impressed the chief engineer. As scary as the rest of the descent was, Rowe felt so much better locked to his seat.

Experimental Otter 3682 test pilot Bob Fowler, between flights on the apron at de Havilland Canada. DHC VIA BOB FOWLER

Landing in the experimental Short Takeoff and Landing (STOL) Otter 3682 was a terrifying experience for the uninitiated. Taking off was fairly bracing, too. But seldom during even the most abrupt of ascents did the question of mortality leap to mind. With the airplane's nose dropping earthward and the jet throttle open, passengers underwent a rediscovery of the positive power of prayer. It was here that Fowler felt the most dramatic improvements in STOL techniques could be realized. The steeper the landing approach, he speculated, the shorter the ground run after touchdown would be. During the early 1960s, he flew the heavily modified experimental Otter 3682 in a five-year program intended to explore the outer limits of safe steep-gradient STOL performance.

On those rare occasions when anyone wanted to fly with him in 3682, Fowler usually advised his passenger to tighten his shoulder belts. But every pilot tells you to tighten your seatbelts. The full significance of his advice did not strike passengers immediately.

So there is still a droll but sympathetic note in Fowler's voice as he describes the reactions of his right-seat companions to the sight of the earth coming up so fast. There was no way to warn anyone, because you had to have done it yourself to believe it. The first few times Fowler did it, he'd had to overcome the same reactions himself.

RCAF Otter 3674, forerunner of the ultimate-STOL X-plane, about to undergo ground effect testing in 1957. Note tufting to show airflow, fully deployed batwing flaps, and engine running to blow flight surfaces. DHC 6952

"What you saw out of the front end was very spectacular. For the most part, your view of the runway didn't change too much," Fowler recalls. Of course, the airplane was descending onto the runway, not flying over it.

"Between 200 and 100 feet you realized that the ground was coming up at you very steeply, at a high rate of speed. Everything on the ground expands. I'd had the advantage of working up to this."

Few experienced test pilots had undergone an 18-degree descent since the prewar days of flying the wings off prototypes in terminal-velocity dives. It seemed to Fowler that veteran pilots often found landing in 682, as the experimental Otter became known to its crew, more unsettling than utter novices. An airliner makes its final approach at a two-and-a-half-, perhaps three-degree slope. A newcomer to the STOL program, such as an engineer eager to see for himself what it was like, didn't necessarily have those comparisons to scare the living daylights out of him.

It felt like freefall. It wasn't; a number of aerodynamic and propulsive forces were at work, some counteracting each other, to make 682's landing performance possible. The negative jet thrust—thrust directed forward—prevented the speed from increasing at such a steep, nose-down pitch attitude. Certainly the angle of descent Fowler could achieve in the experimental 682 would have resulted in a crash in any other airplane. Six-eight-two was built to withstand the occasional crash-landing impact. That was one of its charms.

Nevertheless, Fowler did manage to break the specially designed landing gear once. He broke open two rows of rivets on the float-type undercarriage that was designed to distribute landing impacts between two stout, lever-shock equipped mainwheels instead of the two mainwheels and a tailwheel on standard land-based Otters. The undercarriage was redesigned to take twice the impact.

Moreover, unlike any other DHC-3 Otter anywhere, 682 had a jet engine blasting away in reverse all the way down. The deafening roar of the General Electric J-85 at max revs just behind the cockpit only added to the unsettling effect of having your stomach up somewhere near your throat. But that jet engine was 682's secret. Depending on how Fowler directed the jet's thrust, it could create enough drag—while enhancing the Otter's lift—to actually slow it down as the plane seemed to fall almost vertically toward the runway.

What did passengers do when they found themselves on the ground in one piece, jet whine still ringing in their ears?

"Often," Fowler remembers, "they just laughed right out loud."

Bob Fowler thought the best way to comprehend the steep descent was to see it from outside the airplane: "Eighteen degrees. It has to be seen from the ground to be appreciated." (Fowler has seen it from that angle only in multiple-exposure photographs and movies, in which the airplane has the glideslope of a slow-motion rock.) His early-morning flights in 3682 had become a spectator sport at the DHC facility at Downsview, Ontario, and among those spectators was N. E. Rowe.

Rowe had come to Downsview from England in 1961 to serve as interim chief engineer. Former chief engineer Doug Hunter, who joined DHC from its parent company in Hatfield, England, during the war, had died that year, just when the reorganization of the British aerospace industry made DHC a subsidiary of the giant Hawker Siddeley combine. It was Rowe's task to decide which of DHC's top Canadians, chief design engineer F. H. (Fred) Buller, chief technical engineer R. D. (Dick) Hiscocks, or possibly former Rhodes Scholar Bob McIntyre, should be promoted to head of the department. Rowe quickly concluded that to promote one of the three might would lose the company the others, and accordingly made himself vice-president of engineering.

As such, the Otter 3682 program fell under his aegis, although Hiscocks was DHC's supervisory presence in the program. And Rowe could not watch the ultimate propeller-driven STOL research aircraft drop out of the sky without wondering what it would be like to be inside.

"What do you think it would be like to sit in the other seat?" Fowler remembers Rowe asking. "Do you think a chap like me could come for a ride in that aeroplane? Do you think I'd enjoy it?"

Maybe a little more thrilling than you'd like it to be, Fowler remembers thinking to himself. Sure, is what he said to Nero.[1]

Fixed-wing aircraft were being replaced in many roles by other types of aircraft, Fowler noted in an article he wrote in 1965, late in the Otter 3682 STOL research program. Nevertheless, one strong advantage fixed-wing aircraft still offered was that, as he once wrote, "the basic landing techniques are those first learned by virtually all pilots and have changed little since the advent of powered flight."[2]

Fowler wasn't kidding. One practise he used while developing techniques to shorten both the approach to landing and the aircraft's rollout down the runway was to totally disregard 682's airspeed indicator on final approach. This was utter heresy, and Fowler still takes pride in having defied a long-established aviation convention by returning to a more seat-of-the-pants technique.

For most pilots, airspeed is the critical factor on final approach: if an airplane's airspeed drops below a critical number, the machine will stall, and, if not recovered quickly, depart from controlled flight. The usual technique for recovery from stalls is to drop the airplane's nose and gain airspeed until the wing unstalls. Close to the ground, there may not be enough altitude available to recover.

Instead of focussing on his airspeed indicator, Fowler developed a technique of maintaining the desired lift by relating angle-of-attack (the airplane's nose-up attitude) to jet thrust. Aside from having a jet engine available to create drag—they had oodles of drag—that happens to be the way the Wright brothers landed the first useful powered aircraft. The 1909 Wright Flyer had no airspeed indicator.

With that eyeball technique in mind, Fowler had rigged up a device with a pole and "a few bucks' worth of plywood" that worked like the light-and-mirror centre-the-ball system on an aircraft carrier as an approach angle reference. When the wooden horizontal bar on the ground was lined up with the circular one on a pole between 682 and the bar, Fowler knew he was on the right approach angle. He also had a tuft of wool attached to the wing strut, so he could tell the angle at which the wing was meeting the oncoming air. Looking at the ground was much less helpful, just as looking at a postage stamp–sized carrier somewhere in the vast blue Pacific does not necessarily inspire confidence.

While fixed-wing landing techniques may not have changed "since the advent of powered flight," as Fowler put it, the changes he was demonstrating in Otter 3682 during the early 1960s were in some ways fundamentally contrary to the physics of flight. It is normal neither to steepen angles of approach nor to slow down

N. E. Rowe is briefed by test pilot Bob Fowler before his memorable demonstration flight in the X-Otter 3682, July 1962. DHC 14884
VIA BOB FOWLER

while doing so. Most airplanes gain airspeed as their noses are lowered. In 3682 this could be prevented and the airplane held at the desired lift coefficient—to use the proper engineering term—by the negative jet thrust, while the X-Otter's elevator controlled its approach path angle.

Needless to say, the Otter 3682 STOL research program Fowler was describing in 1965 had attracted wide attention as it unfolded over the previous four years. The program was being underwritten by Canada's Defence Research Board (DRB), based in Ottawa, on the initiative of John L. Orr, who had argued that the unexpected export bonanza of DHC Beavers and Otters to the U.S. military should be underpinned with research and development that could advance the frontiers of STOL.

Johnny Orr was a member of the second class in aeronautical engineering (Engineering Physics, 1939) to graduate in Canada, under Prof. Tom Louden at the University of Toronto. He followed Dick Hiscocks, a member of the inaugural class, through college. Both went to England to begin their engineering careers, Hiscocks with DHC's parent de Havilland company at Hatfield and Orr with Vickers-Supermarine in Southampton, where he was involved in developing later versions of the Spitfire. Both returned to Canada during the war and worked on high-priority defence research projects at the National Research Council (NRC) and the Defence Research Board.

One of Orr's wartime projects at the NRC was finding ways to combat the formation of ice on the wings and propellers of aircraft. He and his intrepid test pilot would fly out over the Atlantic in a Lockheed Hudson patrol bomber in subzero temperatures, purposely icing its wings and propellers, courting disaster while trying out various de-icing techniques. With the end of the war, Orr became a technical advisor to the federal government on flight research projects.[3]

Orr funded and monitored the Otter 3682 DRB-DHC STOL research project. His on-site technical advisor was Alf Gilchrist, also of the DRB, who reviewed reports on the project and assessed proposals for its future direction.

Dick Hiscocks was in his element working with his old friend Orr and the newly recruited Ph.D.s who had joined DHC to work on the STOL research project. Before he rejoined DHC during December 1946—he had spent a summer there as an aero engineering undergraduate—Hiscocks had wondered whether he might not be more of a hindrance than a help with his advanced theoretical background. DHC was a company that, like its English parent and many other aircraft manufacturers, was built upon the primacy of the skilled craftsmen on its shop floor, men who could turn a back-of-an-envelope sketch into an airworthy part.

From DHC's point of view, Hiscocks held overall responsibility for the STOL Otter project, although the program was conceived and directly administered by

Gordon Johnston, DHC's first Ph.D., at his desk around the time of the Otter 3682 steep-approach flights. VIA GORDON JOHNSTON

DHC's Advanced Projects Department under Dr. Gordon Johnston, who in 1955 was the first Ph.D. in aeronautical engineering the company had ever hired. The Royal Canadian Air Force was interested enough in seeing how close a specially prepared Otter could come to being the ultimate STOL research aircraft that they made Otter 3682 available to the cause.

The U.S. Army, which had learned in Vietnam the value of aircraft that can operate close to the shooting from unprepared fields, were especially interested and indirectly helped fund the project with U.S. dollars spent on L-20/U-6 Beavers and U-1 Otters and then redirected into Orr's research and development projects.

At roughly the same time, the Army was directly funding other research projects involving the Otter, including a "Quiet Otter" that could sneak up on enemy troops or drop agents behind their lines, and an Otter with large circular radar installations under the wings for electronic surveillance. Yet another Otter, RCAF 3694, was used for comparison test work in developing the Bell Model 47 helicopter as a simulator for STOL aircraft, which suggested that the versatile Otter was capable of impersonating almost any type of aircraft.[4]

RCAF Otter 3682 in uniform, as a standard Search and Rescue aircraft, twenty-first of the 66 CSR-123 Otters operated by the RCAF, seen at Sea Island, Vancouver, British Columbia, during the 1950s. VIA PETER M. BOWERS

Royal Canadian Air Force aircraft number 3682 was the fortieth de Havilland Canada DHC-3 Otter built. It was delivered on May 27, 1954, becoming the twenty-first of a total of 66 of its type to be operated by the RCAF, which designated its Otters CSR-123s. CSR stood for Canadian Search [and] Rescue, the most frequent role the RCAF envisaged for its Otters.

Otter 3682 could have spent no more than a day or so nominally posted to the Station Flight at Rockcliffe, east of Ottawa, before it was flown the 2,500-odd miles to Vancouver, joining 121 Communications and Rescue Flight at Sea Island in the mouth of the Fraser River where it empties into the Strait of Georgia. Sea Island is the site of Vancouver International Airport, strategically located only a short hop from some of the wildest and most inaccessible mountain and ocean-shore terrain near any major city.

Nearly four years later, 682 returned to the de Havilland of Canada factory at Downsview, where it had been built, arriving on loan to DHC in March 1958. Over the next six years or so 682 would be transformed, step by step, from a standard assembly-line example of one of the most versatile utility aircraft ever designed— the Otter has such remarkable takeoff and landing performance that it was often used in roles normally assigned to helicopters—into one of the more exotic experimental aircraft ever flown in Canada.[5]

Many of the key dates in the STOL Otter 3682 program can only be ascertained through archival photos. This is the Batwing Otter wind-tunnel model, summer 1959. DHC 11111

The 1950s represented a flowering of experimental flight in the United States, the United Kingdom and the Soviet Union. New records for speed, altitude, payload and range were being set weekly, it often seemed, as the major powers demonstrated new breakthroughs in airframe and powerplant technology. And, while those measures are the usual benchmarks of aviation progress, they are not necessarily the most important qualities of aircraft in everyday use.

The most celebrated single aviation milestone of the postwar era was Chuck Yeager's first-ever achievement of supersonic speed in level flight, when he took the Bell X-1 to Mach 1.015, or 1,078 km/hr (670 mph) at 12,800 m (42,000 feet) on October 14, 1947. The speed of sound decreases as the temperature drops, and temperature drops with altitude. Mach 1 at sea level is about 750 mph; at 40,000 feet it is about 660. Yeager's X-1 was a single-purpose, bullet-shaped multi-engine rocket that, while an impressive pioneering accomplishment in that it demonstrated the myth of the much-feared "Sound Barrier," had very little direct application even to practical high-speed flight.

It is in many ways more difficult to make an airplane fly slowly than it is to make it fly fast. Yet the slower the speed at which an aircraft can maintain controlled flight, other things being equal, the safer it should be. It is also more difficult to make an aircraft that can fly slowly and still have the built-in strength to withstand the hard landings that are a fact of aviation life, especially in remote locations. The slower an aircraft can fly, the less likely it is to crash; the more crash-worthy it can be made, the safer it will be when worst comes to worst.

These are issues that the outstanding Canadian flight-test programs of the 1950s addressed. Safety is primal wherever aircraft fly, but it comes closer to the top of the agenda in certain parts of the world. In a far-flung land where by definition most habitations are remote, the coastline is the longest in the world, and the climate varies from the moody wetness of the North Pacific coast to the frozen arctic barrens, safety in aviation is necessarily an obsession.

Otter 3682 became the focus of a program that evolved into the most thorough examination ever of how far the safety advantages of STOL could be pushed with a useful load-carrying airplane. In fact, it was the appearance of the Otter in late 1951 that had suggested the opportunity might be at hand "to explore the subject further, realizing that slow flight stability and control was one of the truly new developments in the design of aircraft since the end of World War 2," as Fred Hotson puts it in *The de Havilland Canada Story*.

The experimental Otter 3682 as flown by George Neal in summer 1959, with bat flaps and temporary drooped outer-wing leading edges, discarded soon afterward. DHC 11153

Conversations had been taking place as early as 1956, Hotson tells us, between DHC and the Defence Research Board on how to further explore the aerodynamic aspects of STOL. Hotson quotes from a report of the time: "The purpose of the DRB-DHC program is to assess the aerodynamic performance, stability and control problems of STOL aircraft with the object of finding new refinements in the art."[6]

Shortly after 682 returned to Downsview in the spring of 1958, it was fitted with a set of flaps so outsized that, with their 45-degree droop, the airplane immediately became known as the Batwing Otter.

Flaps are hinged flight surfaces, usually located at the inner trailing edge of an airplane's wing. The Otter was already endowed with sophisticated double-slotted flaps—flaps that, when deployed by the pilot, increase both lift and drag for shorter, safer landings. So the Otter was already a sprightly short-field performer. The new and even bigger flaps had been designed in accord with the findings of wind-runnel and model studies aimed at determining the effect of slipstream on lift and drag with extreme flap areas and angles for optimum approach and landing performance. Consequently, they were fixed at 15 degrees and could be lowered to a large maximum angle of 45 degrees—although the aircraft could not be landed with them fully extended. (Takeoff was impossible in that mode.)

Gordon Johnston, DHC's new Ph.D., wanted to study both the response of these new flaps in "ground effect," near the ground, and the effects of the diverted slipstream they caused.

In order to study the flap's behaviour in the regime known as ground effect,

682 was mounted on a 20-odd-foot-high steel-tube space frame and rigged at an in-flight attitude, with calibrated balance pickups at each of the three landing gear axle sockets.[7]

This contraption, mounted on wheels, was towed at up to 40 mph up and down runways at Downsview behind a one-ton truck, to quantify the lift and drag induced by the huge flaps. The truck itself disturbed the air behind it, so it was offset to the left (looking from behind) to minimize the effects of the downstream turbulence it generated—although, with various sensors and cameras mounted on platforms rising from the truck's flatbed and front bumper, the rig was anything but aerodynamically clean.

Six-eight-two's engine was run to duplicate the benefits of propwash on the wing roots and flaps. Propwash, like a headwind, adds to the lift and drag produced by flight surfaces and to the "blown" effect of air passing over the flap and wing surfaces. To eliminate downward pressure from redirected air from the flaps on 682's horizontal tail and its influence on the readings at each landing gear pickup point, the tailplane was removed.

Tufts of wool were placed at one-foot intervals in rows along the span of 682's wings to show airflow patterns, and on windy days smokepots were lit and set on the truck-borne platforms to give an even more graphic picture of the Otter's passage through the especially hydroelastic medium of the air at the ground-effect level.

Johnston remembers these tests with some bemusement. With its batflaps, the Otter generated nearly enough lift to leave the runways at 35 to 40 mph, heavy steel test-rig and all. "It didn't fly," he says, "but it came close. It was a sonofagun to steer."

More important, the test data were used, among other purposes, to design a new tail for 682. The new vertical tail was much taller than the standard Otter tail, which had itself been extended during flight-testing in 1952. The new fin and rudder, designed by Ian Gilchrist (no relation to Alf Gilchrist) of DHC's experimental engineering department under the direction of Hiscocks, was more vertical and more effective. This new tail was shaped like a plank to extend up into the undisturbed air above 682, even at nose-up pitch, and to be more effective at slower speeds. Once the Batwing Otter graduated from being a high-tech trailer to actually flying, it would also need a new horizontal tail, or tailplane. Gilchrist's redesigned tailplane, also planklike, angled upward from each side of the fin in a shallow V when seen from head-on, to act upon as much undisturbed air as possible above the downwash caused by the huge flaps.

Another important modification to 682 was the landing gear Gilchrist designed to absorb twice the impact of the already rugged standard Otter undercarriage. Gilchrist came up with a bridgelike structure from which to hang two mainwheels and two nosewheels in place of the standard Otter's three wheels. The twin booms, similar to floats, were in effect aluminum box girders. The booms were internally reinforced with sheet steel, cross-braced to each other with tubes (as floats are), and attached to the normal float mountings on the Otter fuselage by three struts for each boom, arranged in an N-pattern. The multiple, triangulated load paths offered by this modified truss structure allowed it to absorb differential impacts from almost any direction below the aircraft.

The mainwheels were suspended toward the rear ends of these booms from massive forged trailing links that allowed a foot of compression on initial impact of a nose-up flared touchdown. At the fronts of these booms, smaller steerable wheels on oleo-pneumatic struts would sometimes absorb any secondary impact of lowering the nose for the rollout and the nose-down loads of hard braking.

Batwing flap being static-tested, summer 1959. DHC 11034

Phase One Otter 3682 with bat flaps operated by external actuators low on the fuselage, drooped leading edge, and new tail and landing gear, summer 1959. DHC 11153

This was not a particularly sophisticated landing gear arrangement, but it was tremendously strong and reasonably aerodynamic. It was patently designed to withstand controlled crashes—"On the two main wheels, we hoped!" Fowler adds.

(To Gilchrist's credit, when this undercarriage did break, it ruptured only on the side of one boom, due to twisting forces produced by a hard landing on one mainwheel. Gilchrist then reinforced it to again take twice the impact.)

George Neal, DHC's chief test pilot and the man who had taken the Otter prototype into the air, would in all likelihood have made the first flight in the Batwing Otter even if he hadn't been endowed with the ideal temperament for the task.

There was nothing quite like Otter 3682 flying anywhere, and Neal was anything but a daredevil. He took airplanes as they came, attuning himself to their habits and vices, taking their little surprises in stride. He had started at DHC before the war as an engine mechanic, become a flying instructor with the British Commonwealth Air Training Plan during the war, and flown the almost incomprehensible variety of aircraft, from jet Vampire fighters to wartime Lancaster bombers, that passed through Downsview during the early 1950s. Once he and Fowler set out to see how many of the different types available on the Downsview flight line they could fly in one day. Fowler flew nine different types and he thinks Neal flew 10.

Neal started with 682 and its new landing gear by doing taxi runs, and then flew it in short hops along the runway, likely in 1959, and then carefully took it higher, gathering data as he went. He even flew it to Ottawa for a demonstration of what were, for that stage in 682's development, fairly steep landing approaches. The airplane could drop at 1,200 feet per minute, a breathtaking rate of descent. The RCAF and DRB types were impressed.

From Neal's point of view, the biggest danger for a pilot at the controls of the batwing incarnation of 682 was setting the throttle for cruise and forgetting the flaps' limiting speed—the speed at which they could be damaged or ripped off in the slipstream.

What was that speed?

Neal forgets.

One hundred miles per hour? A hundred and twenty? Neal does distinctly remember that 682 would float if you flared going too fast. You had to make yourself fly it slowly—all the time.

George Neal: In 3682, you had to make yourself fly slowly—all the time. VIA BOB FOWLER

Fowler was backup pilot on the Batwing 682, and he discovered that you could obtain outstanding descents in either of two ways. It would float down with low power, "or, if you wanted to descend faster, you could increase to full power." Once you overcame the drag peak at a certain point, Fowler notes, "the airplane would descend with gusto.

"In between, there were flap combinations and power settings that had lift coefficients that were near 3. (That's a lot of lift.) Doing that gave us enormous data bases. As an experimental airplane, it was an amazing thing."

Perhaps that depended on your point of view. As far as Johnston was concerned, the 682 test program had fully milked the advantages of its oversized flaps by then. In retrospect, he doesn't think the program was a success at that point. The airplane was difficult to handle—even for a test pilot like Neal, who was not inclined to complain about any airplane's shortcomings.

"The airplane did not fly extensively," Johnston sums up. "Maybe 10 hours, maybe 20."

The tests terminated in 1960.

Facing page: Phase Two 3682 on final approach with J-85 modulated valves supplying reverse thrust through forward slot, enabling the X-Otter to descend nearly vertically.

DHC 14660/RON NUNNEY VIA BOB FOWLER

CHAPTER TWO

The Otter Jet

To make any further progress, Otter 3682 needed a more effective device than huge flaps to create drag. It was flying as slowly as George Neal could fly and still keep it in the air. A parachute, maybe? Airbrakes? Spoilers might do it; usually located on upper wing surfaces, spoilers open against the slipstream and thus dump lift from the airplane's main lift-generating surfaces.

But Johnston wanted something more powerful, something that would allow use of the smaller, fully retractable flaps 682 would need to cruise. That meant some means of entraining air over or against those flaps, giving them additional effectiveness—something more than the propwash from 682's engine . . . something that would, at the same time, increase drag . . . something variable, something controllable in flight. . . .

Nobody seems to know for sure who came up with the inspiration of installing a jet engine in the Otter's fuselage. There was a series of brain-storming sessions attended by Johnston, Johnston's assistant Doug Henshaw (DHC's second Ph.D.),

Dick Hiscocks, Johnny Orr, and Orr's technical assistant and the immediate Defence Research Board overseer of the project, Alf Gilchrist.

As Johnston remembers those meetings, which convened over a period of months in 1961, Alf Gilchrist may have lit the candle by noting recent European developments in Vertical/Short Takeoff and Landing combat prototypes, powered by separate lift and propulsion jets. The lift jets were small, light powerplants that offered impressive thrust-to-weight ratios (in other words, they were both light and powerful). Rolls-Royce's RB.108 lift jet developed 10 times its weight in thrust—very impressive performance in those days. Some of these lift jets could run for only about an hour between overhauls. Otherwise they were very efficient. Gilchrist was thinking of using lift jets in the normal way, installed vertically in an airplane's fuselage to enable it to take off (and perhaps land) more vertically.[1]

But the group was looking neither for vastly increased lift nor more propulsive thrust, then the accepted uses for jets—which is why the jet idea was such a leap of the imagination. They were looking for drag.

As Johnston recalls the breakthrough idea: "Doug Henshaw and I thought, why not use reverse jet thrust for drag, which would meet the drag requirement. We could use positive lift for takeoff"—thus addressing both sides of the STOL equation, takeoff and landing, at once.

Once the shock wore off, certain facts became clear. The engine would have to be installed at close to 682's centre of gravity to avoid problems with pitch—the tendency for an aircraft to be nose- or tail-heavy. And you couldn't just have the exhaust blast away out the back. The thrust would have to be modulated and able to be directed ahead, for reverse thrust, creating drag, or aft, roughly parallel to the approach angle. It was axiomatic that the engine would have to be very small and light. It was exciting. Put a jet in the Otter? Why not?

There was such a jet engine available—and it would soon be coming to Canada. The General Electric J-85 made possible a reversal of the trend toward heavier, more complex combat aircraft, and eventually the J-85 found its place in executive jets (and as the core of heavy-lift helicopter powerplants, among other applications).

Northrop Corporation of Palmdale, California, had been working on simple, lightweight jet fighter designs since the early 1950s, sending some of its management and engineering people to Third World countries in 1954 to absorb the gritty reality of requirements there for an economical fighter. Northrop, newly revived by an influx of engineers from Convair (Canadair of Montreal's parent, later part of General Dynamics), wanted two engines to power such a fighter in the interests of reliability, making it all the more important the engines be small. At that time, no such engine was thought to exist in the U.S.

Until, that is, a mockup of the J-85 walked in the door of chief engineer William Ballhaus's office at Northrop in mid-1954. GE's Edward Woll, who had started the Small Aircraft Engine Department at the company's Lynn, Massachusetts, plant the previous October, carried a well-built wooden box into the room, checked to see that the door was closed behind him, and showed Ballhaus the highly classified mockup of a jet engine that measured 36 inches in length and 17 inches in diameter.

It was so small Ballhaus thought he was looking at a scale model. The U.S. Air Force had ordered the engine for the Quail decoy missile but had no further use for it. GE had calculated that this little gem could generate 2,500 pounds of thrust and weigh less than 500 pounds. Woll was offering it for a jet-powered drone a Northrop subsidiary was working on.

"Put an afterburner on it," Ballhaus told Woll, "and we will put it in an airplane."[2]

When the brains behind the DHC-DRB STOL research project seized upon the idea of popping a jet into Otter 3682, the J-85 was about to go into licence production at nearby Orenda Aircraft to power the new Canadair CL-41 Tutor jet trainer. Orenda was located at Malton—now Lester B. Pearson International Airport, Toronto—a few miles west of Downsview.[3]

GE made a J-85 available to DHC as a demonstrator, and the DHC Advanced Projects Department moved into the jet age. By the early 1960s the group numbered 10 or so people, including some of the company's most highly regarded technicians.

As audacious as the idea was, the detail engineering was fairly straightforward. The jet had to be as near as possible to the Otter's centre of gravity, and it needed some kind of mechanism to direct its exhaust where the pilot wanted it to go.[4]

One practical ongoing problem for Fowler as pilot was managing separate fuel systems for two entirely different engines. The R-1340 radial used high-octane aviation fuel, carried in underfloor, easy-to-fill tanks. As any Beaver or Otter pilot knows, a constant back-of-the-mind preoccupation is maintaining the airplane's balance by keeping the remaining fuel roughly equal in the forward and aft tanks while never allowing the current tank to go dry. The jet used JP-4, which is a mixture of low-cut gasoline and kerosene, or ordinary coal oil, "and [like all early turbojets], it went through fuel like there was no tomorrow," Fowler says. Ground observers with stopwatches warned Fowler when he was running low on JP-4.

Six-eight-two was now much more than your average Otter. To begin with, it weighed 6,700 pounds empty, compared with a standard single Otter's 4,450. Fowler's first flight in 682 with the J-85 lit was December 18, 1961.[5]

Fowler is a frustrated engineer. His talent as a pilot was recognized from the beginning, and his wartime training was enriched by exposure to a wide range of aircraft types, from Tiger Moth trainers to Lockheed Ventura daylight bombers. He also absorbed special blind-flying and navigation courses—all before he did his 44-trip tour out of Hartfordbridge in RAF Second Tactical Air Force B-25 Mitchells, "a peerless aircraft," he says almost wistfully. With their Mk.XIV gyro stabilized computing bombsights, the B-25s could, he says, reliably bust targets from 10,000 feet.

Long before he joined DHC after the war, Fowler was involved in modifying and flying P-38 Lightning fighters for aerial survey work, and he was curious to learn how engineering decisions played themselves out in the air. Above and beyond filling in the blanks on report sheets, he talked endlessly to the engineers about how each modification worked, often suggesting changes himself. The engineers listened. Today, at 75 years old, Fowler still remembers the names of the STOL Otter project's hangar technicians.[6]

Aside from the plywood angle-of-approach aid Fowler had set up beside the runway at Downsview (George Neal's inspiration), the test pilot was instrumental in developing two other innovations that were critical to 682's success as a mixed-power jet-and-prop experimental airplane.

With the jet came the problem of controlling both the power output and the nozzles through which it exhausted. When the J-85 was first installed, a throttle to govern its power was installed overhead, on the cockpit ceiling. A modulator control to direct the jet's thrust was placed near the inboard side of the pilot's seat. With the trio of radial engine and propeller controls set in the middle of the instrument panel, as they are on all Otters, these additional new jet controls had Fowler reaching up and down, like an orchestral conductor of levers and buttons, just as he came to the critical flare task, where he began to level 682 out about 25 feet from the ground.

Fowler's idea was to integrate these two controls into one handy device, installed where his right hand, when free, would naturally fall. The heart of this new multi-functional control was a horizontal twist-grip throttle, similar in operation to that on a motorcycle. At the inside end of this grip, where his thumb fell, was a friction adjustment that regulated the force necessary to operate the twist-grip. Later, an electric pushbutton was incorporated in the end of the twist-grip throttle handle, which, when pushed by Fowler's thumb just prior to completion of the flare, electrically brought the propeller thrust to idle.

There was one more modification. It was the answer to another issue raised by the jet: how you get the whole thing stopped on the ground. Reverse thrust was available for that purpose—with the J-85, more than a ton of it—but it puts an additional strain on everything connected with it: the mechanism through which it exhausts, the engine mounts, and so on. It would help to have an aerodynamic device that, once 682 was on the ground, could reduce post-touchdown residual lift without undue strain. Johnston and his team decided to employ spoilers that would pop up and block airflow over the upper wing surfaces during the ground roll. By

The J-85 ground-test installation, photographed in June 1961, shows how the jet engine and its intake and exhaust modulator valves were laid out in Otter 3682. The intake was a hole in the cabin roof. DHC 13685

decreasing the lift the wing continued to generate on the ground, the spoilers would also make 682's brakes more effective.

Approaching the flare with the nozzles producing significant reverse thrust, Fowler would pull the control wheel back toward himself in one steady motion with his left hand—"not a jerk," he emphasizes—at a rate that raised the nose just enough for 682 to touch down on the mainwheels, with the nosewheels just clear of the ground. Halfway through the flare, he pulled the nozzle control handle fully aft, to full reverse, and at the same time palmed the J-85 twist-grip throttle forward to full rpm, maximizing the braking effect of the jet engine. Then, when it had been incorporated, he pressed the button on the end of the modulator handle with his thumb, electrically retarding propeller thrust to idle. At touchdown, with the spoilers automatically extended, full brake was applied until the aircraft came to a halt.

"The reason we could do this and not skid the tires was, we used standard Beaver wheels and brakes, which were relatively less effective than the larger Otter ones. Just before the airplane stopped," Fowler says, "the pilot moved the modulator control forward to the zero thrust position, and twisted the J-85 throttle aft, to idle power—in order to prevent the aircraft from backing up."

These additional features worked so well that Fowler needed very little practice to adapt to what was, after all, a radical change in the habits of Otter 3682. The way Fowler described it in 1965, the technique of bringing 682 in with reverse thrust was quite straightforward and so instinctive that his learning curve jumped sharply after half a dozen landings.

The program's target had been to clear a 50-foot obstacle and have 682 stopped within 500 feet. Fowler and 682 had exceeded those criteria with the modulated thrust system. Fowler has a time-lapse photo showing 683 stopped in 362 feet after clearing the 50-foot barrier.

With the nozzle aimed down the approach path, the system could enhance lift because the jet wash augmented the normal downwash off the wing trailing edge and flaps. At minimal weight, as the fuel load decreased, Fowler could almost stop in the air; sustained approach speeds as slow as 58 mph were recorded.

Fowler had flown 200 hours in the jet 682 when Pratt & Whitney Canada announced a new small turboprop engine, the PT6. DHC had been very interested in the engine. The working relationship between P&WC and DHC was so close that a low-cost rental of two PT6s was made available to DHC. Pratt & Whitney Canada obtained the loan of a Beechcraft Model 18 Expeditor (HB109) from the RCAF and made it into a trimotor by designing a system for mounting the PT6 into its nose. Like 682, the trimotor Beech continued to fly in its natural metal and bright red, white and blue RCAF markings: 1,068 hours over 719 flights from May 30, 1961, to June 3, 1980.

Fowler was test pilot, with P&WC PT6 project engineer John Hunt in the right-hand seat for the first and subsequent early flights—three or four of them, as Fowler remembers it—by the time it was apparent that Otter 3682 would become history unless it acquired a further boost. (P&WC's John MacNeil flew on the last flight in the Beech.)

Six-eight-two's last flight with its original P&WC-1340 piston engine was October 10, 1962. The third and climactic stage of the aircraft's remarkable career was about to get off the ground.

CHAPTER THREE

Otter 3682 Points the Way

from the beginning of the STOL research program, Gordon Johnston had considered Otter 3682's nose-mounted engine an aerodynamic liability. The geared R-1340 had been chosen to power the Otter for its power output, size and reliability; and in time, its availability, as Pratt & Whitney Canada tooled up to manufacture it once again. Its rated power was barely adequate, as Dick Hiscocks had recognized, but by gearing its output in order to turn a large propeller more slowly to improve thrust and economy, DHC had given the Otter better takeoff performance than the Beaver.

Unfortunately, the slipstream from the single nose-mounted propeller had been obliged to travel over the forward fuselage before it could sweep the wing roots and, possibly, the innermost surfaces of the flaps, which did not immerse much of the inner wingspan in slipstream. This was no major consideration for Fred Buller and Dick Hiscocks when they designed the Otter in 1948.

But 682 was in a different game now. With the jet nozzles, takeoffs were not an issue. The key to further gains in landing performance, now that the effective drag could be controlled directly, was to somehow further augment slipstream lift so that the landing approach could be performed with higher lift, making a yet lower indicated airspeed possible. One way to do that was to blow more air over the wings, generating more lift independent of airspeed.

Unfortunately, using twin Pratt & Whitney Canada PT6s to accomplish this would increase both lift and drag. The propeller discs, while providing thrust, also cause some drag. The engines would do so at a point where the jet was creating all the drag anybody aiming for steep descents could possibly want. But the engineers hoped that the twin turbines would energize any stagnant air behind them, from the roots of the wing to well out on the spans, producing additional lift that would delay the onset of the stall and allow Fowler to fly 682 even more slowly.

Unlike the J-85 turbojet idea, which was an improvisation to address as directly as possible the drag end of the lift/drag equation, putting twin engines on the wing to blow its flaps had been part of the plan all along. DHC's engineering staff had been working on studies for small twin-engine designs since the early 1950s and were fully aware of their STOL advantages. The problem was the weight of the available piston engines. They were simply too heavy to make a small twin feasible. When a market for a larger twin-engined military transport emerged in 1957, those studies were dusted off and quickly emerged as the DHC-4 Caribou. The Caribou prototype had flown in mid-1958 and was used over a period of time to sell the U.S. Army the sort of tactical transport its commitments required. It was then re-engined with newly developed General Electric YT-64 (Y for service test, T for turbine) turboprops as a flying testbed to explore the problems and advantages of such powerplants for larger aircraft. Thus modified, RCAF Caribou 5303 (the prototype) flew with YT-64 power on September 22, 1961, in Fowler's hands.

Although the period from 1958 to 1961 happens to coincide with the development of Otter 3682 into an increasingly capable experimental STOL aircraft that could be improved only by the adoption of twin engines, there was no connection between 682 and the DHC twins that preceded it (the Caribou and the Buffalo), or the one that succeeded it (the Twin Otter).

Six-eight-two looked a lot like the Twin Otter—aside from the J-85, of course—and while the Twin Otter was infinitely more refined in its detail engineering and aerodynamics, it is difficult to avoid concluding that a project designed to create the ultimate STOL twin resulted, through four years of experimental design and flying, in an airplane with similarities to the one the Twin Otter turned out to be. From a technical point of view, the Otter 682 program took an airplane that had been designed at the outset of the 1950s and gradually developed it into a state-of-the-art flight research vehicle.

Fred Hotson notes, as have others, that "The [Otter 3682] program terminated in 1963, about the time talks started on the design of a twin-engined Otter. The

twin-engine configuration was the most noticeable feature to emerge from the experimental program, even though it was a minor part."

Design engineers who worked at Downsview during those years, such as flight test aerodynamicist Dick Batch, insist there is very little connection between 682 and the Twin Otter, and they make a good case.[1]

DHC management foresaw the Twin Otter project as a straightforward extrapolation of the single-engine Otter, just as they thought the Turbo Beaver would involve a simple engine swap. The detail engineering in both cases turned out to be more involved, and to create more differences between the original and modified airplanes, as the design processes went on. The appearance of the P&WC PT6A turboprop made both the Turbo Beaver and the Twin Otter possible, and it also made them very different from their predecessors.

The conversion of 682 to wing-mounted twin engines for propulsive power had long been planned, and the versatile Ian Gilchrist's powerplant installation design was well along.[2] But somehow—perhaps because of a desire to extract the most from the J-85 installation—the conversion didn't happen until the winter of

The STOL Otter 3682 in its Phase III configuration with the J-85 jet and twin PT6 turboprops replacing its nose-mounted R-1340 radial piston engine, as it appeared in September 1964. The black paint with white X marking was for photographic purposes. DHC 19156

Officially, this was the DRB (for Defence Research Board)-DHC STOL RESEARCH AIRCRAFT Twin (Twin for its twin PT6 turboprops) in May 1963. Note the jet intake between the wing trailing edges and extensive instrumentation sensors at the right wingtip. DHC 15817

1962–63. P&WC, aware of events at DHC, offered to rent DHC a pair of PT6s for the same amount Downsview had budgeted for piston engines—$1,000 a month for both. Their lighter weight did make 682 a sprightlier performer on the straight and level even as it complicated the job of installing them.

For Gilchrist, the design of the new powerplant installations was made more difficult by the outstanding virtue of the new engines: their light weight. A thousand pounds of weight had to be compensated for in the nose of 682, as the PT6s weighed only 230 pounds apiece (in producing 400shp each). Moving the battery forward and adding instrumentation in the nose only partly made up for the loss of the big cast-iron radial. Under the circumstances, it was deemed wise to beef up the wing, especially at the inner and outer wing-strut pickup points.

Again, there was a bonus. Just as the jet, installed mainly to steepen the landing approach, had incidentally offered a takeoff boost, so did the PT6s offer beneficial side effects. To begin with, they simplified the pilot's fuel management task by making the system all JP-4 jet fuel. Also, their reversible props would further curtail a ground roll already made spectacular by reverse thrust from the J-85. Thus did this heavily modified one-time single Otter become the ultimate STOL propeller-driven research airplane.

"It was hot as hell to fly," Fowler remembers, referring to more than airspeed. The J-85 radiated heat from behind, and through the two hot Ontario summers Fowler flew 682 with three engines nearly surrounding him. It made his mind occasionally wander to the question of how he would get out in an emergency. The engineers had thoughtfully installed blow-off doors for a quick exit, but those spinning prop tips passing inches from the doors made that route distinctly hazardous.

By now, early March 1963, it seemed logical to rename the airplane, give it a new identity. At least Fowler thought so. When he logged flights in 682, he began calling it the DHC-85-6A (85 for the jet and 6A for the early-series turboprop engines added to the wings). Lettered on the sides of the newly streamlined nose was the somewhat formal legend D.R.B.-D.H.C. STOL RESEARCH AIRCRAFT. Straightforward and unglamourous, the title was perhaps a cultural artifact of the British and Canadian engineers who had rebuilt almost every component, some of them more than once. We can only imagine what such an aircraft would have been called in the United States.

Edging into the air with what was, by now, a thoroughly transformed Otter gone from one 1930s-technology radial piston engine to three future-era powerplants, Fowler did the first runway skips with the J-85/PT6-powered 682 March 1 and 5, and then took it up for the airframe's fourth first flight two days later, March 7, 1963.[3]

It was a revelation. Most of the benefits from the PT6s, as with the jet, were realized almost immediately. Surprisingly, the reversible props made very little difference to what was already a highly abbreviated ground roll. Fowler loved flying it.

By late 1964 Gordon Johnston was wondering where the ultimate STOL program might lead from this third stage. One way of consolidating the progress Otter 682 had made would be to train new pilots. Bob Fowler had certain reservations about that:

"We were going to look at the idea of checking some non-DHC pilot out [on 682]. I didn't really thrill to the idea, quite frankly. Test pilots stay alive by not biting off one bit more than they know they can safely chew. But they don't like somebody who's done it telling them, 'Oh yeah, but I don't want you to do *that* to begin with.'"

Fowler had an agreement with Johnston that he would accept some of the features of what was, after all, an experimental aircraft, such as two engines fed from a single fuel tank, a far-too-fast elevator trim motor (sized for the batwing 682), and a non-redundant spoiler arming system—"And," Fowler notes, "no real bailout possibility"—if he didn't have to train anyone else to fly 682 at its full capability. Except, he notes, possibly a DHC pilot such as George Neal.

"In some ways," Fowler says, the latest 682 "was trickier to fly with two engines. It was more sensitive. We had to be more careful on the approach."

He understood that by making 3682 a better-known, sexier program, Johnston might get additional funding to take it...where? Maybe a new STOL program? "I didn't blame him," Fowler says today. But he was going to resist as long as he could. Meanwhile, Johnston had a major overhaul of Otter 3682 scheduled.

"And while that was all in flux, this airplane with two engines on was sitting right outside the door where my office came out into the hangar. I was thinking about all this and chewing on it. I liked working with Gord. I didn't want to frustrate him. I went out and I looked at it.

"There was this maintenance stand. They'd been up on it looking at the horn balance on each elevator. The horn balance was made of wood."

An aerodynamic horn balance is a counterweight that helps compensate for the immobilizing effect of air pressure on a hinged control surface in flight, making the surface easier for the pilot to operate. A horn balance is part of any moveable flight control device, such as a rudder or, in this case, an elevator. It is usually located ahead of the hinge line and appears as a forward extension of that flight surface, often wrapping around the tip of the surface to which it is attached.

The tailplane, or horizontal stabilizer, on 682 was specially designed to sweep upward from its mount inside and about halfway up the fin. It was not horizontal at all. Gord Johnston's idea was to mount the tailplane—and the elevators along its trailing edges—into air undisturbed by the big batwing flaps from the previous 682 program, thus avoiding their turbulent downwash when taking off or flaring nose-up at the end of an approach to landing. In those situations, controlling an aircraft's pitch is critical to its safety. Horn balances make it easier to move the elevators and also stabilize the elevators in the presence of gusts or turbulence.

Six-eight-two, unlike every other wheeled Otter, sat with its fuselage horizontal rather than squatting back on its tailwheel, putting the tailplane some distance above Fowler's reach. And, of course, its specially designed tailplane was set higher on the fin anyway and rose from there to its tips.

"It was a V-tail, nothing like an Otter's tail at all," as Fowler describes it.

To inspect this unique piece of engineering, you had to wheel a maintenance

The late Reg Corlett, DHC photographer. Along with Ron Nunney, Reg took most of the photographs that document the career of Otter 3682. Their dated pictures, along with Bob Fowler's logbook, enable us to reconstruct a fascinating chapter in Canadian aviation history. DHC VIA BOB FOWLER

stand over to 682's tail, climb up the stairs, and approach the aircraft from the platform some dozen feet up, higher than a basketball hoop.

On the day in question, Fowler found himself parked beside the maintenance stand. "So I'm standing there picturing the loads. And then I look at the nozzles, they make an awful noise, just shakes the whole airplane, shakes like hell, and noise you wouldn't believe, but they had never peeled back the skin"—on the fin at the elevator mounts—"to look inside. We were going to do that someday, but we never had. And I just thought about that and I got up on the stand that the guys had just left there.

"I grabbed hold of the end of the elevator—of the horn, actually, and I just went up and down"—he demonstrates an arm movement much like lifting barbells over one's head in a standing military press—"and I'd done that on the wings and on the thing before.

"And, geez, when I went like that it just made terrible noises from inside the fin.

"I moved the outer end of the elevator and tailplane up and down. And I wiggled it. Awful noises came from the fin structure to which it was attached.

"A few people in the hangar, a couple of inspectors and a few other people, stood around and watched me. And one of them said, 'What the *hell* is that noise?'

"I said, '*I* think the structure inside there would bear a look . . .'

"And somebody said, 'Yes, we were going to *do* that.'

"We talked about it. Nobody from Engineering was there. But hangar people are very knowledgeable, structurally and all that. Somebody else might remember this differently, but I remember this part *so* well.

"I said, 'I'm going to phone Gord Johnston just to tell him,' and someone said, 'Why don't you do that?' There was an inspector there, see? He was a genius—not a genius, but he was just so good at his job. Bill Wright. Just the smartest guy, and he said, 'With that noise, I would be very hard-pressed to sign that thing out.'

"So I phoned Gord, and he didn't throw a fit. He was very cool. He could take all this stuff in stride. He said, 'Mind if I come over?'

"So Gord came over and he said, 'Oh my God.'

"And this guy Wright came over and said, 'I think we should look in*side* there.'

"Gord said, '*Oh* yes.'

"So they peeled back the skin and opened up the fin. Well, geez, there were cracks galore. Internal fretting, with black edges. All cracks fret. All airplanes crack. That's nothing new. But not like this. This, if you overloaded it or lost an engine on takeoff and put on full rudder, the fin could fail.

"So they looked farther and peeled back more skin, and got in some AID people from the air force"—Aircraft Inspection Detachment, RCAF engineers who oversaw production at contractors' plants—"who owned the airplane, of course. And they said, 'Ooh-oooh.'

"Gord said, 'How much do you think it would cost to repair that?'

"I heard the air force people, one of them said, 'A helluva lot more money than *we* have. Do *you* have some money to repair that?'

"Because you'd have to tear it all out and rebuild the whole fin, and we had no budget for that. Of course. There was a lot of talking, a lot of eyes came and stood on the ground and looked at it, and moved the thing up and down. I thought it probably got weaker through all this. Everybody had to have a push and pull on this thing."

Bob Fowler's inadvertent discovery of the cracking inside the fin of Otter 3682 came as a surprise, but not because wear and tear on the flight surfaces of experimental airplanes—especially airplanes that turn sharp corners and stop on a dime in the sky and are pounded into the ground—is in any way unexpected. The inspection stand was beside 3682's tail for the simple reason that the hangar crew were about to inspect the aircraft for exactly the signs of wear that Fowler happened to find first.

What did come as a surprise was the location of the problem. If anything was going to go wrong on 3682, Fowler and the crew would have expected the modulated jet exhaust outlets to be at fault. The ring cap on the nozzle burned or cracked and sometimes had to be replaced after only a few hours in the air. The job entailed welding on a replacement item. The top and bottom lips within which the modulator moved were subject to high temperatures and very heavy loads and cracked frequently.

But in the end the ring was not the source of the strain. Fowler's opinion is that it may have been sonic fatigue from the jet blast that was responsible.[4]

"And one of the inspectors looked at me and he said, 'Well, Bob, have you enjoyed flying this airplane?'

"I said, 'Yes.' I loved it. 'It was always stimulating.'

"'Good,' he said. 'Because you've flown it for the last time.'"

By rights, Otter 3682 should be restored and enjoying a hero's retirement in a museum somewhere. But, like most experimental aircraft, it was pushed off to the Downsview airfield perimeter, and the engines, instruments, radios and other useful parts removed and disassembled.

Bob Fowler recorded his last flight in Otter 3682—and the airplane's swan song—as July 15, 1965.

Ending the succinct summary of its 13-year life in Karl E. Hayes's *DHC-3 Otter*, 682's epitaph is brief and, in its own spare way, poetic:

"Reduced to spares and scrap March 1967."

CHAPTER FOUR

de Havilland Canada at 20

The origins of de Havilland Canada lie in an airplane that set the company's English parent organization on the road to its unique place in aviation history. De Havilland, the most prolific of aircraft manufacturers and one of the handful of combined aero engine and airframe builders left in the world after the Second World War, dates back to 1914, when Geoffrey de Havilland began designing (and flight-testing) the combat aircraft he produced for DH's forerunner, the Aircraft Manufacturing Co. Ltd., or Airco.

During the interwar period, DH became the most successful builder of light sporting aircraft anywhere. The first of this line was the DH.60 Moth. The Moth first flew February 22, 1925, in the hands of Capt. de Havilland himself, and quickly proved itself to be "a sensational little aerial steed."[1]

It was a two-seat light biplane tough enough to withstand being used as a trainer but comfortable enough for cross-country touring. Best of all, it was powered by one of the first dependable small aero engines, an engine specially designed for it by

Major Frank Halford of Airdisco (the Crown-owned Aircraft Disposal Company, or ADC). Airdisco had 3,000 war-surplus engines in stock during the early 1920s.

"Why don't you take half an Airdisco," de Havilland asked Halford, with whom he had worked since 1916, "mount it on a new crankcase and give me an engine of about 60hp?"[2]

The job took Halford two months in late 1924. He used the pistons and cylinders from one side of the Airdisco air-cooled V/8 engine (itself developed by Halford from a World War One Renault) to develop a new in-line four-cylinder engine with such advanced features as a five main-bearing crankshaft and an aluminum crankcase.[3]

The new ADC Cirrus engine flew for the first time in the Moth prototype. A new engine in a new airframe is a combination fraught with peril, but the spruce-and-plywood Moth (named in honour of Capt. de Havilland's passion for lepidoptera) and its light air-cooled Cirrus, with its four cylinders protruding above the cowl into the slipstream, were the forerunners of a generation of sporty lightweights—Cirrus Moths, Gipsy Moths, Giant Moths, Puss Moths, Fox Moths—and, of course, the Tiger Moths that trained the Battle of Britain's Few. The Moth inspired a national air training program in England and soon equipped five flying clubs. About 100 days after its first flight, the first Moth, G-EBKT, flew Alan Cobham 1,000 miles from London's Croyden airport to Zurich and back in a day.[4]

By 1927 the Moth had won two of the classic King's Cup races in England, and one had been flown the then-unbelievable distance from London to Capetown, South Africa: 8,000 miles. Bert Hinkler flew one from London to Darwin, Australia, setting the following records: longest solo flight to that time, fastest from England to India, first London-Rome nonstop, and longest flight ever in a light aircraft.

On July 25, 1928, Capt. de Havilland used a DH.60G Gipsy Moth, a similar airframe powered by Halford's masterpiece, the 100hp Gipsy, to set a new altitude record for light aircraft of 19,980 feet—with his wife as his passenger.[5]

Six Moths were supplied to the Royal Air Force's Central Flying School. The U.S. Navy bought one for its attache in London. Moths were sold to South Africa, Rhodesia, Ireland, New Zealand, Singapore, Chile, Argentina, Ireland, Germany, Sweden, and Spain; licence-built in Australia and Finland; and assembled in Canada.

The Royal Canadian Air Force bought 23. Ten were ordered by the federal govenment for flying clubs, 1 was supplied to each of Dominion Airways and Western Canada Airways, and the three-year-old Ontario Provincial Air Service (OPAS) bought 4 in 1927 and eventually operated a peak number of 14. The Moths were a quantum performance improvement over the OPAS' lumbering war-surplus Curtiss HS-2L flying boats, or H-boats.[6]

It occurred to the endlessly inventive Francis St. Barbe, de Havilland's director of sales, that Canada might be a good place to locate a subsidiary company. St. Barbe was in Canada in December 1927 to negotiate the federal purchase and found the experience exhilarating.

"In Canada you will find a set of geographical, climatic, economic and social conditions providing aviation with an ideal breeding ground," he wrote in the company publication, the de Havilland *Gazette*. " . . . Splendid openings for the speed of air transportation are everywhere and one of the most encouraging factors in the situation is the Canadian character. Coupled with a measure of good old British caution, you find a people with a big outlook, with imagination and courage. When a Canadian steps, he will step quickly with all the broad-minded enthusiasm of his enterprising nature."[7]

In perhaps one of the first aircraft manufacturing offsets (in which the company exporting the aircraft arranges for significant fabrication or assembly work to be done in the importing country, offsetting the cost of the machines), St. Barbe met

DH.60G Gipsy Moth G-AADV in flight. This was the first amphibious Moth, delivered to John Scott Taggart in February 1929. Short Bros. of Belfast supplied floats for early Moths, including those operated by OPAS. The retractable wheeled gear pivoted on a steel rod running lengthwise through the single centreline float. DHC 12672

with Canadian federal government officials, who were dangling an order for at least a couple dozen Moths—the flying club and RCAF orders—and agreed to establish a Canadian branch of the company as soon as possible. St. Barbe's personal assistant, Bob Loader, was in Toronto the following February with a pair of Cirrus-powered Moths to be donated to the clubs. A narrow two-storey corrugated metal shed, a former vegetable cannery in the Toronto suburb of Mount Dennis, became the first premises of de Havilland Aircraft of Canada Ltd. The site had a railroad siding that carried the traffic of both major Canadian railways, and the flow of crated Moths soon outgrew the business. Across the tracks from the shed was the airfield where Count Jacques de Lesseps flew a Blériot XI during a nine-day airshow that included the first-ever heavier-than-air flight over Toronto, July 13, 1910. A 50 by 50 foot wooden hangar was erected on the airfield, and the facility handled 62 Moths in its first year of operation. A second wooden hangar was constructed in modular fashion at Mount Dennis, dismantled and taken to the 70-acre parcel at Downsview as part of DHC's North Complex plant, occupied in September 1929.[8]

The first Moth ordered and delivered in Canada was G-CAHK, a Cirrus II–powered Moth on floats named "Spirit of the Valley of the Moon," which left Halifax, Nova Scotia, July 27, 1927, on the icebreaker *Stanley* with the Hudson Strait Expedition to study ice patterns near the proposed grain port of Churchill, on the western shore of Hudson Bay. By late August, in 14 hours' flying time, the expedition had selected three base sites, a task that would otherwise have taken weeks. Lowered over the side of the icebreaker on the orders of its captain, who seems to have taken no satisfaction in commanding an icebreaking aircraft carrier, the Moth was wrecked in a gale. So ended the brief but productive career of the first operational DH Moth in Canada.[9]

The ultimate development of the DH.60 Moth, the DH.60T Tiger Moth trainer, which evolved into the DH.82 Tiger Moth trainers in which tens of thousands of Allied airmen won their wings. DHC 12674

The first four OPAS Moths arrived crated at the service's base at Sault Ste. Marie in July 1927. Aside from their impressive performance for the time, the Moths "also embodied another fantastic improvement which must have seemed particularly impressive to the former H-boat pilots who came to fly them," writes Bruce West in his history of OPAS, *The Firebirds*:

"They had a crude but effective intercom system, by which the pilot and passenger could converse. Between the front and rear cockpits extended a length of tubing similar to a garden hose. Into this, the pilot and passenger could yell at each other, listening to the replies on still another set of smaller hoses which were attached to earpieces in their helmets."[10]

Better yet, the Moths came with floats and skis, making them the first OPAS aircraft operable year-round. OPAS was impressed. It was the beginning of a long and mutually rewarding partnership between Ontario's air force and de Havilland.

The Mount Dennis facility was on land owned by mining magnate Frank Trethewey, who as part of his arrangement with the company took delivery of DH.60X Moth G-CANA, in which he took flying lessons from his friend Philip C. Garratt, a wartime Royal Flying Corps fighter pilot.

Garratt, the son of a doctor, was a medical student at the University of Toronto when he became one of the original graduates of the Curtiss Flying School, Toronto, in 1915. He soloed in a Curtiss Jenny that year, enlisted and won his wings April 26, 1916, after three hours and five minutes of instruction in a Maurice Farman Longhorn pusher biplane (becoming holder of Royal Aero Club of the United Kingdom certificate number 2868).[11]

Garratt's widowed mother, living in London, watched him take off from Folkstone in July 1916 to join 70 Squadron at Arras, France. He crashed in a BE.2 being flown from England to the front by another pilot that October. An undated story in the *Toronto Star* headlined "Toronto Airman Not Yet Tired of Thrills" detailed his career up to his period in hospital, where he awoke after his mishap with a concussion. He was posted to the noted Gosport Flying School for the war's duration.

Garratt became a barnstormer after the war (with the Barker-Bishop Flying Company, which failed despite both of the principals being Victoria Cross winners, credited with a combined 122 victories). He was a flight instructor at Camp Borden in 1921–22. But his personal success came between 1923 and 1936 in the chemical business. A New York friend wrote him in August 1922 to congratulate him on quitting flying, "for it gets them all sooner or later that stick to it and while it is darn fascinating there is no future in it."

If Garratt did make such a resolution, the one-time thrill-seeker didn't keep it. He became a volunteer test pilot in his spare time at Mount Dennis soon after the facility was opened, gave Frank Trethewey his flying lessons and made himself valuable to the infant DHC as a business consultant and advisor to Loader and his successor, Lee Murray, a manager from Hatfield who ran DHC from 1933 to 1936.

On September 29, 1929, Garratt and a copilot named Hastings-Trew set out from Toronto Harbour on an 11-hour, 2-stop flight to deliver a Gipsy-powered Moth on floats to the Halifax Aero Club. The *Toronto Star* believed the flight to be the first ever from Toronto to Halifax.[12]

Awarded the peacetime rank of Flight-Lieutenant, the former Capt. Garratt also flew with 110 Auxiliary Squadron, Toronto. Garratt was a fun guy, and one of his pet larks was to fly over the annual outing of the Board of Trade Club—of which he was president during the early 1930s—bombing the picnickers with rubber balls for the kids.[13]

Flying Phil replaced Murray as managing director of DHC on May 21, 1936, which happened to be the twentieth anniversary of his being awarded his RFC

DH.60 Cirrus Moth G-CAUP on skis. This aircraft was owned by Arthur Fecteau of Senterre, Quebec, an early and enthusiastic operator of DHC products. DHC 6750

wings. His management style seems almost quaint today. He hired the best people he could find and backed them when they needed help. He kept himself informed by walking the shop floor every day.

There are many defining moments in the life of an aircraft manufacturing company, and DHC has had its share. Of those, the wartime Mosquito fighter-bomber program presented difficulties the company was ill equipped to deal with but overcame with a stupendous effort.[14]

The parent company at Hatfield specialized in wooden aircraft-building techniques suited to short production runs. Its technical school turned out craftsmen and technicians who could be replied upon to take crude drawings and concepts and turn them into high-quality finished aircraft parts and assemblies.

This was a culture that took de Havilland into the first rank of airframe and engine manufacturers worldwide.

Hatfield was able to transform itself into a mass-production facility with the advent of its DH.98 Mosquito, partly by enlisting cabinetmaker subcontractors to turn out 3,299 of the twin-engine 400-mph speedsters whose appearance over Berlin convinced Hitler he needed his own Moskitos and showed Luftwaffe chief Hermann Goering that the war was lost. Other de Havilland facilities and licence-builders in England accounted for a further 3,150 Mosquitoes. Almost all of them were assembled after mid-1941. But the methods that achieved these totals did not export well to Canada—even though Canada was the source of the raw materials from which Mosquitoes were built.

Under the circumstances—incomplete sets of drawings, damaged pattern aircraft, powerplant conversion to American-built Packard-Merlin engines, mid-production model changes and the North American belief in metalwork over cabinetry in aircraft manufacture—DHC performed one of those production miracles that are almost commonplace in war by turning out 1,133 (or 1,134) Mosquitoes. In the process, DHC transformed itself from one of the smallest, most backward manufacturers in an airplane-building backwater to Canada's biggest, with an engineering staff capable of carrying aircraft projects from concept to production.

The effort cost Phil Garratt his leadership of the company for the war's duration. But it gave him time to think about original designs DHC might undertake once hostilities ceased. He decided the time was right for a new all-metal bush plane. But he knew there was an immediate market for hundreds of modern basic trainers to replace the Tiger Moths that had won the Commonwealth's wings. As the trainer emerged from postwar Downsview's Experimental Shop, he decided to name the new line of DHC designs after the small Canadian mammals that frolicked around his cottage at Lake of Bays, in the Muskoka cottage district north of Toronto. The trainer, which flew May 22, 1946, became known as the DHC-1 Chipmunk. The bush plane, the DHC-2 Beaver, flew August 16, 1947.

A magazine article profiling Garratt appeared after he was presented with the one-thousandth DHC-2 Beaver in 1956. Two photos at the bottom of the title page show PCG, as he was universally known, beside the bulbous nose of the Farman Longhorn biplane in which he trained in 1916, and in the cockpit of a Vampire at Hatfield in 1947, when he became the first grandfather to fly a jet.

He was yet to make his greatest impact. During the 1950s he would twice win Canada's McKee Trans-Canada Trophy for outstanding contributions to aviation.[15]

The most famous personality at the postwar DHC, other than Garratt, was Clennell H. (Punch) Dickins, the legendary bush pilot who made the first flights into the Mackenzie River delta, opening up the western Canadian Arctic to aviation and becoming an early winner of the McKee Trophy. Dickins had organized the RAF's wartime Ferry Command to fly newly built bombers across the Atlantic to England, using Canadian Pacific Air Lines personnel as its core. He replied to DHC

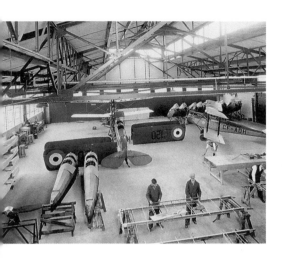

Gypsy Moth assembly in the original DHC plant at Mount Dennis. Wings with roundels are for RCAF Moths. DHC 9521

The DHC-1 Chipmunk was the first of DHC's Canadian-designed and -built airplanes, although many more were built in Britain than in Canada; that made it the first Canadian design licence-built overseas. These are RCAF examples. The Chipmunk first flew May 22, 1946, and the RAF retired its last Chipmunks only during the mid-1990s. DHC 3064

sales manager Sandy MacDonald's questionnaire to bush pilots asking what features they wanted to see in the new DHC-X bush plane that became the Beaver. Dickins made some suggestions that were duly incorporated, liked the concept so much he decided to sell it, and became DHC's director of sales. His colleagues were just as impressive, if lesser-known.

Of the key men who came to Canada during the war to get Mosquito production underway, the one who stayed longest and left the strongest imprint on the company was W. D. (Doug) Hunter, the chief engineer. Hunter's origins reached back to the ancestry of the great Bristol airframe and powerplant organization, as a draftsman at the pioneering Grahame-White Aviation Co. He had been chief technical engineer at Hatfield since 1925. Dick Hiscocks, who held the same title at DHC, thought of Hunter as the quintessential Englishman, reflectively smoking a pipe, almost always agreeing with you by saying "Quite" and exerting a calming presence amid chaos. Hunter was the diplomat who kept some of DHC's raucous egos sitting straight and facing the front of the bus.

Russ Bannock, the Canadian wartime Mosquito night-fighter ace, recruited by St. Barbe in London, became chief test pilot and DHC's phenomenally successful

The first of the 1,100-odd Canadian-built DH-98 Mosquitoes, KB 300, an FB.Mk.VII fighter-bomber that first flew September 24, 1942. The man in overalls may be Ralph Spradbrow, DHC chief test pilot at the time. DHC JH462 VIA PETER M. BOWERS

director of military sales. George Neal, prewar DHC engine mechanic and British Commonwealth Air Training Plan (BCATP) flight instructor, succeeded Bannock as chief test pilot and took the Otter up for its first flight.

Bob McIntyre, who had come from Massey-Harris, a tractor company that built Mosquito wing sets and was the most dependable subcontractor in the program, would go on to head up DHC's naval hydrofoil effort. Bill Burlison, who with his brother George had followed his father to work for Canadian Vickers in Montreal, and who stayed at DHC when George left the company, became superintendent of the Experimental Shop where DHC's prototypes were hand-built.[16]

The key personalities in the engineering department at Downsview were Fred Buller and Dick Hiscocks.

Buller, the chief design engineer and one of the most brilliant men ever to work in Canada's aerospace industry, ran the lofting, drawing and stress departments at DHC after a meteoric wartime rise through the company's ranks. Born in Vancouver, another son of a doctor, self-educated in a wide range of subjects from astronomy to hydrodynamics and shipbuilding, Buller had offered himself to the war effort after becoming chief engineer with Aircraft Repair, an Edmonton BCATP maintenance outfit operated by former OPAS pilot Leigh Brintnell, seemingly overnight. The Canadian government assigned him to a troubled DHC satellite operation, the Mosquito inspection centre at London, Ontario—a bottleneck when he arrived. So quickly did he shape it up that by 1944 he was at Downsview.

Hiscocks, too, had a fulfilling war, but one spent more at the scientific edge of engineering. A graduate of the first class in Engineering Physics (1938)—Canada's first aero engineering course—at the University of Toronto, Hiscocks spent the summer of 1937 at DHC and the following summer at de Havilland's Hatfield plant, working on Hatfield's first all-metal design, the DH.95 Flamingo airliner.

Hiscocks was touring Germany with a U of T student in the following Engineering Physics class, Johnny Orr, just before the war broke out, seeing for himself what was in store for the world. He soon joined Canada's National Research Council to work on such war-related projects as an all-plywood Harvard trainer fuselage and a glider derivative of the tailless Westland Pterodactyl aircraft. The latter project led him to interview Germany's leading exponents of such flying wing aircraft, the Horten brothers, after the war. He credited the Hortens, along with a British aerodynamicist, with influencing the wing section he chose for the DHC-2 Beaver, which he redesigned around a more powerful engine and had prototyped in eight months after he rejoined DHC at the end of 1946.

Hiscocks wondered, when he joined DHC, whether he might not be out of his element in a company where research was secondary to the reservoir of experience on the shop floor and innovation not yet part of the ethos. But de Havilland, at both Hatfield and Downsview, was changing. The company in England was a jet-age pioneer in both airframe and engine development, while in Canada the OPAS requirements for a bush plane that could operate from small northern lakes had taken the Beaver and DHC into a Short Takeoff and Landing niche that was being overlooked elsewhere.

Hiscocks was named chief technical engineer by Garratt in a bid to neatly circumscribe the responsibilities of Hiscocks and Buller. It is often said that the two men fought. But their tasks were such that a creative tension inevitably existed between the two. What Hiscocks needed to have an airplane do, Buller had to figure out a way to get built.

One ongoing source of tension between them was DHC's commitment to STOL aircraft from the Beaver to the Dash-7. All of those designs had high wings for, among other reasons, their high sink rate and lack of float on landing. Low wings are prone to strike docks on float-equipped aircraft. But high wings meant structural problems, such as fuselage-mounted narrow-track landing gear, or (on the Dash-7) longer and thus heavier undercarriage struts, which it was then up to Buller and his staff to devise. There were dozens of these issues to resolve for each of six

Dick Hiscocks, photographed at the forty-eighth anniversary celebration of the first flight of the DHC-2 Beaver, August 16, 1996, at the Harbour Air Seaplanes dock. Two dozen Beavers flew in loose formation over the Flying Beaver bistro. JIM JORGENSON

major design and manufacturing programs they worked on together, and on each of them Fred and Dick had their own viewpoints.

"Gilbert and Sullivan" is how Mike Davy, one of the many English engineers who joined DHC in time for the DHC-3 Otter program, sums up the Hiscocks-Buller partnership.

There was another issue that resurfaced with each program: what standards should DHC's airplanes be designed to? Canada had no national standards for performance or airworthiness during the 20 or so years covered by this account. Whose standards should DHC adopt?

Up to the end of the Second World War, the company was assembling designs certified as airworthy in Britain. DHC's responsibility was simply to make sure the aircraft it was assembling maintained the same specifications as the units certified in Britain.

When the design stages for the Chipmunk and Beaver began, their designers had to face certification procedures that, while new to the company, were relatively simple. Those two aircraft were designed to comply with the requirements of the British Civil Air Regulations (BCAR) code. Since more Chipmunks were built in the United Kingdom than in Canada, the BCAR certification made sense in that case. Nor was the Beaver especially handicapped by its BCAR certification, even though most of those built were delivered to the U.S. and other military air arms. Many upgrades were required by the American armed forces and adopted by others. The question arose again, of course, with the third original DHC design, the Otter.

"It seemed sensible," Dick Hiscocks has recalled, "to adopt the new standards promulgated by the International Civil Aviation Organization, ICAO.

"Unfortunately, this august body was concerned mainly with large multi-engined passenger aircraft and considered single-engined airplanes to be inherently dangerous. As a result, the minimum flight speed under the [ICAO] Category D, which applied to the Otter, was required to be no greater than 56mph. To meet this standard a rather elaborate 'high-lift' double slotted flap system was developed," Hiscocks wrote in a farewell essay on the unique difficulties DHC had overcome to build airplanes for which no airworthiness standards really existed.

On the other hand, Hiscocks said, regulations that didn't really fit had forced him and his colleagues to come up with "one of the most efficient 'utility' airplanes flying. It remains so today, nearly 50 years after the first flight, judging by the numbers that are being fitted with turbine engines to extend their lives yet another decade or two."[17]

Perhaps the most remarkable fact about DHC in its postcolonial phase is that de Havilland's Canadian branch was becoming more British than ever. While the com-

pany was run by a Canadian and its technical staff was headed by Canadians under the quintessentially English chief engineer Doug Hunter, the flood of newcomers attracted to this emerging manufacturer of original STOL high performers included young, talented British engineers with qualifications unobtainable in Canada, such as Ian Gilchrist and Mike Davy. They would go on to higher things with DHC.

Until the great reorganization of the British aircraft industry during the early 1960s, the postwar link between Hatfield and its Canadian branch would grow closer than ever—to the point where Hatfield saved DHC from the fate that had already befallen Avro's Canadian subsidiary. DHC bet the company on the Caribou and Hatfield paid off the bookmakers.

Mass-producing the Mosquito in several different models with various Packard-built Merlin engines involved original detail and production engineering, and transformed DHC from an assembler of kits into a full-fledged industrial organization. DHC 9648

CHAPTER FIVE

Birth of the King Beaver

The Beaver's wholly unexpected sales breakthrough was still not clear to de Havilland Canada three years after it first flew on August 16, 1947. Some 100 Beavers had been delivered. That was impressive enough, but the big sales to the United States military were yet to be announced.

Nevertheless, the success the Beaver was enjoying so far made the direction the company should go with its next design clear enough. DHC and some of its bush operator customers saw the Beaver as a step in the direction of a true freight or passenger hauler. Several customers were urging the company to come up with something that could duplicate the Beaver's short-field performance, but do so with a significantly bigger payload. DHC called the design study for its next bush plane the King Beaver.

One potential market for such an airplane was the Royal Canadian Air Force. The backbone of the RCAF's single-engine utility fleet was the Noorduyn Norseman, introduced in 1935, which flew at a gross weight of 7,400 pounds, compared with the early Beaver's 5,100. Although the last Norsemans were not assembled until 1959,

most of them were built before and during the war. In 1951 DHC foresaw a market for 300 Norseman replacements, counting only those in use with bush operators.[1]

As they had with the Beaver, the OPAS sketched out the basic requirement for the bigger successor by committing the service to buy 20 examples of an airplane that would offer similar performance with twice the Beaver's payload.[2] There were many reasons for the OPAS to want a larger airplane, including one possibility the service's Department of Lands and Forests aerial fire-fighters were not yet fully aware of. One OPAS pilot, Carl E. Crossley, had figured out how to use the floats of a Norseman as airborne water-bomber tanks, although his method had not yet become official OPAS doctrine. Once the details were worked out, Beavers quickly became the favoured forest-fire–fighting weapon for their ability to get into and out of small lakes to reload. Otters could carry that much more water.[3]

We do not know exactly when work began on the project that became the Otter. De Havilland Canada has never begun preliminary design studies for new types of aircraft with much fanfare. So much was new or unproven on the Beaver that flight-testing it, monitoring its use by the OPAS and its other early users, designing such modifications as its roof and belly hatches, and adapting it for military and civil roles never contemplated by its designers fully preoccupied the approximately 40 members of DHC's engineering department for at least two years after the airplane first flew. It soon became obvious, however, that the basic principles of the Beaver design, such as its high-lift wing profile with interlinked flaps and ailerons and its easy-to-fill belly-mounted fuel tanks, were sound.

To pinpoint the exact moment when someone either at DHC or in a customer organization first thought of applying those principles to a bigger airplane is probably impossible. The other shoe simply had to drop.

Often new projects at DHC got underway and gained momentum as engineers involved with other projects were released from those duties. Fred Hotson, author of the definitive company history *The de Havilland Canada Story*, tells us that the basic concept had evolved by 1950.[4] The lead designers of the Beaver, chief design engineer Fred Buller and chief technical engineer Dick Hiscocks, dated the beginning of design work on the Beaver's successor at roughly the same time.[5] As usual, though, in an era when the follow-up work of detailed design was done on paper from calculations usually done on slide rules, those tasks would have awaited the arrival of enough hands to do them.

DHC's parent, the de Havilland Aircraft Co. Ltd. of Hatfield Aerodrome, Hertfordshire, was at the time the most advanced manufacturer of airframes and aero engines in the world. In 1949, Hatfield was developing three new types of aircraft, each a world-beater in its category. The DH.114 Heron was a four-engine development of the immediate postwar Dove feeder airliner, economical to operate and able to fly out of unimproved airfields. The DH.106 Comet was, of course, the world's first jet airliner to fly.[6] The DH.113 Vampire N.F.Mk.10 was a two-seat development of the Vampire 5, the most recent version of Britain's second operational jet fighter.

Each of these projects required the labours of battalions of engineers. When the call for help came from England during the post-Beaver period, Downsview responded with some of its brightest talent, talent polished by DHC's wide variety of postwar overhaul work (Lancasters, Mitchells and Cansos, among others) and by the company's first two original designs, the Chipmunk basic trainer and the Beaver.

Charlie Bishop, Jack Greeniaus, Bill Heaslip (a future vice-president of engineering), George Luesby, Al Marten and John Mazur worked on the Vampire night-fighter at Hatfield. Judging by the N.F.10's first flight date of October 1949, the DHC loaner engineers would have made the prototype, which was modified with a two-seat Mosquito cockpit, ready for production. They toiled there under the direction of Wsiewolod J. (Jaki) Jakimiuk, the Second World War Polish émigré who had developed that country's front-line fighter at the dawn of the war, the PZL P-11C. Jakimiuk had supervised the design of the Chipmunk and an early, smaller concept for the airplane that became the Beaver. A cultured, polyglot man of the world, he left the group during their stay in England to accept an offer from Sud Aviation of France.

The others returned to Downsview in September 1950, becoming available for detail design on the King Beaver. Indeed, *Time* magazine's story announcing the new "Bush Pilot's Workhorse," which appeared about three months into flight-testing, set the beginning of engineering work on the project at November 1950.[7] Presumably, *Time*'s date refers to the onset of detailed engineering, such as the design of individual parts and the specifics of, for example, the powerplant installation.

Essentially, the King Beaver concept was a scaled-up Beaver, with the same takeoff performance and twice the payload—a one-ton truck to the Beaver's flying half-ton pickup—with cabin volume to be increased two and a half times. "This was a formidable challenge," Fred Hotson notes dryly, "considering that there was only 33.3 per cent more power to do all these wonderful things."[8]

The King Beaver project stepped squarely into a void in the range of horsepower available from the proven powerplants left over from the war. The 450hp Pratt & Whitney R-985 Wasp Jr. air-cooled radial, which powers the Beaver, was widely manufactured during the war for use on instructional aircraft, often on twin-engine navigation trainers. There was a gap between the low to midrange power class typified by the R-985 and the 1,000+hp engines that emerged under the stress of wartime. Engines in the midrange power category were pretty much leapfrogged during the conflict, and their successors, some of them capable of up to 3,500hp, were in any event being replaced by much more powerful turbojet engines by the 1950s.

Virtually the only aero engine left in this class was the Pratt & Whitney R-1340 Wasp, a 550/600hp radial piston engine that had powered first-line combat aircraft before the war and was still widely used, notably in AT-6/Harvard trainers and the Norseman, but was barely in production by 1950.

The nine-cylinder R-1340 Wasp (R for radial, denoting the layout of its cylinders, which radiate outward from its crankcase and are cooled by air passing over them; 1340 for the number of cubic inches—actually 1,344) is a classic among aero engines—the engine upon which the great Pratt & Whitney Aircraft organization was founded in 1925. It was designed by the brilliant partnership of MIT-trained George Mead and Andy Wilgoos, of whom it was said that he could "think with his fingertips," so sure was his sense of the rightness of a design.

Mead, in his earlier capacity as Wright Aeronautical's chief engineer, and Wilgoos, the same company's chief designer, had perfected the first reliable radial engine, the 200hp Wright J-4 Whirlwind, a later version of which powered Charles Lindberg's solo flight in the *Spirit of St. Louis* across the Atlantic in May 1927. Wright's board of directors, happy with the J-4 and its development potential, were unwilling to invest in more powerful engines for the future.

But Frederick Rentschler, Wright's president, knew there was a market for a 400hp radial to power the fighters required for the U.S. Navy's two new aircraft carriers, *Saratoga* and *Lexington*. The Navy was sold on radial engines, which present their finned cylinders to the airstream for cooling and thus dispense with the weight of radiators, coolant and their associated plumbing. Radials also resist battle damage better. It is possible to multiply the power ratings of radials by adding further rows of cylinders—up to four—as was done through the 1940s in developing powerplants for the last generation of piston-engine airliners.

So Rentschler, Mead and Wilgoos left Wright and had their future engine project underwritten by a small tool company in Hartford, the Pratt & Whitney division of Niles-Bement-Pond Company (founded in 1860 by two skilled machinists who had worked in the Colt pistol factory in the same city). In June of 1925 Mead and Wilgoos settled into Wilgoos's two-car garage in Montclair, New Jersey, not far from Mead's house on the same street, and the two created an aviation milestone.

They started with nothing more than the requirements for a reliable 400hp and a maximum weight of 650 pounds. Neither had ever before started an engine with a clean sheet of paper. (The Wright J-4 was developed from a concept by Charles Lawrance that Lawrance was ill equipped to improve and manufacture.) Mead and Wilgoos designed an engine that would run reliably at higher revolutions per minute, be simpler to assemble, and cool better with more and thinner fins cast into the cylinders. Mead devised a rotary induction system that replaced three carburetors with one and added an impeller, somewhat similar to that of the fans of modern jet engines, to force air into the engine. This was an early step toward supercharging radial engines for more power at higher altitudes, addressing a weakness of radials.

There were many innovations small and large in the R-1340, the prototype of which was completed late the night of December 24, 1925. In fact, it was built too well and had to be torn down during its test runs to make its piston rings a looser fit, "because," as piston aero engine historian Hershel Smith writes, "the oil consumption was too low!"

The prototype R-1340 ran easily at 380hp. Next it developed 410 with no strain. On its third run it put out 425. It swept through the 50-hour Navy test at full throttle, pumping out between 410 and 425hp. After these labours, the first R-1340 went directly to a museum. Another preproduction model flew May 5, 1926. "Within a year," the unnamed author of a twenty-fifth anniversary commemoration of Pratt & Whitney tells us, "the Wasp shattered its first world record and went on to smash existing standards for both landplanes and seaplanes for the next seven years, carrying airframes and pilots higher, farther, and faster than ever before."[9]

The U.S. Navy immediately ordered Wasps installed in its first-line fighters, the Curtiss Hawk and the Boeing F2B, both of which had been designed for water-cooled in-line engines and flew with Wasps that summer. The Navy had its new scout, the Vought O2U-1 Corsair, flying on Wasp power that fall. That October the Navy ordered 200 R-1340s, the first of many thousands. In the Curtiss and Boeing fighters, the Wasp installation saved between 250 and 300 pounds of empty weight. By 1929 Wasps (and P&W's next new engine, the larger Hornet) powered 90 per cent of American commercial transport aircraft and every one of the 200 warplanes based aboard the carriers *Lexington* and *Saratoga*.

As the Wasp was improved and equipped with supercharging and gear drives, it moved above the 500hp output level. The 450hp R-985 Wasp Jr. was born in 1930 to compete in the 300/400hp market, which the Wasp was outgrowing. By the onset of war, the Wasp Jr. was being installed, singly and in pairs, in a wide variety of training aircraft. Meanwhile, the Wasp, aviation milestone that it was, had been eclipsed by two- and even four-row radials as a powerplant for new airliners and front-line combat types. Its principal application during the Second World War was in the 18,000-odd AT-6/SNJ/Harvard advanced trainers built in the United States and Canada up to 1953. Still in service with air arms throughout the free world during the King Beaver's design process, few of those engines were available for use in DHC's new big bush plane.[10]

Nevertheless, the R-1340 was the heart of the powerplant Dick Hiscocks selected to power the King Beaver. Availability was not the problem.

As distinguished and fully proven as the R-1340 was with nearly 25 years of use behind it in 1950, and as nearly unique as it was in its midrange power class, the powerplant installation would be the most second-guessed single engineering decision of the many such decisions that went into the design that became the DHC-3 Otter. The engine seldom gave trouble in military Otters, which were seldom overloaded and often maintained to higher standards than civil ones. Ditto for the R-1340s in Harvard trainers and, by and large, in Norsemans. The same engine also contributed to the Otter's phenomenal trouble-free mileage totals when it was used as a survey aircraft. But in high-frequency, low-maintenance backwoods use, its engine became the Otter's most criticized feature.[11]

There was one alternative. This was the Wright R-1300, an engine designed in 1942 and called the Cyclone 7. The various nine-cylinder models of Cyclone had

reestablished Wright as a first-rank supplier of aero engines, powering most DC-3/C-47 transports and almost all Boeing B-17 bombers during the war. (The Cyclone G was the first nine-cylinder radial to produce 1,000hp.) Production Cyclone 7 engines pumped out 800hp, at the cost of their weight of 919 pounds.[12]

With the Wright engine, DHC calculated that the King Beaver could weigh 8,200 pounds fully loaded and carry 2,500 pounds over 500 miles, or 700 pounds all-up and 500 pounds payload over the same airplane with the P&W Wasp—significant initial improvements, but not much greater than subsequent increased weights and loads the Otter was cleared for. It is intriguing to speculate that the Wright engine might have given the Otter a slightly greater margin of power, which could have increased its reliability in arduous backwoods use.[13]

Hiscocks tells us that he chose the R-1340 for efficiency. Other voices spoke out in favour of the R-1340 for other reasons. They included the highly influential Punch Dickins, who as DHC director of civil aircraft sales thought that a powerplant installation compatible with the direct-drive R-1340 of the Norseman would be a good sales point with operators. Given DHC managing director Phil Garratt's close working friendship with P&WC's Jim Young, whom Garratt knew wanted to get into engine manufacture, the question of engine and parts availability seemed capable of solution.

In Hiscocks and Fred Buller's *Engineering Journal* article on the Otter, the King Beaver project's lead designers call the Wasp "a conservatively rated engine of proven reliability." It is inherent in an efficient powerplant choice that the engine and its associated mechanisms are intended to work hard. Hiscocks understood the engine's limitations, and he made further conceptual layout decisions that were intended to fully maximize the engine's propulsive thrust.

"As an engine proportionately more powerful than that of the Beaver was not available, it was necessary to carry aerodynamic and structural refinements somewhat further in order to assure a comparable performance," Hiscocks and Buller wrote. "This was not considered to be a serious drawback, because if the difficulties could be overcome, it would result in a more efficient aeroplane."[14]

First, Hiscocks chose the geared R-1340 H version, which would swing a bigger three-bladed propeller more slowly than its crankshaft turned. The bigger prop would give better takeoff performance. For the King Beaver propeller Hiscocks turned to perhaps the most widely available model, the Hamilton-Standard DC-3/C-47 prop, minus three inches from each of the three blade tips.

Secondly, Hiscocks specified an exhaust ejector system that would use the engine's heated exhaust to provide extra cooling and some direct thrust from its pipes. Since the bigger plane would not climb as quickly as a Beaver, it was foreseen

Facing page: The Otter instrument panel. Centre: the throttle, propeller and mixture controls; above these are the engine instruments. Left, behind the control column, the flight instrument panel. Below that, left, the starter panel; and beside it, the fire extinguisher switch panel. Right, radios; below, electrical switch panel. Knurled knob below headset: fuel and oil emergency shut-off control. Base of centre windshield column: flap indicator. DHC 3570

that a possible lack of cooling air might subject the engine to overheating when it was working hardest. So heated exhaust air, in effect, sucks cooler air flowing around the engine's cylinders into four mixing tubes that sheath the exhaust pipes paired on the lower sides of the fuselage behind the firewall—heating and thus expanding the air and creating a measure of thrust, sort of a jet effect.

Choosing the R-1340, which had been in production for many of the years between its introduction and the end of the war, was one thing. It was another thing entirely to find them in sufficient quantity—especially the rare geared ones. Compared with other engines, such as the direct-drive Wasp itself and the Wasp Jr., relatively few had been manufactured during the war, and those were mainly intended for a stopgap Australian fighter, the Whirraway, developed from the Harvard trainer.

"A world search was conducted," Fred Hotson tells us, "with the aid of Pratt & Whitney and a used aircraft entrepreneur, Charlie Babb. The search covered four continents and took on all the aspects of a detective mystery. Fifty engines were found in Sweden, and, although it was not enough for a production program, it was sufficient for a start."[15]

From the first 50 on, P&WC would overhaul used R-1340s and fabricate gearbox conversion kits to add to those Wasps intended for use in the bigger Beaver that, by the time of the November 1950 factory order to buy materials for 15 airplanes, was officially known as the DHC-3 Otter.

Mike Davy joined DHC one month after the six Downsview veterans returned from Hatfield. That was during October 1950, when, as he remembers it, the Engineering Department was starting work on the King Beaver mockup. They were also building jigs to accelerate Beaver production—and to the consternation of many, making them out of wood.[16]

Davy brought an impressive résumé with him: a year of engineering at Cambridge before he joined the Royal Air Force in 1942, flight training in the British Commonwealth Air Training Plan near Calgary and at Estevan and Summerside in Canada, and operational training in Nassau, the Bahamas, perhaps the most enjoyable place in the world to learn to fly B-24 Liberator bombers. (Davy's pilot's licence, kept current ever since, is still in effect.) After his tour of duty, Davy completed his degree in aeronautical engineering at London University in 1949 and returned to Canada for a holiday. Deciding to stay, Davy went to work for A.V. Roe at Malton, several miles west of Downsview, where he was involved with the Avro Jetliner and the CF-100 Canuck interceptor, still the only indigenous fighter to be produced in Canada.

Perhaps because of his impressive record for a junior engineer, Davy found himself honoured with an intimate look at virtually every part that went into the Otter prototype. He quickly became Fred Buller's right-hand man (and social convenor), the 10 years' difference in their ages seemingly ideal for a mentor-type working arrangement. They even lived close together.

"Believe it or not," Davy says, "I weighed every part of that aeroplane"—the Otter prototype.

"And when we weighed the assembled aeroplane, there was a 41-pound differential from what we calculated. Only 41 pounds." That's 41 pounds out of the early Otter's empty weight of 4,431 pounds.

Most DHC engineers who worked on both programs define the Otter as a bigger and infinitely more sophisticated Beaver. The Beaver, as Dick Hiscocks often pointed out, was a compromise between the smaller, more elegant 330hp Gipsy Queen inline-powered DHC-X project designed by Jaki Jakimiuk and Waclaw Czerwinski at the end of the war, and the brawnier, squared-off, snub-nosed airplane Hiscocks reshaped and Buller restructured around the 450hp Wasp Jr. radial. The redesign was done in nine months flat. There wasn't time to smooth out all the wrinkles.

"The Beaver was in trouble," Davy says. "There was a mistake made in the Beaver weights and balances, and it went undetected for some time. The aircraft's centre of gravity with the Gipsy Queen was impossibly nose-heavy, necessitating a redesign in which the engine was moved aft. In this new position it interfered with the ideal placement of the pilot, who had to sit under the wing with a restricted view.

"Meanwhile, the Gipsy Queen was having developmental problems in England. The dilemma was brilliantly resolved with the switch from the Queen to the P&W R-985. With the radial being stubbier, the aircraft's centre of gravity was not so far forward, and it balanced out the aircraft. At the same time, the R-985 produced a reliable 120hp more than the Queen. This chapter of accidents was probably the biggest single factor in the success of the Beaver . . .

"The Otter had some beautiful corners in it. Mostly in the wing. Fred Buller added a stub spar near the leading edge," which added rigidity to a very large, squared-off wing that would be subject to bending loads when its full-span flaps were deployed. The stub spar enabled Buller to move the wing's main spar—its primary structural support—back from where it was on the Beaver to 35 per cent chord, or more than one-third of the distance from leading to trailing edge, adding further rigidity.

For yet further torsional, or twisting, resistance, "[Buller] added corrugations rivetted to the inside of the upper wing skin. He worshipped at Douglas's shrine"—that is, he admired the cellular construction of the everlasting Douglas DC-3 wing conceived by John Northrop, one of the greatest wing designers ever.

Like the Beaver, the Otter would have lift-enhancing devices along the entire span of its wing's trailing edge. But they, too, would be carried further than on the Beaver. There would be double-slotted flaps that were carefully designed to allow air through spanwise openings to enhance their lift-producing properties during takeoff and landing. In short, the R-1340 would get more help to carry the burden it was being asked to shoulder.[17]

The vital outer wing strut attachment was pure Fred Buller, another of his hidden signature moments—designed almost purposely to elicit skepticism so he could make a memorable demonstration of its amazing properties. The strut-to-fuselage attachment was quite similar to that of the Beaver at its front and back, where loads from the wing were transferred to the fuselage structure, clearly capable of carrying the loads that would be asked of it.

But Buller proposed a smaller fitting to take the loads out at the other end of the strut, at a point about one-third out along the wing's span. Here, it would have to withstand different types of loads during different manoeuvres. Davy and the other engineers eyeballed the fitting and made their doubts known.

Buller's surviving portraits show an unsmiling, almost grim fellow, straining under the responsibility that came with his calling, hands joined behind his back with almost military rigour. But he did have a sense of humour, a subtle one that showed up at times like this.

Davy explains: "Fred made a rubber model of the fitting. And he showed how it was arranged so the loads on it tended to cancel each other out. The rubber didn't bend. The idea became visual. The thing was the office joke."

In their article on the design of the Otter, Hiscocks and Buller explained how they avoided the kind of weight crisis that often afflicts new designs as they progress from paper to metal.

"In general," they wrote, "it is Company practise to treat simple or determinate structures and mechanisms by straight analysis, with supplementary tests of course to cover castings or unusual parts. For very indeterminate or diffuse structures, however, reliance is placed principally on tests of complete units. Analysis is used in a simplified form as a guide in design proportion—coupled with engineering judgement. However, a conscious attempt is made to design light, particularly with regard to stiffeners and skin gauges"—that is, the thickness of metal used for outer surfaces—"and to patch and modify on test where necessary. The degree to which parts are designed light depends on a number of things—the probability of catastrophic failure on test, and the accessibility of the part for examination and repair during test.

"The amount of reinforcing required with this philosophy usually turns out to be surprisingly small. In the case of the Otter fuselage, which was thought to be designed very light, the total weight added during tests was only about 15 lb., or about 2 per cent of the original weight. . . ."[18]

From an engineering point of view, the outstanding, immediately visible difference between the Beaver and the Otter, aside from size, is the Otter's fuselage, which is slightly curved down the sides where the Beaver's is flat. An English writer who asked about the change was told it was to prevent the "tin-canning" or sheet-metal buckling that Russ Bannock heard so clearly when he switched off the oil-deprived engine of the Beaver prototype on its first flight.[19]

Speaking on the forty-eighth anniversary of the Beaver's first flight, Hiscocks spoke of the most difficult aspect of its design being the addition of so many openings to its fuselage that it became questionable in engineering terms whether they were working with a structure or a mechanism. The same happened with the Otter, and this time he and Buller were prepared.

"The most noteworthy feature (of the fuselage) from a structural point of view is the number and size of the cutouts.

"The main cargo opening seemed like a forbidding problem at first. . . . It was designed much lighter than analysis would dictate, in the expectation that a great deal would be learned about this type of problem as successive reinforcements were added during testing.

"As it turned out, the only addition required was the increase in gauge of two stiffening members. The weight increase was about 3 ounces."

Ian Gilchrist, the DH technical school grad who worked as half of a two-man stress office on the Otter fuselage, calls it "a very complicated piece of stress engineering." The other member of the office was Bob Klein, future chief of airworthiness. Later, Dick Batch, an aerodynamicist by trade, joined them.

Marin C. Faure, author of a textbook on floatplane aviation (who added a chapter on the Otter to the third edition of his classic *Flying a Floatplane*) calls the Otter fuselage "tank-like."

Then again, there were some fairly crude additions—testimonials, perhaps, to the deadline pressure that comes with any attempt to follow up on success in timely fashion. Eight stiffening strakes, or parallel ridges, were added to the belly from the rear landing gear struts to the door. These add strength to the already strong fuselage shell to resist the bending loads imposed in the all-too-common event of a one-mainwheel landing. The strakes are on the outside so that the fuselage skin can present a smooth surface to the three fuel tanks just inside.

Nevertheless, the engineers at Downsview, working on their third original design since the war, pretty much got it right the first time.

Still current as pilots, Otter test pilot George Neal *(left)* and Mike Davy each brought an aircraft to a recent Family Day celebration at DHC. Neal arrived in a DH.87 Hornet Moth biplane he had restored; Davy attended in a Rebel homebuilt he constructed in 1992–96.
VIA MIKE DAVY

Facing page: Philippine Air Lines Otter air-to-air, March 1955. Aircraft registration is not yet added, but it could be the third of three Otters for that operator, PI-C53, which was being flight-tested that March before being delivered on the eighteenth. It returned to Canada with Thomas Lamb Airways, The Pas, Manitoba, as CF-XUX, in August 1968, and was written off at Nahanni Park, NWT, July 1972, with B.C.–Yukon Air Services Ltd. DHC 1613 VIA PETER M. BOWERS

CHAPTER SIX

The Otter Flies

The striking paint job in which the Otter was rolled out on December 10, 1951, reflected the extra measure of confidence the authors of the Beaver had in its successor. The Beaver prototype, CF-FHB-X, had appeared from Bill Burlison's Experimental Shop with its bare aluminum polished but unadorned except for the anti-glare panel ahead of its windshield and the registration on its fin. The Beaver had to earn its stripes. The Otter was awarded its stripes before it ever flew.

This time Fred Buller, Dick Hiscocks and their rapidly growing staffs of engineers had started with a clean sheet of paper. The Beaver had been redesigned around a new engine, and the bigger, bulkier fuselage that resulted was filled with small compromises. By 1951 the DHC team realized that they were creating an original line of bush planes, and that their expanding talent base was capable of more ambitious projects. For now, the group had the satisfaction of knowing the Otter was as good as they could make it.[1]

When CF-DYK-X, the Otter prototype, emerged from the Experimental Shop, it was painted in a scheme very close to the Ontario Provincial Air Service's colours:

brilliant yellow overall, with a royal blue (rather than OPAS black) speed line that started as a ring around the leading edge of the engine cowl and gathered itself into a broad tapering stripe running under the pilot's windows and the four underwing passenger windows, passing over the cargo door on the left side, and petering out at the trailing edge of the fin. The blue was bordered by a neat pinstripe. The words "de Havilland Otter," with Otter rendered in the same bold brush-type script as the Beaver trademark, stood out against the blue on the pilot's door. A similar but nontapering stripe carried the registration a little more than halfway up the vertical tail. And a barely discernable stripe with the same pinstripe outline defined the leading edge of the fin and its dorsal extension forward along the top centreline of the rear fuselage.

The statement was clear: the Otter will fly with OPAS, among many other customers. We know there's a big market for this airplane.[2]

There was a more subtle message in the registration letters themselves. DYK-X was registered to honour the man who had shaped it, Dick Hiscocks. In fact, the salute to him was too subtle for Hiscocks, who didn't notice until it was brought to his attention that DYK was the only way, with the three letters available, that the first Otter could bear his first name. He was humbled.

DYK-X made one statement or another to each of the hardy souls who braved the windy but snow-free DHC apron at Downsview on that cold pre-Christmas day in their flapping overcoats and pulled-down fedoras. But the new prototype was another long day's work for the man who would fly it first. Chief test pilot George Neal, similarly bundled up against the Great Lakes wind chill but alone in wearing his signature mechanic's peaked baseball cap, was aware of the excitement the Otter prototype had generated within the Engineering and Experimental departments as he watched it being assembled.

But for Neal, no first-flight date was that much of a red-letter day. Leading up to this occasion, he had been busy with first flights of modified search-and-rescue Avro Lancaster bombers and Consolidated PBY Canso amphibians, B-25 Mitchells fitted out as survey aircraft, and hot newly assembled Vampire jet fighters for the postwar RCAF. On top of all those, there was a de Havilland Dove commuter airliner from Hatfield to be demonstrated by the sales staff all over the continent.[3]

All of those aircraft save the Vampires were larger than the Otter. Nevertheless, Neal's first impression of the Otter in the outdoors as he stood directly in front of it, hands jammed into his overcoat pockets and peering at the three-bladed propeller, was that it was big. "And," he laughs in recalling that day, "it *is* a big aeroplane."

Underlying his impression were his three years of work with the Beaver: certifying it for operation on floats, flying the tricky tests that defined its forward and

aft-most centres of gravity, and then production flight-testing most of the first hundred or so Beavers off the line. During that time he had become quite intimate with the DHC-2, no lightweight itself.

That rudder is too pointed, was another of his first thoughts, although he kept that one to himself. No question, the vertical tail *was* rather pointed. Ugly, in fact, by de Havilland standards, although Neal was not exercising his judgement as an esthete. Until he got DYK-X into the air, Neal would avoid reaching conclusions about the Otter's fin and rudder. But it is amazing how often such immediate reactions by test pilots result in the addition of sheet metal—especially to the tails—of prototype airplanes.

The big snag in taxi testing turned out to be, of all things, the Otter's tailwheel. Actually, there were problems with all three wheels. But the stiffness in the tailwheel controls, perhaps due to the effect of the cold on the wires running most of the

Otter CF-GCV-X, the second prototype, used to attain certification for operation on floats, photographed in 1952 during flight-testing. The aircraft has the original pointed Otter vertical tail, with new leading edge and dorsal fin sheet metal added.
JACK MCNULTY VIA PETER M. BOWERS

length of the fuselage, was a particular pain, what with all the manoeuvring—U-turns, for example—that runway testing entails. Mike Davy remembers Neal breaking a tailwheel early in the test flight program before the controls were tuned to his satisfaction.

The mainwheel headache-producer was a peculiar rolling gait, "as though the wheels were hitting bumps on the runway," as Neal remembers it. "I said [to the engineers], 'It's like a rabbit. It jumps.'" It is normal for tires to lose their roundness in cold weather, but these responded not to being warmed up by use but to increased speed. Neal observed that the hopping behaviour lessened and then disappeared as he gathered velocity on his taxi runs. As the Otter picked up speed and the landing gear unloaded, the loss of weight pulled the struts inward, and the thumping disappeared. As Neal backed off, the struts would resume their normal track, and the airplane would go hipetty-hop. The technicians from the Experimental Shop looked over the main landing gear and concluded that it had been assembled with a few degrees of toe-in.

DYK-X did two days of taxi tests, the second day to confirm the impressions Neal had noted on the first and to test the realigned main wheels. The problem was taken seriously. While it was easy to fix, nobody wanted Neal to be wondering on final approach from the first flight whether his main gear would roll smoothly.

The cold weather kept the air-cooled R-1340 Wasp engine a little cooler than Neal and Jim Houston, the powerplant engineer, would have liked. With the indicated oil temperature a bit low, Neal felt he had to keep an eye on the cylinder head temperatures and be careful about throttling the engine back at the end of each taxi run.

Neal noticed one other thing during his high-speed runs on December 10 and 11: the Otter wanted to fly. Of course, he notes, it was practically empty and balanced to a neutral centre of gravity. Still, the Otter was a homesick angel. "It was very eager to get airborne," Neal remembers.

Neal also remembers Fred Buller's single piece of pre–first flight advice: watch for aileron flutter. In retrospect, none of the surviving engineers who worked on the Otter have any idea why Buller might have been worried about turbulence of sufficient intensity at the outer trailing edges of the wing to make the ailerons vibrate. Flutter is a constant concern of aircraft structural engineers, and some who were there speculate that his warning to George Neal was simply good procedure.

The Otter wing was an extrapolation, size-wise, of the Beaver wing, and perhaps Buller and Hiscocks were worried about the scale effects—changes of behaviour due mainly to a difference in size—on the bigger wing. They would have worried especially about any additional spanwise, or outward, airflow. One concern would

Designed to have nearly three times the interior space of an unmodified Beaver, the Otter has a total of 260 cu. ft. of interior space. DHC 3567

have been the interconnected operation of the flaps and ailerons. Although the mechanism Buller had designed to droop both flaps and ailerons was fully proven on the Beaver, the Otter had proportionately much bigger flaps.

In fact, Hiscocks and Buller referred to them as full-span flaps "divided into inboard and outboard sections of approximately the same length."[4] The outboard flaps simply acted as ailerons when operated differentially by the pilot. The rearmost trailing portions of the double-slotted inner flaps, fully deployed, deflected all of 60 degrees. The consequences of such a pronounced flap angle were partially unexplored territory for DHC. It would have been prudent of Buller to have some concerns about outward air spillage from inner flap to outer flap under sideslip conditions or in turns. "It was new for us," Neal says today, "and it was new for Fred Buller."

A bigger aerodynamic issue the Otter wing and its flaps presented was the fore-and-aft trim change that could be expected when its big double-slotted flaps were deployed. All other things being equal, the downward deployment of a hinged flight surface on a wing trailing edge should cause a nose-down change in pitch. The bigger the flaps, the greater the nose-down effect. A pilot, anticipating this nose-down moment, trims the horizontal stabilizer, or tailplane, nose-up to compensate for the anticipated pitch change.

On the Otter, the effect of deploying the big flaps was just the opposite of what Neal might otherwise have expected. Deploying the flaps caused a pronounced *nose-up* trim change in pitch. The reason for this was the redirection of the fast-moving underwing airstream downward by the flaps and the spillage of that air onto the upper surfaces of the tailplane. This downward air pressure on the tailplane caused the nose to pitch up.

George Neal is the consummate hands-on test pilot. His early experience with building engines and airframes—he was a mechanic before he was a pilot—and his vast firsthand knowledge of widely varying types of airplanes made him a great seat-of-the-pants airman. He says he anticipated the nose-up pitch change that would accompany his deployment of the Otter's flaps and fully understood the forces at work. The engineers had warned him. From a procedural point of view, Neal simply resolved that any time the flaps were deployed during the first flight, he would use the ailerons "tenderly."[5]

Neal solved the problem of the flap-actuated pitch change by accomplishing his first takeoff in the Otter prototype December 12, 1951, without using the flaps. He didn't need them. He and CF-DYK-X left the ground from the same 600 feet of runway the Beaver normally used. This was immediate confirmation to the engineers that they had succeeded in matching the Beaver's STOL performance.

With the seven passenger seats folded, the cabin of an Otter was cavernous in 1956. Today's turbine Otter can seat 16 in a high-density layout. DHC 3566

"I could feel the airplane just sort of lift up," Neal recalls. "You could feel it extend the undercarriage and it climbed into the air."

Neal set the Otter in level flight cruise—a little over 130 mph—and settled into getting the feel of it. He did some stalls. Stall speed—the speed at which the Otter is not moving forward fast enough to sustain controlled flight—is about 58 mph on the production Otter, and less than that when so lightly loaded. These stalls, "which I gently approached," says Neal, were neither sudden in their onset nor difficult to recover from.

He deployed the flaps, "and I could see the nose position change quite drastically—which I expected. For that middle centre of gravity, it handled very well." Neal spent a little over an hour in the air.

"The only thing was, it was so noisy. But that was to be expected because of the augmenter tubes," which extracted exhaust from the engine's cylinders and added to the exhaust flow's velocity in the exhaust pipes to add a small jet-like thrust bonus. Otter pilots are universal in their opinion that the airplane is loud, but they have argued for nearly 50 years about whether the extractor (or augmenter) tubes make any difference whatsoever. Neal's impression was that they did.

One of Neal's minor worries was low oil-pressure in the engine, although nothing like the plummetting oil-pressure reading Russ Bannock got on the first flight of the Beaver, compelling him to end it with a dead-stick landing. Although it was a very cold day, the Otter's cabin was kept warm by the engine oil tank located directly underneath Neal's feet.

On approach to his first Otter landing, Neal was thinking about that darned (nary a curse escapes George Neal's lips) tailwheel. "I didn't want to do a three-wheel landing," he says now—no matter how impressive it would look.

"I had to watch whether I was going to veer off suddenly," he recalls, "as the tailwheel was still in question. I just did a wheels-on landing, main wheels, then tail down. Just no problem at all."

Neal doesn't remember what he said to the frozen multitudes waiting on the ground. It would not have been like him to say anything that sounded even mildly pretentious stepping out of a cockpit. With the extractor exhaust bark still ringing in his ears, it is unlikely he could have heard himself speak anyway.

Of course, how you felt about the first flight of the de Havilland DHC-3 Otter depended on where you stood. Mike Davy, for one, as a newcomer from England, could not believe how long Neal stayed airborne on what Davy thought was supposed to be a brief first flight. Nor could he quite believe how frigid he became awaiting the Otter's return.

Neal does remember what he said at his debrief in chief engineer Doug Hunter's

office. Present among others were Hunter, chief design engineer Buller, chief technical engineer Hiscocks, powerplant engineer Jim Houston and Bill Heaslip, one of the men who had returned from Hatfield just over a year before to do the Otter detail design. Neal remembers the room being crowded. Phil Garratt might have been there. He mentioned the low cylinder head temperatures, which were fixed following the meeting with a higher-temperature oil cooler thermostat. And, of course, the tailwheel. Aside from that, what ringing endorsement did he offer this distinguished audience?

"I said the airplane was good enough that we could continue testing," Neal recalls. There was a lot of work to do.[6]

Its designers felt that the outstanding feature of the Otter fuselage was the number and size of its openings. Otters have flown with entire wings from other Otters inside the cabin. DHC 10566

CHAPTER SEVEN

Reviews and Improvements

George Neal's log records a total of two and a quarter hours spent flying DYK-X on December 13, the day following the first flight. Included is a 10-minute hop that, while he can't be specific, seems likely to him to have been a demonstration.

It was during these winter demonstrations that Neal showed how the Otter could take advantage of the appalling conditions in which it was designed to operate. In mid-January, before Canada's defence minister, Neal nosed DYK-X into a 20-mile-per-hour headwind—a barely noticeable breeze in the lee of the Great Lakes—and was off the ground in 90 feet, or less than one-third the length of a Canadian football field. It was at 2,000 feet in a minute. The landing was accomplished "in something under 60 feet." To top off his account, the *Globe and Mail*'s knowledgeable aviation reporter James Hornick warmed Canadian hearts by recording for posterity that "some of the U.S. observers expressed unreserved astonishment."[1]

In early February, in front of a *Time* magazine reporter, among others, Neal got the Otter off the ground in about 80 feet (with no mention of a headwind). The

Time writer quotes "an impressionable newsman" present as saying out loud that the Otter's climb performance was that of "a single-engined transport with the performance of a helicopter." Rash as this fellow must have seemed, he was onto something: it would be the Otter's ability to outperform the helicopters of the time that would persuade the U.S. Army to buy 190 of them. To the gimlet-eyed man from *Time*, the Otter's landing run "seemed even shorter than its abrupt takeoff," as incredible as that, too, must have seemed. It *was* even shorter.[2]

Another distinguished visitor to these early 1952 demonstrations was the world's foremost pioneer of rotary-wing flight. Igor Sikorsky found himself on one of Downsview's runways accompanied by Russ Bannock and Phil Garratt, whose presence must have assured him that he was safe only a few hundred yards from Otter DYK-X as it rushed toward them, committed to takeoff. Of course the Otter was already well overhead when it passed them. The reaction of the father of the helicopter consisted of a single word: "Competition."

But the flight that was, on the face of it at least, the most amazing, was an inadvertent demonstration. This was the time Neal stopped the Otter in midair, backed up and had pedestrians in downtown Toronto craning skyward, wondering when he would crash. Neal was at 7,000 feet, flying at 65 mph, a safe margin over the Otter's stall speed, especially in its lightly loaded flight-test configuration. What the onlookers didn't know was that Neal was purposely flying into a 75-mph headwind. Both the police department and the newspaper that ran the story, the *Toronto Telegram*, were "deluged" with calls. Neal explained to the *Telegram* reporter that the tests were routine: he was merely determining rudder loads and the effects of deploying the double-slotted flaps while flying the Otter backwards in relation to the ground. Nothing to it, really.[3]

On January 4, Neal finally found a moment in his busy flight-test schedule to take Doug Hunter, Hiscocks and Punch Dickins up in the Otter. Had they been nagging him?

"Oh yes. They wanted to go."

No wonder, considering what an impression the Otter was making on one aviation writer who had come a long way to experience it.

The Otter's welcome into the aviation world was warmer than we might remember from a late-century viewpoint. Otters still offer nearly unique performance. Otters are still very much in demand. But they are not necessarily recalled as the leap forward that James Hay Stevens saw when he wrote about the newest DHC product in the April 11, 1952, issue of *Flight*:

"The Otter is a remarkable aircraft, far more remarkable than its somewhat simple outlines would suggest.

"It is usually regarded rather as an enlarged Beaver, but it is very much more than this and is, in fact, an entirely new design by its makers. . . . it has been born out of experience with the Beaver, itself the epitome of a generation of practical bush flying, but apart from the adoption of a similar high-wing layout the two types have very little in common.

"Good as is the low-speed performance of the Beaver, the Otter was designed to better it and, in particular, to reverse an unusual characteristic of the former. The Beaver needs slightly more space for landing than for take-off and it was decided that the Otter must be able to enter any clearing it could leave. . . . This objective has been attained and the land plane can be taken off in 400 yards over a 50-foot obstacle in still air. Actually this figure gives no idea of the extraordinarily short run achieved under normal wind conditions, when the Otter just seems to waddle along for a few yards before lifting off and climbing steeply."[4]

After giving detailed performance figures and the conditions under which they were recorded, Stevens sums up his impressions of the first Otter:

"Altogether an outstanding aircraft; the all-round performance is excellent for 600hp and to be able to carry a ton payload at over 160mph *and* at only 50mph is good by any standard."

As good a salesman as George Neal was in the cockpit, by spring 1952 he was keenly aware of the prototype's two main limitations—one of them fairly easily fixable, the other not.

The Otter prototype, CF-DYK-X, with its vertical tail modified to the production standard, October 21, 1952. Note the redefined fin leading edge and taller rudder, its tip barely visible. Sandbags would have been used to determine centre-of-gravity limits. JACK MCNULTY VIA PETER M. BOWERS

The first confirmed Neal's initial suspicions upon seeing the Otter assembled and in the open—the overly pointed vertical tail created a stability problem. An airplane's vertical tail, the flight surface composed of the fin and rudder, enables it to fly straight, sideslip under control or, in conjunction with the airplane's ailerons, make a co-ordinated, rolling turn. Too much vertical tail generates drag, acts as a sail in crosswinds and makes an airplane difficult to handle. Too little makes for a lack of directional stability and difficulty keeping the airplane on course. Adding sheet metal is a relatively simple solution; the trick is to add it in the right places.

It wasn't that the Otter wouldn't fly straight. But there are many forces at work when an aircraft flies. The game is to make them balance each other out. On the Otter, it all begins with a propeller spinning at the front, making the airplane sideslip. This is a torque, or twisting force. The Otter wants to turn left.

Floats have a further destabilizing effect on an airplane simply because large masses are hung below the fuselage, creating differential drag and turbulence, especially in crosswinds and turns. This is why floatplanes have additional fixed surfaces, usually attached to the underside of the rear fuselage. Adding such a ventral fin would compensate for the Otter's floats, but it would also make the airplane more vulnerable to crosswinds. Neal remembers Adam Davidson and the flight-test staff working with various combinations of additions to the fixed and hinged surfaces, adding to the area of the fin and/or rudder.

They did manage to counteract the effects of the floats. But when Neal started flying with floats *and* the bush pilot's time-honoured canoe tied to the float struts on one side, stability was marginal again.

"You design and develop it so that it just passes," Neal explains. DHC design philosophy was to minimize the size of flight surfaces in the name of efficiency—just as structural weights were simplified and minimized—and add reinforcement or area as the need was proven.

"You don't have bags in reserve. It was okay with straight floats. When we put a canoe on it, it became marginal again. While [DYK-X] was on floats, we made the changes to the fin."

In April 1952 DYK-X was on floats, bringing the directional stability problems to light over the next few months. Neal believes the second prototype, CF-GCV, was used to get the Otter's float certification. GCV flew for the first time May 2, 1952, and was fitted with floats June 13.[5]

There were many advantages to having two flight-test airplanes, entirely aside from being able to do different tests simultaneously. There was a saving in wear and tear on each, and the opportunity to do before and after tests of modifications by making the changes to only one. The most obvious benefit was the ability to continue

Another Otter milestone: CF-HXY-X, the prototype amphibian, was the sixty-seventh Otter built. It was photographed January 22, 1956. JACK MCNULTY VIA PETER M. BOWERS

testing while one prototype was undergoing the extensive maintenance required of a new design—a design for which shop manuals are being written on the go.

Another benefit was that a second Otter demonstrator was now available. Despite defence minister Brooke Claxton's interest in the Otter, expressed at George Neal's demonstration January 18, the Royal Canadian Air Force had made no move toward a firm order as summer set in. Russ Bannock, DHC's director of military sales, had been in Ottawa for many of the intervening weekends, and the line from RCAF procurement officers was that the 35 or so Norsemans (of the 100 that served with the RCAF altogether) still in the inventory would take care of their needs for 10 to 15 years. But Bannock was tipped that the RCAF's top brass would be at Goose Bay in July for a week's salmon fishing on the Eagle River. Bannock and the brand-new float-equipped GCV were there and waiting.

"It was a very hot day, 90° F. They loaded a group of eight people and their gear into a Norseman. The bay was flat calm, and this Norseman failed to get airborne after going for two or three miles and then coming back, and I invited the whole group into the Otter—in fact, there were nine people and their gear came aboard. We took off in a matter of a thousand feet or so even though it was glassy water and a hot day.

"We went to the camp and I landed on a portion of the river which they never even attempted to land on in the Norseman. They usually landed in a bay at the mouth of the river and then walked a mile and a half to the camp. Where I landed with the Otter it was only a 500- or 600-yard walk to where they'd set up this tent camp. It was just below a major rapids. They fished for salmon below the rapids. After five or six days of fishing I flew them off this river and back to Goose Bay.

"When we got back there, the chief of the air staff turned to one of his senior officers and said, 'This is a better airplane than the Norseman. We should buy six of these.' The contract didn't appear until the end of that fiscal year, at the end of March 1953."

Mike Davy remembers the additions to the Otter's vertical tail coming about 18 months after its first flight, which would make it June 1953—rather late in the prototype's development, with the Otter certified for use as a passenger transport the previous November, and, with 16 Otters built and most of those delivered to customers, a highly expensive retrofit to those and the new ones coming off the line. Davy feels the order to make the changes was a tribute to Dick Hiscocks's objectivity as an engineer. Hiscocks simply accepted the recommendation that the Otter's vertical tail be almost doubled in area. "I give Dick one hundred percent credit for doing that," Davy says. "For him, it wasn't a big problem. Just put it on and get back to him."[6]

Another engineer who worked there suspects that one of Fred Buller's mechanical engineers, Charlie Bishop, pulled out a compass with a pencil stub and a set of french curves and drew up the new tail, probably over lunch, and had Davidson's airframe mechanics cut the metal that afternoon. Things were simpler then. The remark is a salute to an improvisation that transformed the only truly ugly part of the original Otter. The angular leading edge of the fin and its straight dorsal extension became a continuous concave curve which, extended to the top of the fin and the horn at the rudder's tip, became convex, adding the needed surface area and, incidentally, producing a new variation of the graceful trademark de Havilland S-shaped tail to the Otter. Ironically, Bishop, a religious man and a notorious worrywart, quick to find fault in himself, agonized about his tail modifications once Otters started crashing.

The lack of directional stability—the Otter's reluctance to fly where it was pointed under certain conditions—was amenable to a simple cure: more vertical tail, added in the right places. Smart pilots could do themselves a favour by lashing canoes on the starboard float struts, to counteract the leftward torque forces of the engine, rather than on the port side, where they traditionally carried canoes so they could keep an eye on them from the left-hand seat.

The engine was another matter.

"Really," Neal acknowledges, "the Otter needs higher power. Anything with flaps down and a full load [was marginal]. The Otter, with floats, would get out of the water but it wouldn't climb very well. You had to be careful. You had to fly well ahead of you."

Answers to that issue were longer in coming. A small industry exists today to convert Otters to lighter, more powerful gas turbine engines. The result may be the perfect big single-engine bush plane, the Turbo Otter.

Otter bound for Wideroes Flyveselskap, Norway, in shipping crate, January 1957. Wideroes operated seven Otters along Norway's rugged coastline north of the Arctic Circle, and the Royal Norwegian Air Force used 10. DHC 4878

Neal's most famous demonstration of the Otter was to Max Ward. Ward was still flying the DH.83 Fox Moth biplane he had bought from DHC shortly after the war, modified for Canadian conditions by the addition of a neat bubble canopy, or "coupe top," and a slightly more powerful Gipsy Major Ic engine with domed pistons that used leaded gas to pump out an extra 12hp (for a grand total of 142). The Fox Moth, like most of Hatfield's prewar designs, was a lightly built airplane that, if not robust, was a good performer.[7]

Ward, a practical businessman-pilot, had heard via the airman's grapevine that the Otter was "something of a miracle," even at $100,000, "about two and a half times the average cost of a bush plane at the time."[8] Ward related best to direct comparisons. The Otter had three times the Fox Moth's range, and it could carry 8 to 14 passengers to the Fox Moth's 3 or 4. Ward would have visited the Downsview factory during the spring of 1953, when he had yet to secure more than the $25,000 guarantee he had from a gold mining company, and was still two applications short of his air transport licence. Nevertheless, he met his bush-flying hero, Punch Dickins, DHC's Vice-President, Sales, and Dickins introduced him to George Neal.

"George took me on my first Otter flight, and I'll never forget it," Ward wrote in his memoir, *The Max Ward Story*.

"We were lined up outside the de Havilland hangar at Downsview, pointing directly at the hangar, which, to my eyes, seemed about 10 feet away, when George hit the throttle. I thought to myself that we were probably going to have a short, nasty flight when that Otter just sort of leaped up in the air, jumped over the hangar, and soared.[9]

"I lusted after that aircraft something terrible. It could carry 14 passengers or two thousand pounds of freight, could go anywhere, had a fair turn of speed, handled well, and, I came to discover, would revolutionize not only flying in the North, but the way of life in the North itself."

Although each of George Neal's Otter airshows was carried out with sales very much in mind, his heart-stopping demonstration for Max Ward was part of the transition from the 11-month program of test-flying that certified the Otter for commercial use November 5, 1952, to the task of selling the Otters that were being built even before the first one flew.

That hop was confirmation of a partnership between the flying entrepreneur and DHC that lasted until Wardair was bought out by Pacific Western Airlines in 1989. As Wardair grew, it bought successively bigger DHC bush planes and regional airliners. Even now, long after the demise of Wardair, the partnership continues. Max Ward still flies his personal Twin Otter many times a year between Edmonton and Yellowknife.

Facing page: Amphibious Otter RCAF 3685 being overhauled, June 1957. 685 (46) had just finished an assignment to 103 Rescue Unit, Greenwood, Nova Scotia, when it was returned to DHC before being posted to the Cold Lake (Alberta) Station Flight. By spring 1959 it would be back at Greenwood. DHC 6407

CHAPTER EIGHT

Military Otters: Triumph and Tragedy

flight-testing revealed that the Otter's short-field and fast and slow performance characteristics were in a class by themselves among fixed-wing aircraft and impressive even by the standards of the heavy-lift helicopters of the time. The comparison between the Otter's capabilities and those of helicopters crossed the minds of almost anyone who saw an Otter demonstration. The comparison was almost exact: assuming both carry maximum loads, a helicopter must execute a rolling takeoff much like that of the Otter. It cannot use its vertical liftoff advantage when burdened with its maximum payload.

Russ Bannock, who remained director of flight-test operations even as he flew Otter demonstrations in his role as director of military sales, had shown the new Otter to U.S. Army Aviation staff at the Pentagon, at Continental Army Command (CONARC) and at the Army Aviation Section Test Centre, Fort Bragg, North Carolina, where in 1950 Bannock had made a lasting impression by landing a Beaver on a sandy road the army considered unusable as a landing strip. Bannock had become worried about taking off when he saw an air-dropped howitzer's parachute fail to deploy and the artillery piece disappear into the soft loam. But he took off from the spongy surface nevertheless, with the very definition of a useful military load—five senior officers—aboard.

Later the Beaver, with Bannock at the controls, won formal flyoffs at Fort Rucker and Wright-Patterson Air Force Base, winning Army and Air Force contracts against a dozen-odd American types by landing in less than half the distance required by its closest competitor.

Brass from NATO air arms shop at DHC for military applications of the Otter in April 1957, possibly wondering about roles for the ground-effects Otter 3674 and the Quiet Otter 3692. DHC 5286

Back at some of the same bases in 1953 with the Otter, Bannock knew he could improve on the Beaver's exploits. The problem for DHC, once again, was that their newest product was doing things no military mind had yet thought of asking fixed-wing aircraft to do. "Everyone seemed impressed with the 'bigger' Beaver but could not see a requirement at the time," Bannock wrote years later.[1]

"In general," Lt.-Gen. (ret'd) Robert R. Williams, later director of army aviation, has written, "Army interest was lukewarm. An exception was Bob Rawls, in the office of the Chief of Engineers. Bob was responsible for supporting the 30th Engineer Group doing a survey of Alaska north of the Brooks Range"—Alaska's Arctic Ocean coast, America's final frontier.

"The Otter seemed ideal, in a seaplane configuration, to carry out local logistics, particularly supplying fuel for the 30th's helicopters. The engineers submitted a request for six Otters. By the summer of 1953," Williams recalls, "six months from the identification of the requirements, de Havilland had an order from the Army for six Otters for the Engineers, plus 60 more for the Army. The order very quickly grew to 240."[2]

So, as with the Beaver, the first U.S. Army order for the Otter came from an Alaska-based unit, in this case a survey team of the Army Corps of Engineers. But the breakthrough from the initial sale to further orders came with Bannock's inspiration to volunteer the Otter for a helicopter exercise.

Exercise Skydrop II was designed to evaluate the second-generation helicopters the U.S. Army was using during the early 1950s and see whether they were capable of supplying troops in the field for a sustained period.

The prime competitors were the Sikorsky H-34 Choctaw and the Piasecki H-21 Shawnee. The H-21, often referred to as the Flying Banana, was a single-engine, twin-rotor design with a shallow V-shaped fuselage profile—hence the nickname—that could carry three and a half tons. Sikorsky's H-34 was a development of its classic S-55/S-58 series, the most widely produced helicopters of their time, with more than 2,400 built in the U.S., Britain, France and Japan. The H-34 could carry

about two and a half tons. Bannock offered to have an Otter compete at DHC expense under the same rules as the helicopters.[3]

The two types of helicopters were to fly a 100-mile stage daily in company strength (21 aircraft) for the month of April 1953 at Fort Bragg, and the Army would find out which could carry the most cargo over that time. Maintainability was the key. While the helicopters and the Otter were powered by similar piston radial engines, the H-21s drove two rotors through complicated transmission units and driveshafts. The Sikorsky's powerplant installation was simpler and its payload lighter than the H-21s, but, as Bannock remembers the exercise, the H-34s had "consistent unserviceability problems."

DHC sent an early-production Otter, flown by test and demonstration pilot Doug Givens, to fly its ton daily over the 100-mile stage—an almost absurdly relaxed schedule for a working Otter. A company engineer, Bob Irving, did routine maintenance, but nothing more. Photos of the exercise show row upon row of identical H-21s, easily recognizable for their distinctive shape, and the single Otter, looking

U.S. Army U-1A Otters and H-21 Shawnees at Ft. Riley, Kansas, February 1957. Otters did the same tasks helicopters did, more reliably. DHC 4917 overwhelmed under the canopy of rotors, two sets per H-21. But the Otter carried five times as much as any helicopter that month. It simply did not break down.[4]

"The Army were impressed," Bannock recalls, "and CONARC wrote a requirement."

As sales of the Otter to the U.S. military mounted, the problem of training the first cadre of American pilots on the type arose. An "Otter College" was founded at Downsview. Production test pilots would check out the first batches of army aviators, who would return to such bases as Bragg and Rucker and pass on their techniques.

One of these production test pilots was Bill Ferderber.

It was Ferderber who had recommended Bob Fowler to Russ Bannock for a job in the flight-test department at DHC. Fowler had done a similar favour for Ferderber earlier. The two had run into each other at the southeast corner of Wellington and Bay streets in downtown Toronto, probably in 1947, and Ferderber had asked about a flying job with the surveying outfit Fowler was working for, Dominion Gulf. Fowler was happy to recommend him: "Bill was a gem of a pilot." And he was likeable—"a young, good-looking, blue-eyed blond."

Ferderber had come to Canada at 10 as an immigrant from Austria. He flew Spitfire 21s late in the war, and he never lost his yen for high-performance aircraft. To keep his hand in, and with the idea of possibly using it as a high-speed survey aircraft, Ferderber bought a de Havilland Sea Hornet carrier fighter at RCAF Station Namao, where it had finished being cold-weather tested, and flew it from Edmonton to Ottawa. He also flew a twin-engine P-38 Lockheed Lightning, which had

The first of 190 U.S. Army Otters. YU-1 52973, the forty-third Otter built, was delivered on the last day of February 1955, duded up in white and insignia red for Alaskan duty. VIA PETER M. BOWERS

been modified for survey work with Spartan Air Services and had survived having an engine fail, a condition that usually caused a disastrous snap-roll when it happened to an unwary pilot. Arthur Fecteau, an early Beaver customer and purchaser of Otter Number 3, who supplied Dominion Gulf's base at Chibougamau, northern Quebec, honoured Ferderber with the nickname "Le Petit Ferderber."

Spartan took over Dominion Gulf's survey contracts, and Fowler and Ferderber worked together for the first time in the spring of 1948 when Fowler checked his friend out on Spartan's Grumman Goose amphibian. Fowler ended up flying the Lightning for Spartan out of Dawson City, Yukon (with the legendary Weldy Phipps, who put DC-3 wheels on a Beaver to operate off arctic tundra), while Ferderber won a contract to fly the Sea Hornet, registered CF-GUO, doing mapping for the same firm during the 1951 season. The advantage former fighters had over such prosaic survey aircraft as the Avro Anson was that survey work became more cost-effective with higher altitudes, where each photo could cover more ground. For the two veteran combat pilots, flying disarmed, lightened twin-engine World War II fighters was like reliving the excitement of wartime without the bother of being shot at.

That season, 1951, was the last big survey period. But Ferderber was offered a job in DHC's flight-test and demonstration department by Buck Buchanan, who worked for Bannock and became one of the company's ace salesmen and aircraft delivery specialists.

As it turned out, Bannock and Bob Fowler had run into each other a number of times during the war in London. When Ferderber was introduced to Bannock, the head of flight-test asked him, "Is Bob Fowler still with Spartan? Do you think he would like this sort of work?"

It was Ferderber's considered opinion that Fowler would enjoy test-flying with DHC. In time, Fowler introduced Ferderber to his future wife and was the best man at his wedding.

There was also an immediate affinity between Ferderber and George Neal, who brought Ferderber into the Otter program. "George liked him," Fowler says. "They were a good team."[5]

U.S. Army U-1A 53250 (88) pioneered air-to-air refuelling techniques, making it possible for an H-21 helicopter to make the first transcontinental rotary-wing non-stop flight.
VIA PETER M. BOWERS

In the early afternoon of Tuesday, February 14, 1956, Ferderber was 3,000 feet over Downsview in Otter Number 92, Army serial 55-3252, with three pilots who had arrived there from Fort Riley, Kansas, the day before. It was the Otter's delivery day. Ferderber had spent the morning with Maj. A. G. Aticisson and Capts. J. P. Dowling and C. E. Durand, briefing them on the Otter in preparation for their familiarization flight.

They had, Fred Hotson tells us, been in the air for about an hour when security guards saw a wing panel separate from the Otter and the rest of the airplane spin to earth: "The fact that it came apart in the air was extremely serious, in view of the fine record and the 75,000 hours of flying time Otters had accumulated in service." All four men were killed.[6]

This was the first time a DHC-built aircraft had crashed at Downsview. The tragedy triggered an emergency response and investigation unlike any the company had yet experienced. Every engineering feature of the Otter was second-guessed by its authors, who were worried stiff lest it was during their labours that the flaw had been overlooked. Forty members of the DHC engineering staff, headed by Dick Hiscocks and Fred Buller, were reassigned to their Otter design teams. The accident changed the life of every DHC engineer involved, and, while Buller had always been noticeably serious about his responsibilities as an aircraft engineer (even at home; a glance at any portrait of the man is convincing), the fact of a catastrophic structural failure on Number 92 made him the dynamo at the centre of the search for the cause.

They were joined by accident investigation specialists from the Royal Canadian Air Force, which had the largest commitment to the Otter—38 delivered so far, of an eventual total of 69 ordered—among the 100 or so flying by then; Canada's Department of Transport and National Research Council; the USAF and U.S. Army; and the National Advisory Committee for Aeronautics, the predecessor of the National Air and Space Administration. The chief detective was Fred Jones of the Royal Aircraft Establishment, Farnborough, England.

Aside from the painstaking examination of wreckage and debris, an important, if hazardous, direction of inquiry was a series of flights undertaken by Neal and Fowler to try to duplicate the conditions the ill-fated Number 92 had encountered. They used a specially reinforced Otter with extra instrumentation to measure loads on flight surfaces and wore parachutes. An early assumption was that Otter 92 had suffered a failure somewhere within its flap system, causing an inadvertent release of the flaps. With the elevator trimmed almost fully nose-down, when the flaps suddenly retracted, they caused the nose to drop without warning. A sudden dive that becomes steeper, as in the beginning of an outside loop, is called a "bunt." If the bunt continued to the point where the Otter passed the vertical, the negative-G load on the wing, which is stressed more for positive-G and is stronger in that direction, would in moments cause structural failure of the wing by negative bending.

Neal found the strengthened Otter would bunt violently when the flaps were merely selected "up" on a signal from the copilot.[7]

With a relatively sophisticated instrument package in the test aircraft the engineers were able to analyse the negative-G forces that would result if the flaps retracted almost entirely with the aircraft trimmed almost fully nose-down at very near the flap limit speed. Mere selecting of the flap "up" position would not normally cause the flaps to retract instantly.

RCAF CSR-132 3680 (38) spent 10 years with 121 Communications and Rescue Flight, Sea Island, Vancouver, before joining the Royal Canadian Mounted Police as CF-MPK. It crashed at Goose Bay as C-FEBX in 1981 but was repaired. VIA PETER M. BOWERS

The DHC test-flight department, October 12, 1954, in front of U-6 53-2845, the 661st Beaver built. *Left to right:* Chief test pilot George Neal, Bill Ferderber, Bob Fowler and Doug Givens. DHC VIA BOB FOWLER

"After a series of these flights Neal reasoned that, although recovery was within the capability of the pilot anticipating the manoeuvre, the abnormality of the original case, coupled with the surprise element, would render recovery out of the question.

"A contributing factor at the time of the accident would undoubtedly be the forward centre-of-gravity condition due to the fact that it was a training flight. It is not difficult to picture three keen students, one in the copilot's seat and two by the cockpit door, looking over his shoulder."

There was now a believable theory of how the accident had happened. But what had gone wrong?

Hotson tells us that the investigation was proceeding around the clock when a second, similar accident occurred with an Otter on a test flight near Goose Bay, Labrador, having a replacement flap checked. Hiscocks and Buller flew to the scene; Hiscocks later described his first action on arrival as falling out of the airplane into deep snow and having to be rescued while Buller hit the ground running.[8]

As awful as the second fatal accident was, it did provide a second helping of evidence. The theory about a sudden retraction of the big double-slotted flaps seemed confirmed. Fred Jones traced the malfunction to a "ratchet valve," so-called because it was designed to allow hydraulic fluid to flow only one way, thus maintaining pressure in the flap actuation system that locked the flaps down in the face of tremendous pressure from the airstream. The Otter wing was built by Canadian Car and Foundry of Fort William, a company that had built Hurricane fighters during the war. Continuing investigation revealed that in machining these valves, a CCF supplier had allowed microscopic metal particles to remain within some of the valves. These impurities circulated within the hydraulic system until the fateful moment when one of these minuscule bits prevented the flap's closure.

As far as we can tell from reconstructing the events of the afternoon of February 14, 1956, when Ferberder selected Flaps Up, the hydraulic system that operates the Otter flaps lost pressure instantly. The airstream blew the flaps flat instead of raising them gradually as the fluid bled back to its reservoir, as would normally have happened. With the aircraft trimmed fully nose-down, Otter Number 92's nose pitched down with a force that two men at its wheel could not have counteracted unless they had reacted in less than two seconds. As it tumbled through the vertical plane and onto its back, one wing panel failed and wrapped itself around the underside of the fuselage with such violence that it sheared off the airplane's tail section.

The major modification to the 90 some Otters delivered up to then and units following on the assembly line was a linkage between the flaps and the horizontal stabilizer that maintains the stabilizer's setting at an appropriate angle matching the flap position. Thus, even if the flaps suddenly retract, the stabilizer moves to a position that ensures longitudinal control "without," Hotson explains, "any input from the pilot. The same device was used later in the Twin Otter." The valve was modified to introduce a sharp chamfered edge that could cut through any contamination, ensuring that it would close.

The Otter soldiered on with the U.S. Army, often in a supporting role. One Otter enabled a CH-21 helicopter, one of the types it had outperformed at Fort Bragg, to make the first nonstop transcontinental flight by a helicopter, from San Diego to the Pentagon, Washington, August 23–24, 1956.

This CH-21 became famous as "Amblin Anny" for covering 2,610 miles in 37 hours. The Otter that refuelled it in flight has been almost forgotten. Lt.-Gen. Williams has called the Otter "the unglamourous, ignored workhorse of Army Aviation" before and during his term as director, which began in 1966.

Otter 53250, the eighty-eighth built, was fitted with a large fuel tank that took up much of its interior, connected to a flexible pipe with a funnel on its trailing end that was extended from the drop hatch. The helicopter had a probe that extended forward on the pilot's (left) side of the fuselage. The probe-and-drogue equipment, and the expertise to use it, was supplied by Flight Refuelling Ltd., the British pioneer of a procedure that is a critical factor in the use of global airpower today.

But there were unusual hazards to be surmounted. The CH-21 had a rotor at each end of its fuselage—driven by a single rear-mounted radial engine—meaning that almost half of the 41-foot front rotor diameter extended ahead of the glazed cockpit in the nose. The hose had to clear the rotor disc. Both aircraft had to be flown with intense concentration during the refuelling cycle, which lasted 22 minutes.[9]

"The H-21 and its crew, Gaddis, Givens and Bowman, were highly publicized," Lt.-Gen. Williams told his U.S. Army Otter and Caribou Association listeners during their 1990 reunion in Dallas.

"Few words have been said about the Otter that refuelled the H-21 in flight. June Stebbins was the pilot of the Otter.... His was the really tough job."[10]

DHC managing director Phil Garratt (left) with a visiting RAF air marshall and the air commodore who was then Britain's air attaché to Washington, posing in front of the RCAF's second Otter, 3662, delivered March 28, 1953. The Otter was still current in 1980 in Whitehorse, Yukon Territory, as C-FSUB. DHC 10556

The H-21's transcontinental flight was not the only helicopter performance record aided and abetted by the best fixed-wing near-helicopter the U.S. Army had. During the early 1960s the Army was very proud of the rotary-wing aircraft that was to set new standards for battlefield helicopter operations in Vietnam, the new Bell UH-1D Huey. The Huey first flew October 22, 1956, and during its subsequent service-testing period the Army wanted to set new time-to-climb and 100-mile closed-circuit speed records with the new turbine-powered helicopter. It was entirely logical to support these record attempts with Otters.

A Canadian Army exchange test pilot at the Army Aviation centre at Fort Rucker, Alabama, then-Lt. K. Randall Mattocks, was assigned to fly support missions for the record attempts. As preparations unfolded, Mattocks found himself shuttling back and forth in Otters from Rucker to the Bell Helicopter plant at Fort Worth, Texas.

How far was this flight? "About seven hours," Mattocks chuckles. "Chug, chug, there's the Mississippi River, chug, chug . . ."

Mattocks's assignment during the actual record attempts was to circle not far from Longview, Texas, and keep an eye out for the speeding Huey. The idea, of course, was to fly slowly: in the 75–80 mph range with full flap and a lot of power. And, oh yes, it had to be done at night, when the cool temperatures and thicker air were more conducive to high-performance rotary-wing operations.

"For that sort of job, when you're cruising and on a taxi route just waiting for something to happen, you want to make the best use of your fuel. Certainly it wasn't at high cruise. You wouldn't be counting the blades going by, but it would be at lower rpm. If he [the Huey] squeaked, I could light his area so he could land somewhere safely."[11]

It didn't happen. Sometime during the early 1960s, military helicopters began reliably carrying their own weight. They no longer required Otters to help them along.

CHAPTER NINE

The Trans Antarctic Otter

In keeping with the outsized dimensions of its ambition—peaceful co-operation and research into the world we share—the International Geophysical Year lasted a year and a half: the 18 months from the first of July 1957 to the end of 1958. IGY was "a world crusade by 60 nations against man's ignorance of planet Earth," writes Al Muenchen in *Flying the Midnight Sun: The Exploration of Antarctica by Air*. The job simply could not be done in a normal year. Indeed, many of its studies continue today.

The world's smallest and most inhospitable continent would become not only a below-zero scientific laboratory; it would, the IGY's sponsors hoped, also be an experiment in cooling the world's tensions. That may have been IGY's outstanding achievement. People who might have been shooting at each other elsewhere would find a way to get along on what some called the Peace Continent. All too briefly, the Cold War chilled out. "Ideological differences seem to have evaporated at 50 to 60 degrees below zero," Basil Clarke writes in *Polar Flight*, a history of aerial exploration of the world's top and bottom. One thing peoples from widely separated parts of the world had in common when they convened in Antarctica was the Otter.

Shortly after the U.S. Army ordered the Otter in quantity, Russ Bannock was tipped at the Pentagon that the U.S. Navy had a dirty, dangerous and miserably cold job to be done. Bannock thought the Otter might be just the ticket. Otter demonstrations were carried out before naval personnel at installations in Norfolk, Virginia, and Washington. Army Aviation supported DHC's bid by supplying data on the Otter's performance on the Corps of Engineers Alaska surveys.

By 1956, 40 nations were committed to exploring Antarctica as part of the IGY. The American effort, the most extensive of any single nation, was labelled Operation Deepfreeze, and was to be organized by the U.S. Navy. Naval Air Development Squadron Six (VX-6) was assigned the aviation task. When the call for volunteers for Antarctic duty was circulated, so many stepped forward that only one out of 16 was accepted. VX-6 was a versatile crew, credited in one account with having the best fliers and ground crews in the Navy. They started Operation Deepfreeze in 1955 with naval versions of the four-engine C-54 (DC-4) and twin-engine C-47 (DC-3) transports, plus long-range Lockheed Neptunes and Grumman Albatross amphibians—along with four Otters, among the earliest the U.S. military ordered. VX-6 soon added nine more.

Of those first four Navy Otters, three were recently delivered RCAF examples (Numbers 60, 62 and 66) donated to replace Otters delayed by the strike at DHC in 1955. They were based at the McMurdo Sound air operations centre, located at the eastern corner of the Ross Ice Shelf.

VX-6's operational plan was to support the establishment of bases at, first, Little America, 400 miles west of McMurdo at Kainan Bay, near sites occupied previously by four earlier Little Americas. There a fuel farm and airstrip would be constructed. From there, land elements would drive southwest and inland to the site of another base, to be named Byrd Station, after pioneer polar aviator Rear Adm. Richard Byrd, a U.S. Navy hero (still alive at the time), who, on a previous trip, had named the territory west of the ice shelf where Byrd Base would be established Marie Byrd Land, after his wife.

Otters would scout land routes to each site, supply travelling parties moving along those routes and, of course, conduct search-and-rescue (SAR) operations— sometimes looking for another Otter. Ground parties travelled by tractor trains, which were subject to countless unseen but deep crevasses, mazes of them, between Little America and Byrd Station. Pilots were only slightly less vulnerable than tractor and bulldozer drivers. Aircraft were consumed by whiteouts and wrenched out of control by sudden winds and downdrafts generated by Antarctica's unexplored mountain ranges.

VX-6's sixth Otter loss: BuNo 142427 (79) took a party of scientists from McMurdo to Cape Chocolate, a distance of 30 miles, and taxied back after its fuselage buckled October 22, 1958. VIA PETER M. BOWERS

The first Otter delivered to the Navy, 142424 (DHC Number 76), crashed within days of its arrival, December 22, 1955, striking its tail on the ice so hard on takeoff that a passenger was thrown out of the airplane. The following February two more were lost.

One of those went down February 3, 1956, with six aboard, after straying off course in a whiteout. After days of waiting, pilot Paul Streich and his passengers decided they might be beyond rescue, and set out to walk the 100 miles to the coast. vx-6's Doug Cordiner searched every day but found only the engineless hulk of Byrd's Fokker trimotor, left there in 1929. When an SAR Otter was unable to land at Little America because of bad weather and returned to McMurdo, Deepfreeze commander Rear-Adm. George Dufek ordered it loaded aboard an icebreaker and shipped there. As it was being unloaded, a cable broke and the Otter was damaged

Russ Bannock (far left) and Punch Dickins (far right) flank U.S. Navy officers from Squadron vx-6 and an unidentified civilian U.S. naval Bureau of Weapons buyer in front of Otters bound for the Antarctic, October 1956. The Otter behind Punch Dickins, BuNo 144670, was still active with the Navy in the early 1990s. DHC 4351

The Trans Antarctic Otter, May 1958. Otters left outdoors in any degree of wind want to fly, so Royal Air Force XL 710 (126) was buried for the 1958 Antarctic winter after making its historic flight across the continent earlier that year. DHC 8192

beyond repair. (The crisis deepened further when a Neptune carrying a parachute rescue team from Naval Air Station Patuxent River, Maryland, to Antarctica crashed in the Venezuelan jungle along the Orinoco River, precipitating another SAR operation to find the would-be rescuers.)

One account of the week-long search credits a helicopter off-course in another whiteout with stumbling over the party, but Hayes says it was the fourth VX-6 Otter that found the Streich Otter party 40 miles from the crash site. Three of VX-6's four Otters were thus written off during the first few months of Deepfreeze, including one with only 29 hours in the air.

VX-6's three strike-delayed Otters were delivered in March 1956, and an order for six more was filled in September and October 1956. That makes 13 VX-6 Otters, of the 14 Otters the U.S. Navy operated.[1]

That fourteenth Otter is the most famous Otter ever. It joined vx-6 in July 1958 after service with a Royal Air Force crew supporting the British Commonwealth Trans Antarctic Expedition that aimed to cross the continent on the ground for the first time, from the Weddell Sea to the Ross Sea, under Sir Vivian Fuchs, an experienced Antarctic explorer.

Thus they would fulfill the dream of Sir Ernest Shackleton. The expedition was a joint venture by Britain, New Zealand, Australia and South Africa. New Zealand's contribution included the famous Trans Antarctic Beaver and a contingent under Sir Edmund Hillary (recent Everest conqueror), who would supervise stocking the depots for Fuchs's party from the South Pole to Scott Base on McMurdo Sound. The Royal Air Force contributed a couple of Auster light aircraft, communication equipment and four aircrew led by Squadron Leader John Lewis. But Austers carry only a pilot and passenger and a lunch bag for each. To stock caches and supply the trekkers, a bigger aircraft would be required. After studying its requirements, the expedition bought an Otter and turned it over to the RAF.[2]

Otter Number 126, the only Otter ever operated by the RAF, was painted orange and delivered to Lewis at Downsview July 11, 1956, equipped with a 177-gallon long-distance tank that brought its fuel capacity to 355 gallons and doubled its nominal range to 1,600 miles. It was ferried to Hatfield by Lewis and Flt. Lt. Gordon Haslop and their two ground crewmen via Greenland, Iceland and Prestwick, Scotland. At Hatfield it was, quote, winterized, unquote: there is no mention of a heater or de-icing equipment, but it was given a heavy-duty battery, upgraded from 12- to 24-volt electrics and fitted with radio altimeter and compass, Search and Rescue Aircraft Homing (SARAH) beacon and receiver direction-finding equipment, and Bendix polar compass and gyro system. Number 126 was serialled RAF aircraft XL 710 and crated.

That gear, valuable as it would be, hardly transformed XL 710 from a Visual Flight Rules (clear weather) airplane into one equipped for blind flying. In aviation, as in life, it is often better to be lucky than good. Often in Antarctica it was impossible to see when cloud merged with snow-covered terrain, as was the case on a flight into Shackleton Base on the Weddell Sea shortly after XL 710 arrived there. Guided by its SARAH radio beacon, the Otter began to descend, only to strike something with its skis and rebound upward. The unseen ridge became known as the Touchdown Hills.

Part of the expedition's 1957 program was to close down Shackleton Base and move inland to South Ice Base. One of the XL 710's more memorable accomplishments was to move an entire hut, the weight of which apparently exceeded the Otter's maximum payload, from Shackleton to South Ice. Another trip involved carrying a 12-foot sledge, 10 dogs—which seem to have enjoyed flying in the Otter—and supplies for two men for 30 days.[3]

The eighth U.S. Navy Otter of 14, BuNo 144699 (148), pictured here during flight-testing in September 1956, survived its arduous Antarctic duties with the Americans and was turned over to the Belgians in late 1965, only to be written off by them at Sanae Station, Antarctica, on February 9, 1970. DHC 4269

One Antarctic distance that was fairly well known was the mileage from South Ice over the South Pole to Scott Base (near McMurdo on the Ross Sea), the route XL 710 was scheduled to cover late in 1957 to survey what lay ahead of the trans-Antarctic trekkers setting out from South Ice. The distance is 1,450 miles, which, even with this special Otter's extended 14-hour range (in still air, at that), "places a premium on exact navigation," as Hayes so delicately puts it. Hayes goes on to detail the airmanship that went into the attempt at a first single-engine trans-Antarctic flight:

An astro compass was mounted on the instrument panel coaming in front of the copilot, "and with this the true course could be checked using the sun. The Bendix Polar Path gyro acted as the master directional indicator, checked for heading precision every 20 minutes with the astro compass. An ordinary directional gyro calibrated for 80 degrees South acted as a standby gyro. A drift sight mounted on the inside of the cockpit door, used in conjunction with the radio altimeter, gave drift and ground speed."

"Only those with an adventurous turn of mind would have wished to be on that flight," Basil Clarke writes. Yes, they could have set down in an emergency at the pole—if the weather was right. (The South Pole is at approximately 10,000 feet above sea level.) Yes, the Americans or New Zealanders would have rescued them in the event of an unscheduled stop, "but the experience, to put it mildly, would have been unpleasant."

There was no shortage of bad omens. The trip was scheduled for December 29, 1957. The ground expedition had left South Ice for the Pole. When the Otter and its four-man RAF crew took off that day, South Ice was deserted. But bad weather and low cloud made it impossible to survey the conditions the Fuchs ground party would encounter. Worse, the Otter's wings were icing up. "The somewhat demoralized crew," as Hayes describes them, turned back. Finding South Ice under those conditions was no sure bet until they spotted the tracks of Fuchs's outbound tractors and landed in 100-yard visibility. Then they reopened the coccooned base. The abortive seven-hour flight had used up much of the Otter's overall fuel reserve. What remained at South Ice left no margin.

The Americans at Ellsworth, some 50 miles along the coast from Shackleton, agreed to fly aviation gasoline to South Ice but were prevented from doing so by the weather until January 6, 1958. Weather forecasts from Fuchs and the Pole for that day were encouraging, so Lewis and Haslop and their engineers, Peter Weston and Taffy Williams, took off for a second time at 11:48 p.m., flew in clear weather and passed the Fuchs party barely more than two hours later. They arrived at the South Pole at 4:28 p.m., spotting the station there from 2,000 feet, and although they were still less than halfway to their destination at Scott Base, XL 710 and the four RAF flyers circled the pole, making a three-minute flight around the world by crossing

The last active U.S. Navy Otter, NU-1B BuNo 144670 (151), looking well used at the Naval Test Pilot School, NAS Patuxent River, during the early 1990s. In September 1996 this aircraft was 40 years old. BOB FOWLER VIA WAYNE MUTZA

every meridian and flying from Tuesday to Wednesday and back to Tuesday again.[4]

On approach to Scott Base, XL 710 was escorted down to the runway by two Otters from McMurdo, which peeled away as the RAF Otter touched down. XL 710 had covered 1,430 statute miles in 11 hours and one minute.[5]

When Fuchs arrived at Scott Base, Otter XL 710's immediate task was finished. After further service with the New Zealand Antarctic flight alongside the equally well-known Trans Antarctic Beaver, XL 710 joined the U.S. Navy in July 1958, becoming naval aviation Bureau No. 147574.

It flew 148 hours with VX-6 to April 1960. In response to an appeal from New Zealand to replace its Trans Antarctic Beaver, which was lost January 15, 1960, in a whiteout on the Beardmore Glacier, VX-6 turned BuNo 147574 over to the Kiwis.

VX-6 was still flying Otters in Antarctica during the early 1960s, but by the early 1970s the squadron had been honoured with having its unit identity promoted to Antarctic Development Squadron VXE-6 and its equipment upgraded and standardized with turbine-powered four-engine Lockheed C-130 Hercules transports on ski/wheels and twin-turbine Huey Iroquois helicopters. The military's most sincere compliment to a retired aircraft type is often the quality of its successors: it seems fair to observe that it took Hueys and Hercules transports to replace Otters in the Antarctic.

One of three RCAF Otters passed on to the U.S. Navy's Antarctic expedition, in transit to the south polar region. BuNo 144259 (60) was written off February 3, 1956, when it became lost and went down in a white-out after just 29 flying hours. Another Otter was lost during the search. DHC 5855

Number 126 became known as the Trans Antarctic Otter after a complete overhaul by de Havilland Aircraft of New Zealand (Wellington), but it never returned to the continent for which it was named. Tendered for sale with the closing of New Zealand's Antarctic flight detachment with 508 hard-working hours on its airframe, 126 was bought sight unseen by Georgian Bay Airlines and shipped to Parry Sound, Ontario, where, as CF-PNV on amphibious floats, it spent the summer of 1964 working along the subarctic coasts of Hudson Bay and James Bay.[6]

In returning to civilian life in Canada, PNV once again pioneered. Most of the Otters that survived military life have since returned to Canada or become the backbone of short-haul civil aviation in Alaska.

The Trans Antarctic Otter's story is representative of the 22 other Otters and Beavers that supported IGY in the harshest flying conditions anywhere. Seven nations involved with the IGY explorations of Antarctica used Beavers or Otters: Australia, Britain, Chile, Japan (their Beavers blessed in a Shinto ceremony), New Zealand, Norway and the United States.

Norway's pair of Otters, from the Royal Norwegian Air Force, flew 36,000 miles and were the platforms from which 3,000 aerial photos were taken of Antarctica's Queen Maud Land. The Norwegian base was called Otter Bay. Although Canada sent no expedition to Antarctic, de Havilland of Canada made a fairly decent contribution to IGY on its own.[7]

CHAPTER TEN

Civil Otters: Firebirds, Peacekeepers and Wardair

Nineteen-fifty-three was a year of important aviation innovations: the first production supersonic fighters to go into service flew that year, and the Boeing Airplane Company was building the Dash-80 prototype that led to its revolutionary 707 airliner. The 707 set intercontinental city-to-city scheduled service times that are reduced by very little today.[1]

At the same time humankind was being treated to the mixed blessings of aircraft that could fly faster, airplanes that could fly (and land) more slowly were bringing more tangible benefits to some of those who needed them the most: the natives of Canada's Arctic and Alaska, and the prospectors searching for mineral wealth in the world's hot and cold hinterlands.

Even as military minds created new combat roles for Otters, those same airplanes were being painted white, their sides lettered UNITED NATIONS, and they were enforcing fragile ceasefires in the Middle East, Kashmir, Yemen, the Congo and New Guinea. Survivors of these wars were often their most wretched victims.

Otters evacuated refugees and flew in the Red Cross before any other form of transport could get to them. The Otter became synonymous with the new post-Suez concept of peacekeeping: the U.N. operated 14 repainted Royal Canadian Air Force Otters and eight of its own (two of those donated by Norway).

Max Ward's Otter began scheduled services in the Far North and wrought a lifestyle change as significant as any since the Inuit had moved out of their igloos.

In the Far North, as in cities all over North America and Europe, one of the fundamental architectural ideas of the time was the modular building—a structure that could be built to almost any size simply by adding the requisite number of four-by-eight-foot panels, often of simple plywood. Entire settlements in Canada's Far North were built in modular fashion. The first of these modular buildings were constructed there in 1953. They were assembled on-site from sheets of four-by-eight plywood brought in by Max Ward in Otter CF-GBY, the first aircraft that could carry such bulky cargo into such remote settlements as mining sites, and the only one of its kind in that part of the North until well into the late 1950s. GBY could also carry 16-foot two-by-four lumber for framing buildings, and Ward notes that many contractors and mining companies ordered boards in that length "just for the novelty of it, even if they were going to cut it afterwards."

Ever since, Ward has said, he could date any building in the North constructed with four-by-eight plywood panels: it had to have been built after 1953.

Perhaps the most significant benefit of the Otter was in the daily lives of miners and prospectors. Suddenly they could afford the very basics of life. Proper framing materials made possible bigger tents in which a man could stand up on a board floor, and the availability of cots consigned the normal bedding of pine boughs back to the outdoors. The flat floors made good, solid tables useable for the first time in mining camps. Stoves that could burn safely all night made their appearance in places where overnight temperatures routinely dropped to -50°F. Not to mention foodstuffs: prospectors could now eat food that came in neither cans nor sacks.

Ward allows that the same or larger cargo could have been carried north in the aerial workhorse of that era, the DC-3, or in its more plentiful war-surplus military C-47 variant, many of which had huge double cargo doors. Chartering a DC-3 was an expensive proposition, though. Only government bodies and large mining companies could afford that luxury. And, of course, you could hardly land a DC-3 on the Mackenzie River or a small snow-covered airstrip. The arrival of the Otter gave shippers and mines a freight-rate alternative that cut air shipping costs by two-thirds.[2]

Even in Yellowknife, a big settlement at the time, the Otter had a notable impact. Yellowknife, today the capital and only city of the western Northwest Territories, is

named after the aboriginal people who lived there when Europeans arrived. It is located on the north arm of Great Slave Lake, 621 air miles north of Edmonton. During the slack 1953–54 winter period, Ward demonstrated the new possibilities by renovating his office shack into what he would refer to as "a genuine airline building," with a proper waiting room, dispatcher's office and two other offices:

"The executive suite was only ten-by-ten, but it had a big window cut into it. In fact, the windows I cut around that building caused quite a stir in that town. A number of the oldtimers who came by gave me a blast because I would lose so much heat out the windows, and when I explained that I had double-glazed them, they looked at me as if I had taken leave of my senses. Small windows are what you have in the North, anybody knows that."

Ward, like most pioneers something of an iconoclast, went so far as to paint the walls of his headquarters in pastel colours, since paint was now available in Yellowknife. He took static for that, too.

Max Ward with his first airplane, a postwar DH.83 Fox Moth he bought in 1946: it cost $10,000 with wheels, floats, skis and—merciful heavens—a sheltering DHC-designed canopy. DHC 10951

When Constable Donald P. Mattocks of the Royal Canadian Mounted Police saw Ward fly into Aklavik, on the West Channel of the Mackenzie River delta not far from the Yukon border, in August 1954, at the controls of the biggest single-engine airplane Mattocks had ever set eyes on, he knew that a new era had dawned. The Otter looked like the right airplane to open up that part of the Arctic.

Aklavik defined remote: 674 miles by air north of Yellowknife and about 62 miles south of the Beaufort Sea. But little did the constable know that the Otter would do more than connect Aklavik more reliably with civilization.

On that late-summer flight, made at a time of year when the sun shines nearly 24 hours a day, Ward was carrying, among others, Pierre Berton, a best-selling Canadian author and native of the North, then a journalist on assignment; Jean Lesage, a future premier of Quebec; and Gordon Robertson, a future federal cabinet secretary. Lesage and Robertson's mission was to scout around Aklavik to look for new townsites as the town, melting the permafrost underneath it, sank into the mud and was threatened by flooding from the mighty Mackenzie. A new site was found to the east on the Mackenzie delta, and the work of constructing the new town began during

The first Quantas Otter of four, VH-EAW (241), being refuelled in Papua New Guinea in 1959. Despite having been delivered in early 1958 (as an amphibian), the airplane still looks new. DHC 9496

the late 1950s. That flight was the beginning of today's capital of the western Northwest Territories and of the largest settlement north of the Arctic Circle, Inuvik (Inuit for "place of man"). The Otter was instrumental in the founding of Inuvik.

So when Max Ward says the Otter changed life as it is lived in the Far North, he is hardly exaggerating. It changed his life as well. Ward's former partnership, Yellowknife Airways, had gone bankrupt in 1949. With help from the Canadian government's Business Development Bank, he had CF-GBY, the fifth Otter off the line, committed before, strictly speaking, he had his air transport licence.

Wardair eventually operated four Otters, moving medical personnel, missionaries, geologists and prospectors around the upper Arctic and hauling furs, building materials and other less likely cargoes. Ward flew dairy cows from Hay River, on lower Great Slave Lake, to Yellowknife; one of his pilots helped capture three muskoxen by buzzing their defensive circle and flew them south for an ill-fated experiment in crossbreeding them with Aberdeen cattle; and Wardair flew beavers from Prince Albert, Saskatchewan, to Fort Rae in a failed attempt to start a beaver colony in the Northwest Territories.

"In short," Ward writes, "we would fly anything anywhere, and frequently did. On one trip, I flew an upright piano, which I covered with canvas and tied to the float of the Otter, from Yellowknife to the Discovery Mines [whose owners had put up the first $25,000 of the price of GBY]. One of the pilots, Hank Hicks, was playing the piano when we lashed it to the float. The landing, with about fifteen hundred pounds of piano on one side"—hopefully the right side—"had to be very slick indeed, or we would have struck a sour note."

Of course the police were regular clients of Wardair's. (In time, Ward bought a fifth Otter from the RCMP: C-FMPY, the 324th built). Ward also kept in touch with the Mounties to let them know about unusual movements. Once he was unloading a passenger's unusually heavy baggage and asked, "My God, what have you got in there, gold bricks?" The passenger laughed but made no comment. The kicker is that, of course, they *were* gold bricks. The regular weekly two-brick shipment from the Consolidated Mine was in his bag, and the regular mine bag contained "two bars of the finest-quality lead." The thief escaped to Cuba.

There was a swashbuckling quality to almost everyone who lived in the North at that time. Mattocks remembers one of Wardair's Otters being flown by a character named Rowdy Rutherford.[3]

The Otter made Wardair. By 1957 Ward was operating a Bristol 170 Freighter (and four more soon after), and by 1961 he had a DC-6, which he put to use during the summer season flying fun-seekers to Europe. Ward was a launch customer for the Twin Otter in 1963, by which time his bush outfit was Canada's third-largest airline, already flying big jets and poised to rise into the DC-10/747 league.[4]

The sophistication of the Otter's powerplant installation and double-slotted flap-aileron systems belie the simplicity and ruggedness of its basic design. Like the Beaver, it was intended for use in wilderness and arctic conditions, and it shared many of the Beaver's little bush-pilot conveniences, such as the underfloor fuel tanks that could be filled—unlike wing tanks—by a person standing on the ground. And it was fixable in the field.

In 1958 Max Ward's first Otter, GBY, was on Baffin Island supplying a Distant Early Warning (DEW) Line construction site. Baffin Island, certainly distant, was a long way from GBY's home tundra, the western Arctic, but the DEW-Line project drew every flyable tramp transport, from ancient Junkers W34s to Curtiss C-46s, into its whatever-it-costs Cold War orbit. Far from Yellowknife, GBY came to grief.

An overnight gale-force wind blew the Otter backwards onto a boulder-strewn knoll. The vertical tail was pounded to junk down to the dorsal fin, and the port wing was ripped to shreds outboard of the flap. There were countless dents and gouges, but it was the damage to the tail and wing that led most of the radar site contractor's personnel to conclude that it would never fly again.

The same Karl Frisk who joined DHC in 1951—in time to work that summer on the third Otter prototype, Arthur Fecteau's CF-ODH—had continued his nomadic wanderings within the aircraft industry, on one notable occasion quitting a job at lunchtime and finding himself rebuilding a Cessna with its belly ripped out in another company's Vancouver South Airport hangar at 1:00 p.m. No matter how hard he tried, Frisk could not keep himself unemployed.

It was that restlessness that took him and Denny McCartney to Baffin Island to save CF-GBY. McCartney was a foreman at Vancouver's Boeing plant during the war, licence-building PBY-5A Canso amphibians for the U.S. and Royal navies, then bomb-bays for B-29 Superforts. McCartney had 11 children: he would fix anything for a buck. Frisk was the same, but for no reason anyone could think of. They made a good duo.

Along with the major assemblies they picked up at Downsview on their way north, Frisk acquired a bottle of rye whiskey. Neither he nor McCartney was much of a drinker. In fact, McCartney, perhaps because he was Irish, objected. But Frisk, who in his engineering career on two continents had acquired tools in British, metric and North American sizes, thought the firewater might come in handy.

The bane of any remote aircraft rebuild is usually not major parts. The major parts needed are usually obvious. Where rescuers run short is on the nickel-and-dime stuff: fabric and dope, sheet-metal, glue, rivets. Frisk and McCartney used proper aircraft-grade fasteners and rivets until they ran out of those; then they used sheet-metal screws they found on-site; and finally they resorted to wood screws and stove bolts and nuts to hold everything in more or less one piece.

One of the first of an eventual 15 RCAF Otters to see United Nations service in three hot spots, this one is loading mail in Egypt in April 1957. Others supported peacekeepers in Kashmir and New Guinea. DHC 5299

One of the most critical structural components on an airplane is its wing spar. It turned out to be the simplest part to repair on GBY. Frisk took strips of steel and welded them to the inner surfaces of the inboard wing-spar box, possibly doubling its strength where the box was double-walled and depending on the strength of the added steel to absorb the tortional, or twisting, loads imposed by the double-slotted flaps and especially the ailerons out near the tips.

Karl Frisk still has the flap-aileron centre bracket he hammered from sheet steel stock, blacksmith-style, with a bolt-and-nut crosspiece offset with washers to the correct position to take the control loads and transmit them to the rods and bell-cranks that actuate the wing's moveable surfaces. It was crude, but it worked.[5]

This photo is dated October 1957, so presumably this Otter is an RCAF machine, since there were no direct U.N. Otter procurements at that time. It is an early-series DHC-3 with counterweight prop. Seven RCAF Otters served at El Arish with the U.N. Emergency Force's 115 Air Transport Unit, El Arish, four of them from December 1956. DHC 4670

The final step was to have the boulder-strewn field into which GBY had been blown bulldozed. The heavy-equipment operators at this DEW-line site were not being paid to remove boulders, but neither were they permitted to consume alcohol. The prohibition against whiskey only made Frisk's bottle more desirable to the operators. Soon GBY had a runway as good as any on Baffin Island. GBY flew out—although, the amazed pilot said, the left wingtip tended to fly a little low.

The Ontario Department of Lands and Forests, a prime user of the provincial air service's flying equipment, had been working on systems for water-bombing forest fires since before the end of the war. It was the Otter that, for the first time, married adequate load-carrying performance with the ability to fill its tanks while still on the step on small lakes and then get away over the timber that usually surrounds them, bringing theories about quick-response fire-fighting that had been dreamed of for decades to fruition.

Carl C. Crossley, a veteran Ontario Provincial Air Service pilot, had a conversation one day in 1944 with Pete Marchildon, the district forester at North Bay, who had read about the Allied strategic bombing campaign in Europe that was reaching its peak at the time. Marchildon wondered whether, instead of raining down fire and brimstone, OPAS' airplanes might not put out forest fires by water-bombing them. "At first," writes Bruce West in *The Firebirds*, a history of OPAS, "Carl Crossley thought Pete's suggestion was a little far-fetched."[6]

But Crossley kept thinking about it. He fitted a tank into the open cockpit of a Fairchild KR-34 and ran some complicated plumbing down to the water rudders on its floats to create a drop pattern in the KR-34's wake, but that airplane never seemed

Air Fecteau Ltee operated the world's largest commercial Otter fleet at one time, a total of a dozen passing through the outfit's hands, starting with the third one built, C-FODH. This picture was taken in July 1957, when Fecteau had owned his second Otter, CF-JUH (214)—possibly this one—for two months. DHC 6735

to create enough pressure at the uptake to fill the tank. Nevertheless, it was with this rig that Crossley first water-bombed a fire (after pumping water into the tank on land). Frank MacDougall, the flying deputy minister of lands and forests, who had a habit of dropping in unannounced on the many remote outposts of his department, offered Crossley the key inspiration: skip the tank in the cockpit, he said, and use the floats as your tanks.

Crossley's next experiments involved equipping a Noorduyn Norseman, which he considered the most suitable testbed with its 600hp R-1340 engine, with specially modified floats that could scoop up more than 54 gallons of water each while taxiing on a lake and then release it over fires in nine seconds flat. He worked on perfecting the pickup and release equipment through the final winter of the war at the air service shops in Sault Ste. Marie. Crossley's drawings and a set of pontoons were shipped to the MacDonald Brothers plant in Winnipeg, modified and installed. The release controls were added at the Noorduyn factory in Montreal. Crossley's system had the water drop from an outlet at the rear of the floats, near the water rudder.

As soon as the Norseman was ready, Crossley flew it to the OPAS Timagami base, where that same day, August 26, 1945, he extinguished a lightning fire in a hilly, inaccessible area in the Elk Lake district with three passes in his Norseman.

Just as this technique of using floats as water tanks for fire-bombing was proven, it was promptly abandoned, in favour of filling paper bags with water and dropping those—despite the fact that a 35-pound bag of water sometimes scored a direct hit only to scatter the embers, setting new fires in the underbrush. The Beaver's ventral hatch was an OPAS requirement, ordered with water-bag bombing and fish planting in mind. Needless to say, there were too many things that could go wrong at too many points with the bag method, and it almost killed off interest in quick-response fire-bombing through the early 1950s.

Most forest fire suppression was being done by such big war-surplus bombers as Consolidated PBY Canso amphibians, modified by specialist firms like Field Aviation to drop water rather than depth charges. Grumman Avengers, B-17 Flying Fortresses and other warbirds were converted for water-bombing in other parts of Canada, but they needed bases with concrete runways, and the Cansos needed big bodies of water to load. The plumbing for these strategic water-bombers was being developed by Field Aviation's chief engineer, Knox Hawkshaw. But the concept of a smaller, tactical water-bomber awaited the right vehicle.

The problem for OPAS was that the northernmost reaches of Ontario are far from concrete runways and dotted with small lakes. Often, putting water on a fire as soon as possible was the difference between a small outbreak and the kind of major conflagration that sucks up armies of smoke-eaters. OPAS was still committed to dropping bags on fires as a quick-response strategy when the Beaver appeared. The Otter opened up new possibilities.

Although the OPAS was interested in a bigger Beaver for other reasons, the availability of its doubled payload (more than that, compared with the Norseman) revived the float-tank water-bomber idea in 1957. Thomas Cooke, another ingenious OPAS pilot-engineer, revived the idea. Cooke was concerned with dropping enough water in a single mass to make extinguishing a blaze likely. He followed Crossley's path from a tank within the airplane—at the Otter's centre of gravity—to focussing on the floats. An engineer named George Gill mentioned to Cooke over coffee, at the same OPAS station where Crossley developed his system, that tubular open-top tanks on top of each pontoon could be made to roll sideways to dump their load and then be returned by lead counterweights to the upright position for the next refill. The rolling tanks were soon perfected for installation on Otters earmarked for the quick-response forest fire-fighting role. Each tank could take on 80 gallons, or 800 pounds, of water, which could be picked up in a 600-foot run.[7]

That July Cooke held a mile-long strip of fire at bay in the Sudbury District, performing continuous drops from the first fire-fighting Otter while crews made their way to the blaze. By 1958 all OPAS Otters and Beavers had been modified with the float-mounted tanks, which had already been improved by being rigged to roll inward, toward each other, thus consolidating their drop pattern. A further upgrade was to install a single, larger 210-gallon tank between the Otter floats, cleaning up their aerodynamics and making the tops of the floats available once again as walkways during docking.

Two days' work during consecutive summers show how far the OPAS had pushed the aerial fire-fighting state of the art. The service's Otters were on call to anywhere in Canada they could fly in time to be useful. Newfoundland was three days' seat-of-the-pants flying for Otter CF-ODL, piloted by Tom Cooke and George Beauchene without navaids through high winds, fog and rainstorms in August 1961. (Cooke's report on the mission, otherwise glowing, requested automatic direction finder equipment for the OPAS Otters.) Their first day, August 14, assigned to protect fishing outports from the 400,000-acre fire near Traverse Brook, ODL dropped 38 loads in six hours, 40 minutes. The next day, assigned to a three-mile section of fire line in a combined assault with ground crews, they flew 10 hours and 45 minutes, dropping 94 loads. The following June 9, called to a fire near Maniwaki, Quebec, OPAS Otter CF-ODW, with Cooke at the controls and a three-and-a-half-minute turnaround from a lake one mile from the fire, dropped 108 loads (or 17,280 gallons) in eight hours, five minutes.

Commuter pioneer: Taxi Air Group Otter N96T, an amphibian for Detroit-Cleveland intercity service most of the year, was refitted with wheels by winter for Miami–Florida Keys service. TAG operated Otters from 1956 to 1959. DHC 3256 VIA PETER M. BOWERS

The advent of the Turbo Beaver in 1965 inspired another reversal in water-bombing technology—a return to the Carl Crossley technique of using the floats themselves as tanks (after the 210-gallon belly tank had become standard on Otters). Field Aviation had by then developed pickup and discharge systems that used doors in the inner planing surfaces of the floats to concentrate the 140-gallon drop—not as much as an Otter could manage, but in a faster, shorter-STOL package that could load up in five to eight seconds and 400 feet. It was the turbo's power increase that made this quicker quick-response possible. West informs us that Beauchene once extinguished four separate small fires while flying an entirely unrelated mission.[8]

Later, Twin Otters duplicated the Turbo Beaver's fire-fighting exploits, but with the same Field Aviation equipment that enables them to be used for everyday utility flying and fire-fighting without making changes, they are able to load at the rate of 450 gallons in the same five to eight seconds, over 525 feet. That makes 4,500 pounds of water per trip. Since the Twin Otter (like any aircraft) has a rising payload as the weight of the fuel in its tanks declines, OPAS Twin Otters are equipped with a Field innovation "Dial-O-Matic" cockpit control designed by Hawkshaw that retracts the underwater probe at any desired gross weight as it taxis, enabling the pilot to fly with maximum loads every time.[9]

Facing page: Early stealth technology: RCAF Otter 3692, the Quiet Otter, with its new prop and mufflers, as modified in March 1957. Later a bigger muffler was installed in the cabin, making the Quiet Otter even sneakier. DHC 5073

CHAPTER ELEVEN

Altered Otters

Until very recently, Bob Bator was the chief engineer of Harbour Air Seaplanes, which flies the world's largest fleet of de Havilland Beavers out of its facility at the mouth of the Fraser River, south of Vancouver, British Columbia. Bator was happy to tell me the identities, histories and idiosyncrasies of the dozen-plus Harbour Air Beavers, which have become emblematic of the operation as a whole.

"But," Bob said, pointing to an air-to-air colour photo of one of Harbour Air's pair of Turbo Otters, "*this* is my favourite airplane. If you want to know anything about these, just come by the hangar."

So I did. Bob was pleased. "It's a nice airplane," he said, understating his affection for the Otter much as a coach with the best goalkeeper in the league might call him "a good goalie."

"It's come a long way in its lifetime."

To say the least. And Bob Bator has had a lot to do with the improvements.[1]

Two-thirds of the 466 DHC-3 Otters built were delivered to military air arms. This is a remarkable figure for an airplane that, like the Beaver, is hardly an instrument of mass destruction.[2]

One might ask what the military saw in the Otter. But the military mind does not always get full credit for its creativity. For some personnel in U.S. Army and Navy aviation, the Otter was a kind of blank canvas onto which almost any wartime wish (except for speed) could be projected. Only aircraft that are easy to fly get to be disfigured in all the ways the Otter was. There was, to cite an example almost at random, a joint Army-Navy program to see how the Otter would fare as a water-skiplane. And thus was it proven: the Otter could walk—or at least taxi—on water.[3]

If the Otter's versatility needed further demonstration, Otter spyplanes made the point yet one more time. There were many Otter intelligence-gathering platforms, but the most picturesque and well documented are the Quiet Otter and the Radar Otter. Both appeared early during the Otter's career with the U.S. Army, around 1957.[4]

In May of that year DHC modified RCAF Otter 3692 to see how quietly an Otter could be made to fly. The engineering was less conceptual than a relentless suppression of whatever noise was left after the last modification. The changes began with the Otter's loud powerplant.

First, a five-wooden-blade propeller, with each blade paddle width and the pitch fixed at a fine, nearly flat setting, was installed. (Test pilot Bob Fowler believes the hub for this prop came from a Hawker Sea Fury, and its five large blades were custom-built of wood.) Downstream effects of what looked from the cockpit like a solid flickering disc when it was spinning were revealed by taping tufts to the aft end of the engine cowling. The pitch had to be manually adjusted on the ground between flights to find the optimum angle. The penalty of the five fine-pitch paddle-bladed airscrew was poor takeoff performance and low cruise speed.

Two huge automobile-type mufflers were hung on each side of the fuselage, the extractor exhausts were removed, and a single narrow pipe was run from the engine's manifold, through the mufflers, to pipes that ran back to the freight door. Later the mufflers were relocated into the airplane cabin, and a different gearbox was tried on the engine.

Various small aerodynamic experiments were carried out on the leading edges of Otter 3692's wing, including stall bars taped about three feet out from the cockpit on each side.

"It was loads of fun," Fowler says, adding that he once test-flew the Quiet Otter over Lake Simcoe, north of Toronto. With the sun behind him and reflecting off the lake, he had a psychedelic experience: the intense light, glinting back at him from

This photo of the revised in-cabin muffler installation in the Quiet Otter was taken in October 1958, more than a year and a half after the rest of 3692's modifications were made. DHC 9011

each wide, laminated and polished blade, had a strobe effect "that," he says, "was really weird." *Really* weird.

But not as strange as the sensation of sitting on the ground in a normally quite loud airplane, listening to internal moving parts inside the engine—gears, pistons, tappets, connecting rods, their sounds normally overwhelmed by combustion and propeller noise—clicking and tapping merrily away.

The tests were held at (as Neal remembers it) Naval Air Station Patuxent River. Neal was ordered to approach sound equipment on the ground from a certain angle, at various altitudes, some as low as 200 feet. But he felt these demonstration guidelines failed to show what the airplane could do. Why not sneak up on these guys?

So Neal, not the sort to be regimented, changed the approach angle. Trees ringed three-quarters of the test area diameter, and he used them to screen his turn as he flew. "And they never heard me until I was right over them. I could see how much I startled them."

The Radar Otter still confounds aviation historians. And yet the four- to five-foot-diameter spheres that were hung well outboard under the wing of U.S. Army serial 55-3272 made more sense as external payload than a lot of items Otters have carried in flight. At least they balanced each other out.

Top secret: The Otter could walk on water—as long as it kept moving. U.S. Army U-1A 53318 being tested on hydro-skis, somewhere in the U.S.A., November 1958.
VIA PETER M. BOWERS

Before its time: Officially destroyed in 1973, the former CF-MES, later prototype Cox DHC-3T Turbo Otter first flew in September 1978 but was still not certificated when seen at Renton airport in 1981. PETER M. BOWERS

"So much drag," Neal reflects. The round spheres contained radar in its pre-transistor, vacuum-tube form. But apparently the round shape enabled the Radar Otter to make a 360-degree sweep of the ground the Otter was flying over.

"It was still manoeuvrable," Neal says, ever forgiving of the idiosyncrasies of aircraft. "It was easy to handle. It just didn't have the speed."[5]

The malady that Neal observed when he flight-tested the Otter in 1952—lack of power—has been the subject of clinical research since 1971–72, when Downsview took up the question. It has been treatable since 1982, and curable in an increasing number of ways since then. Aside from the standard R-1340's weight and lack of horsepower, the passing years have meant parts have become more scarce and overhauls more expensive.

By 1971, 10 years after it appeared, increasingly powerful developments of the PT6 turbine engine were becoming available. The PT6A-34 was sized right for the Otter, and DHC's Advanced Design devised a factory conversion. Their studies showed worthwhile performance gains, but the price of a new PT6 was not much less than that of a complete standard Otter, which cost around $80,000 at that point. DHC's experience with the Turbo Beaver—60 sold between 1961 and the end of production in 1967—showed there was a limit to what the average owner-operator could afford, no matter how impressive the takeoff, how long the time-between-overhauls (TBO), or how easily available the cheap turbine fuel, kerosene. Downsview dropped the project.[6]

Shortly afterward, the first attempt was made to mate an Otter with a turbine, at Western Rotorcraft Ltd. of Seattle. The turbine was a Garrett AiResearch TPE331, the Otter was N3904 (54) and the marriage did not take. Restored to R-1340 power, N3904 went to Alaska.

Bob Bator, retired in 1998 as chief engineer of Harbour Air Seaplanes, Vancouver, and originator of a dozen Otter modifications, photographed at the controls of his favourite airplane. HARBOUR AIR VIA CALVIN REICH

In 1975 the idea of a turbine-powered Otter was revived by Ray Cox, an Edmonton-based specialist in recovering crashed aircraft from out-of-the-way places. Enough of these recoveries were Otters for Cox to be aware that the airframe could last indefinitely, but the original powerplant was driving the airplane into retirement. Cox saw the PT6A-27 as the answer.

One of Cox's wrecks was CF-MES (421), classified destroyed in August 1973 after an engine failure at Cambridge Bay, Northwest Territories. This became the prototype Cox Turbo Otter. Cox enlisted the help of an engineer named Aimo Pitkanen; making MES flyable again, an ambitious goal in itself, was the least of their worries.

"Many problems were encountered," Karl Hayes summarizes, "mostly to do with weight and balance. It is typical of aeronautical engineering that every solution seems to create new problems and aggravate old ones, until, in time, the total solution falls into place."[7]

The 42-gallon rear tank was relocated ahead of the cockpit bulkhead, and a new 40-gallon gravity-feed tank ahead of the engine bulkhead not only addressed the centre-of-gravity problem caused by the loss of 700 pounds' worth of engine, but would keep the engine running in the event of an electrical failure. The -27 turbine offered 662shp, more than the R-1340 at its best, freeing up the 700 pounds to become increased payload on short trips. One real improvement for water handling was the new Hartzell four-bladed prop, which was fully reversible.

CF-MES-X flew September 26, 1978, the product of more than a million dollars' (pre-inflation) worth of design and development. But that was all there was in the till. Cox and CF-MES-X moved to Renton, near Seattle, re-registered the Turbo Otter as N4247A, and re-engined it with a higher-powered 750shp PT6A-135, which realizes its output at lower rpm's than earlier PT6s. Cox Aircraft Corp., as the American company became known, acquired the historic wreck of the Trans Antarctic Otter, the former XL 710 (Number 126), intending for it to become the second Turbo Otter prototype.

Meanwhile, the estimated cost of the conversion had gone from $CDN200,000 in 1977 to $US410,000 in 1982. Hayes says they had 27 firm orders, but Cox ran out of money again shortly thereafter. The airplane Ray Cox was left with, Otter N427A, was an unfinished concerto awaiting someone to compose the last few bars.

A more modest conversion, and the first certified as airworthy, was an eventual outcome of the transfer in 1952 of responsibility for manufacturing Russian piston aero engines to the Polish engine and aircraft builder PZL Kalisz, which not long thereafter became the only source of new-build radial replacement engines anywhere. In 1980, well before the breakup of the Soviet Union, Bogdan Wolski, founder of Airtech Canada Aviation Services Ltd. of Peterborough, Ontario, made available the Polish PZL-3 seven-cylinder radial for installation in Otters. It took a bilateral agreement between Poland and Canada for the transfers to occur. The PZL gave the same power as the R-1340 for 528 pounds less installed weight and claimed fuel savings of seven gallons per hour. The conversion cost $76,000 with no structural changes to the Otter, and Airtech did eight of those, the first being C-FWJB (183).

Three years later, Airtech made available another PZL engine approved for use in Canada, the 1,000hp PZL ASZ-621R, a derivative of the Russian radial that powers the only equivalent of the Otter in the world, the Antonov An-2 "Colt." Airtech refers to this radial as "reminiscent of the Wright R-1820 Cyclone" which powered almost all prewar DC-3s. This combination of engine and airframe mates the best from Communism's utility best-seller (close to 20,000 built) with the only airplane of its kind in the West. As it does on the An-2, the Polish engine drives a four-blade prop, shortened on the Otter to a diameter of 10 feet, 10 inches.[8]

People who have flown "Polish Otters," as these aircraft became known, rave about them. "It's a fun plane to fly," says one pilot, presumably one of very few who feel that way about the Otter. Another actually claimed the PZL-engined Otter would outperform a Turbo Otter "in certain respects."

"It'll beat the turbine off the water any time," says Bob Polinuk of Selkirk Air, Manitoba, whose outfit owns two of the 15 Polish Otters so far and operates in a region of small lakes. "The turbine's faster from then on," he allows. And the PZL installation is easier on gas: 10 to 20 gallons less an hour, depending on many factors.[9]

But the most favourable comparisons are with the Otter's original powerplant, and the most telling of those is the unidentified voice on Airtech's videotape, which says, "You're flying, you're not staggering."

Katmai Air, Anchorage, Otter first-time start-up with its new Airtech 1000hp engine, June 1998. N491K (434) is the fifteenth "Polish Otter." Lighter ovoid area ahead of the landing gear struts is where the extractor-tube housing has been removed.
BERNIE LAFRANCE/AIRTECH CANADA

Watching his floatplane C-GGSL taxiing, Polinuk says the PZL power is a match for crosswinds, the Otter's bugaboo on water: "It can overcome the wind."

Bob Jackson of Eagle Aviation claims 15-second takeoffs and a 200-foot-per-minute improvement in climb. Some pilots can't make up their minds which they like most: the better performance or the increased reliability. Says Nick Zahorodny, a Selkirk pilot, "I was always preparing for a forced landing [with the R-1340]." He says he once had three deadstick [no power] landings in one season. As for performance, it's "thrilling." Ed Gaffney of Eagle Aviation calculates that two Polish Otters are the operational equal of three standard airplanes because of their higher cruise speed, faster turnarounds and higher TBOs—now officially 1,550 hours but past 2,000 on four early Airtech conversions.[10]

A particularly astute observation by Jack Green, owner of Green Airways of Red Lake, Ontario, is that the shortened takeoff and more uniform, speedier propwash from the PZL results in less wear on the horizontal tail, which takes a real beating on takeoff with the flaps deployed.

Airtech's biggest advantage is price. The conversion, which Airtech calls the DHC-3/1000, costs $US136,000. At a time when standard Otters are worth twice that and some are insured for more than $1 million, the Airtech conversion qualifies as a quick, less expensive pick-me-up.

Small-unit AWACS: This experimental installation on U.S. Army U-1A 53272, the Radar Otter, offered overlapping 360-degree coverage. VIA PETER M. BOWERS

In 1990 Marin C. Faure, the authority on floatplane operations, felt that "the most impressive turbine floatplane of all" was the Vazar Dash-3, a PT6A-135 Otter conversion.[11]

Faure quotes logging contractor Irvin Olsen of Campbell River, British Columbia, on why he converted his Otters to turbine power:

"It'd get off the ground right away but then it wouldn't climb. You'd stand there and watch this thing struggle off toward the horizon, wondering if it was even going to clear the trees at the end of the field. Now, with the turbine, it takes off and just keeps going up. I used to worry about the plane blowing a cylinder and having it go down in the woods with my men on board. Now I don't worry when I send a crew out to camp. I know they'll get there."

"For Olsen," writes Faure, "the Vazar Dash-3 turbine conversion kit represents the solution to a problem which has plagued Otter operators ever since the plane went into production in 1952: the unreliability of its 600-horsepower engine. Aft of the firewall, the Otter is a remarkable airplane. Its long, high-lift wing and slotted flaps will get it into the air in slightly over 700 feet. Even its smaller brother, the DHC-2 Beaver, can't beat Otter's STOL performance. An Otter can lift off at an airspeed of 42 miles an hour."[12]

Like so many Otter operations and improvements, the Vazar Dash-3 evolved from a prospector's requirements. In this case Dara Wilder, a gold miner, pilot, manufacturer of mining and oil-extraction equipment used worldwide, and tireless inventor, was quick to see the advantages of the big single-engine hauler and wanted to address its power shortcomings as simply as possible. Wilder, born into a timber-mill family in B.C.'s Kootenay region, zero-timed a Beaver in 1979 for exploration purposes and re-engined it with an early version of the new Orenda V/8 aero engine, but after six months of effort switched to the larger-capacity Otter. The prototype Vazar Dash-3 opened the 1989 Abbotsford Air Show by landing in less than 100 feet with the reverse thrust of its Hartzell propeller, then taking off in the same distance.[13]

One of Wilder's guidelines in his quest for simplicity was to avoid airframe changes behind the firewall, enabling him to supply his turbine conversion as a bolt-on kit that could be installed in the field. The 730-pound difference in weight between the original R-1340 and the PT6 meant that getting full-forward centre of gravity, an FAA requirement, would have involved an even longer nose. So one compromise that keeps the Otter's new pointed nose to a reasonable length is to use ballast ahead of the firewall if the trip requires heavy single items to be carried at the extreme rear of the cabin. That is seldom the case. TBO: 3,500 hours.[14]

Dash-3 conversion kits cost $US198,000, which, Vazar marketing manager Shawna Vaughan points out, is a bargain considering P&WC's retail price for a 750shp PT6A-135 of $US380,000. The price of a complete Dash-3, assuming the basis is a used Otter valued at $180,000, was $US658,000 in 1990. Vazar, located just below the Canadian border in Bellingham, Washington, has approval to re-engine Beavers with PT6s and is contemplating a Dash-3 upgrade to the 850shp PT6A-40.

There are now 45 Vazar Dash-3s in service, including a pair with Vazar bubble windows doing sight-seeing tours of the Grand Canyon; five with Seattle's Kenmore Harbor Air; and the Harbour Air airplane Bob Bator is so fond of, C-GUTW. In the air-to-air picture on Bob's wall and at the wharf, UTW looks like a million dollars. Like its stablemate OPP, UTW spends the summer season flying out of the Harbour Air base at Prince Rupert, B.C. The two aircraft generate higher passenger-density counts than the company's Beavers.

Facing page: The ultimate Otter? Vazar Dash-3 Turbo Otter (405) served with the United Nations in Kashmir and New Guinea, yet was second-lowest-time among its retirement batch (less than 6,000 hours) when sold to Harbour Air. Conversion to 16-seat Dash-3 January-March 1992 overseen by Doug Hamerton; first flight as turbo April 1, 1992, with Peter Evans. It has since had its floats extended to 7535s by Bob Bator, certified by Leo Galvin of Transport Canada, May 6, 1997. HARBOUR AIR VIA BOB BATOR

One component of the Otter few have ever complained about is the wing. It could be improved structurally, as the Twin Otter proves, but its aerodynamics are little changed, aside from the double-slotted flaps, from the Beaver to the Twin Otter. AOG Air Support of Kelowna, B.C., thought they could make those wings safer, and they did so with Dick Hiscocks's encouragement.

AOG Air Support manufactures kits that droop the blunt leading edges of DHC wings, giving them a greater curve over the upper surfaces and lessening their characteristic wingtip droop. Testing has shown that the best flap angle on takeoff for 1340, Polish or turbine Otters is a mere 10 degrees. That is the setting for climb on a standard Otter. In other words, with AOG's Baron STOL kit you take off with the flaps already at the climb setting. "That's all you need," says AOG pilot-president Dave Barron.[15]

This means, of course, less drag while the airfoil itself is developing more lift. No need to hold the nose down and hang in ground effect. Barron says he has pulled the control wheel back to the stop, raising the nose, on takeoff—the opposite of what you would normally do—with 30-year Otter veterans in the left-hand seat ready to jump out until Barron pointed to the airspeed indicator showing 100 mph already. It is difficult to convince them to use so little flap, he says. Doing so lessens the conflicting forces at work on the Otter airframe: the drag of 35-degree flap and the downwash on the tail, and the consequent necessity to fight the downwash by keeping the nose down while trying to climb.

AOG claims a 30 per cent increase in lift, better fuel consumption and higher payloads from its STOL kits, which consist of the new leading edges and tips. About 100 of these kits have been installed on Beavers and Otters (with a new Twin Otter kit available), out of a potential market AOG estimates at 3,700 de Havilland aircraft.

In an effort to become a comprehensive Otter supplier, AOG has bought seven or eight certificated modifications from Harbour Air—mods developed with back-of-envelope drawings in Bob Bator's office—from a 400-pound upgross wing-strut sleeve (that Hiscocks helped certify), to cabin cargo nets to prevent payload shifting, to 16-place high-density seating, to a float stretch kit that took 400 manhours to build the first time and can be pushed onto an existing float in 40 hours.

The humble float is the Otter's true Achilles heel. The aircraft was designed to use an easily available float of the time, the Norseman's Edo 7170 float, licence-built by MacDonald Brothers in Winnipeg (now Bristol Aerospace). The 7170 was never really big enough, and it is a real gross-weight limitation for Otter floatplanes: what cannot be supported by the floats cannot go into the cabin. While a smaller float is nice to fly with, its handling qualities on water only exacerbate the big Otter tail's weather-cocking tendencies.[16]

Originally delivered to the Tanzanian Air Force in 1966, N9707B was returned to Canada in 1972 as CF-DIV and became the Vazar Dash-3 prototype a dozen years later. After four years of engineering and testing, it was certified in the U.S. November 1988.
VAZAR AEROSPACE

AOG's float extension for the 7170 was worked out by Bob Bator in 1993. But a better solution for Harbour Air's Otters was based on the DHC-specified amphibious float from MacDonald's, the 7490. Bator's idea was to remove the wheels and their associated plumbing and wheel-wells, and get it certified into what he calls "a long, long 7490." That float modification was tested by Transport Canada test pilot Leo Galvin May 6, 1997. But not every Otter owner wants to go to all that trouble.

There are new floats available from a pioneer of many Beaver and Otter modifications, Wipair of Minneapolis, although they are built for the Cessna Caravan. They are 7000s, but then again they are new.

By the way, the Cox Turbo Otter has found its finisher. Dave Curtis takes the turbine Otter story back to its origins at Downsview. Curtis presides over the fortunes of Viking Air, the fast-growing Victoria, B.C., aircraft rebuilder and authorized DHC parts manufacturer that has certified a 6,000-pound gross weight Turbo Beaver and has been working for a couple of years on a Turbo Otter that it aims to certificate at 9,000 pounds, with that additional half-ton abetted by the essentials of the powerplant conversion developed by Ray Cox.

A U.S. Navy VX-6 Antarctica veteran, the former BuNo 142425 (77), Jim Harkey's N129JH is more capable than ever: Baron STOL 8367 upgross wing, Vazar Dash-3 power, Wipline 8000 amphibious floats. DAVE BARRON

As Viking did with the Beaver, it has comprehensively re-engineered an Otter as the conversion prototype and has a privately owned one committed as a first production unit.

"We wanted to make it into a true turbine airplane—not a piston airplane with a turbine bolted on—a true turbine design," Curtis says. Three principles governed the redesign:

"We wanted to keep it as short as possible. Our airplane is one foot shorter than the Vazar. We wanted to keep the same centre of gravity range.

"We wanted to keep the same zero thrust-line, identical to the piston Otter." The Vazar engine is canted five degrees downward, its designer has noted, for performance gains. Curtis feels these gains may be realized on the wheeled taildragging Otter but doubts there is any advantage on floats, with the airplane level.

"We increased the fuel by 50 per cent," partly by retaining Cox's header tank ahead of the firewall but making it a separate (rather than flow-through) tank with the redundance of gravity-feed. That additional tank also helps balance the airplane.

Another worthwhile inheritance from the earlier project is the flutter analysis Cox had done. Viking will add a dynamic balance system of weights set into the airstream to help the elevator cope with the flap's downstream forces. Curtis foresees keeping the full-flap capability, mostly for STOL landing purposes.[17]

One advantage Curtis has over Cox is that the time is right: a standard piston Otter costs several hundred thousand dollars. Converted, a turbine Otter can be worth more than a million. At those prices, the airplane might as well be reliable.[18]

CHAPTER TWELVE

DHC Survives the DHC-4

In the dozen years or so since the Otter had first flown, de Havilland of Canada had become a different company. In 1963 Phil Garratt was still running the place in his personal hands-on way, walking the shop floor every morning, chatting with the supervisors and foremen.[1] But it was a different place: a bigger plant in a new location, a more sophisticated operation and a magnet for talent, especially from overseas. By then, too, the organization had been tempered by misfortune. It had become more mature as a result.

DHC had begun to run out of room at its old wartime factory by 1952, with Otters joining the Beavers on the assembly lines and overhaul work overflowing the rest of the hangar spaces. In a singular example of serendipity between the public sector and private industry, the Canadian government, which still owned most of the land surrounding the DHC plant, offered to acquire the company's facilities at the north end of the site for an RCAF base. DHC would get $5.5 million and a lease on a 96-acre parcel at the southwest corner (and still have access to the runways the company had always used). The company built a bigger 10.5-acre, $8-million complex, creating most of the DHC of today, and became connected to the north Toronto suburb of Downsview by a road it named Garratt Boulevard.[2]

The misfortunes included the Otter crashes that killed Bill Ferderber and several military pilots, and an unexpectedly arduous certification process for the Otter's successor, the twin-engine DHC-4 Caribou. A test-model Caribou crashed as well, fortunately without loss of life, when George Neal and his Department of Transport test-pilot colleague, Walter Gadzos, hit the silk. DHC lost its innocence during the mid- to late 1950s as the company dedicated itself with the Caribou program to lifting three tons—three times the Otter's payload—from that same 725-foot unimproved strip, and landing with an even shorter ground run. The strain of following up its previous achievements took DHC to the brink of bankruptcy.

The success of the Otter immediately suggested the outline of its successor: twin-engine reliability and a doubled payload with the same short-field performance. It would also be nice, customers said, to find some way of alleviating the crosswind problems that came with tail-dragger landing gear, and the same difficulties with the increased vertical flight surfaces the Otter required while operating on floats. One other thing was clear: more takeoff power was essential.

This was a pretty simple formula. So transparent was the requirement that the 15-year effort DHC undertook to design an Otter successor seems, on the face of it, unbelievable. Had DHC lost its touch?

The origins of the Twin Otter go back so far that the first studies seem almost prehistoric. There were at least three distinct starts on a project that was intended to produce what DHC called, more and more wistfully with time, a "Light Twin." In its efforts to accomplish what looks in retrospect to be a straightforward engineering challenge, DHC actually designed and built a more ambitious twin-engine transport, the Caribou (and re-engined it to create the yet-higher-payload DHC-5 Buffalo).

As we know now, too, the ultimate-STOL Otter 3682, as it evolved into a twin-turbine jet-assisted dive-bomber, came so close to the eventual Twin Otter design as to look like the Light Twin's prototype. But as obvious as the resemblance between Otter 3682 in its final form and the eventual Twin Otter is from 35 years on, one did not lead to the other.

Otter 3682, worn out, was hauled to the Downsview perimeter and discarded as one of a kind, a project unto itself, an engineering dead end. But the false starts and diversions on the road to a Light Twin had the cumulative effect of testing the confidence the company had earned for itself in designing and developing five original designs that sustained impressive manufacturing programs. DHC became a better company in the effort.

DHC's wind tunnel: Otter prototype 3667-X carrying a DHC-4 model in flight. The Otter prototype's original registration, CF-DYK-X, was changed when the RCAF acquired the aircraft and then loaned it indefinitely to DHC. VIA PETER M. BOWERS

Sometime during 1954 one of the first studies for a possible twin-engine Otter successor was underway. Fred Hotson refers specifically to a 13,000-pound gross weight project with two of the engines that power the Otter, Pratt & Whitney R-1340s.[3] This airplane existed only on paper, because doubling the number of powerplants did not add enough to the design's payload to make it worthwhile.

The problem was that any twin piston-engine design with a decent payload worked out to be too heavy to survive the engine-out case. The two engines themselves were too much dead weight for one of them to carry. The safety regulations that require twins to be able to continue a takeoff on one engine meant that, if an engine failed at the worst possible time, the engine still running would be keeping two and a half more tons aloft than on a fully loaded Otter, where the available power was already marginal.[4]

The Light Twin studies kept producing heavier and heavier designs in an effort to carry a worthwhile payload.

By doubling the horsepower with two of the readily available radial engines in the 1,200hp class, a further study concluded that a 22,000-pound all-up weight airplane with full transport category certification was possible—but, alas, not commercially attractive.[5]

But then the U.S. Army, fully satisfied with its Beavers and Otters, began hinting at a bigger, next-generation tactical transport. Russ Bannock, director of military sales, divined that what he was hearing was a highly unofficial wish for a three-ton-payload STOL transport with rear loading. Such a payload resolved some of the questions that had remained unanswered by the Light Twin studies.

In 1956, the design staff schemed out a bigger twin with 1,450hp P&W R-2000 engines, which would give a maximum weight of 26,000 pounds. At that all-up weight, suddenly the combined masses of the R-2000s, at 3,200 pounds for the pair, became a smaller factor in the overall equation. It worked. Russ Bannock took the draft specifications and preliminary design to the U.S. Army at the Pentagon in September.

The biggest prototype DHC's Experimental Shop had ever built up to that time, KTK-X is under construction during early summer, 1958. The second prototype, CF-LAN-X, is also well underway. DHC 8280

He was asked to stick around Washington for a few days. The director of Army Aviation and the chief of research and development asked Bannock how soon five test aircraft could be available and at what price.

Bannock telephoned Doug Hunter, then DHC's chief engineer, from a pay telephone in a corridor of the Pentagon—by then he knew his way around the biggest military building in the world. He suggested to Hunter what the answers should be.

"Less than an hour later," Bannock recalled, "I had a reply to the effect that the five aircraft could be delivered at the rate of one a month commencing 22 months from contract go-ahead. The price was established at $US550,000 per aircraft with no up-front development costs." Lt.-Gen. Robert R. Williams (U.S. Army ret.) is a former director of Army Aviation. He relished telling his side of this story and credited his superior officers with being the only ones who "could have accomplished this miracle." His audience was the U.S. Army Otter and Caribou Association meeting in Dallas, Texas, August 17, 1990. This organization exists so that thousands of retired military pilots can refresh fond memories of flying DHC products in war zones. Lt.-Gen. Williams summed up: "The company received a Letter of Intent within a month and the project was underway, to be known as the Caribou AC-I. . . . The opposition was caught completely asleep. The Army purchased 165 Caribous."[6]

DHC's bridge from single-engine bush planes to complex multi-engine aircraft: one of the 100 Grumman CS2F Trackers licence-built for the Royal Canadian Navy. DHC 7651

"If ever the Canadian de Havilland company wants to look back for the period it came of age, the answer is somewhere in the Caribou program," Fred Hotson tells us. "In the wake of earlier successes, the decision to move into the big league with a large twin-engine design was accepted without a qualm by everyone concerned. Certainly the drama began with a formidable cast of players, but much was to be learned before the box office tallied the receipts or the final curtain fell. No project came closer to bankrupting the company, yet the Caribou is credited with setting de Havilland Canada on the trail to its present world status in the industry."[7]

The leap from single-engine, one-ton payload Otter to three-ton Caribou would have seemed almost foolhardy had DHC not surprisingly won a bid for the licence to supply 100 twin-engine Grumman S2F anti-submarine patrol aircraft to the Royal Canadian Navy, thus giving the company multi-engine experience. The surprise was in the fact that DHC, unlike Canadair (for example), had never built multi-engine aircraft other than by assembling twins designed at Hatfield, although it had overhauled and modified many such aircraft. By the end of May 1956, George Neal and Tony Verrico had flown the first CS2F-I Tracker—"the largest and most complicated aircraft DHC has undertaken," Phil Garratt told *Canadian Aviation* magazine—and the new plant was already becoming a tight fit.[8]

But DHC had not been required to certify the Tracker as airworthy. The company had only to build it to specifications already certified in the U.S. by Grumman.

For political reasons, as a military aircraft being procured from a foreign source, the Caribou had to meet not only U.S. Army requirements, but the tougher airworthiness standards for civil transports. "Never before," writes F. A. (Ted) Johnson, the former Royal Air Force airman to whom fell the task of performing hundreds of dangerous stalls as Fowler's copilot in the Caribou, "had anyone certificated a STOL aircraft under these stringent rules."[9]

The first prototype Caribou, CF-KTK-X, was flown for the first time by George Neal, Hans Brinkman and Dave Fairbanks July 30, 1958—at about 18 of the 22 months DHC had allowed itself to make the first delivery—after an intense all-out effort to complete it. A second prototype, CF-LAX-X, joined the first and by 1961 was being used by Nordair for arctic tests.

One measure of the U.S. Army's eagerness to get its hands on Caribous is the fact that the type was ordered off the drawing board rather than the order being contingent upon successful flight-testing. To enable all the necessary testing to take place before production models began to appear, the next five Caribous were YAC-I service test models, delivered in October and November of 1958. (At this point there were 22 Caribous at various stages of assembly along the line.)

It was the first of these service test models, the Number 3 Caribou (U.S. Army serial 57-3079), that was modified by the addition of a 42-inch fuselage plug ahead of the wing. The thinking behind this change was that the longer fuselage would give greater fore-and-aft centre of gravity limits, and thus more flexibility in loading under operational conditions. This airplane was therefore required to repeat its terminal velocity dive test. (Terminal velocity is the highest speed an aircraft can attain in a dive, the speed at which it ceases to accelerate.)

On March 23, 1959, this longer Caribou encountered flutter in the elevator during a dive (at 280 mph, the Caribou's design dive limit) with Neal at the controls, assisted by Department of Transport test pilot Walter Gadzos. Neal managed to get the big transport slowed to 180 mph, but the flutter continued until the two heard the port elevator fail. Reducing speed further did not help, and neither did switching off the engines. Neal and Gadzos jumped, but only after Neal coolly returned to the cockpit to switch off the YAC-I's fuel and electrical systems, averting a fire at the crash site. Neal touched down and found a telephone and dialled Dick Batch in DHC's Flight Test office to inform him of the loss of the third Caribou.[10]

As an analysis of Caribou Number 3's tailplane flutter confirmed, the insertion of the plug to lengthen the prototype's fuselage changed the natural frequencies of portions of the airplane's tail assembly, which caused flutter in an elevator spring tab and then in the elevator itself.

Every part of an aircraft has its own vibrational frequency when it is in the air. The frequencies of those parts that were lengthened changed, and so did those of

Facing page: The prototype Caribou CF-KTK-X. The open hatch above the pilot's seat was George Neal's escape route from the stricken Number 3 Caribou in March 1959. DHC 8635

The DHC-4 Caribou prototype takes to the air for the first time, July 30, 1958. The main landing gear doors were not yet installed on KTK-X that day. DHC 8665

some parts one might have thought would be unaffected. Certain speeds generate certain frequencies, and when the right speed excites the right frequency in a part, that part begins to vibrate, or flutter.

Lengthening the fuselage necessarily lengthened the control circuits running from the cockpit to, among other flight surfaces, the elevators. That changed the frequencies of the circuits. And it so happened that the spring tabs at the trailing edges of the elevators, which make the elevators easier to operate, were now susceptible to flutter in the region of 270–280 mph—the design dive speed, and the speed at which Neal was diving the airplane.

Finding the answer involved commissioning an analysis at Ohio State University. Changes were made to the elevator control circuit to move its resonent frequencies to values well beyond the speed envelope of the Caribou.

Another interesting flight-test program involved modifying Caribou prototypes to lower their one engine-out minimum control speed to conform with the design figure. In an effort to make the tactical transport fly five or six knots slower on one engine, a very complex airflow study was done to determine the downstream effects of the upswept belly. Disturbed air from the belly kink was swirling up over the fin and rudder, robbing them of effectiveness in a situation where they are vital to longitudinal stability. Part of the solution was ridges, or strakes, along the lower edges of the fuselage sidewalls where they meet the upswept underside.

While the tail flutter problem was a case of a structural flutter under high-speed conditions, and complex but straightforward to fix, the Caribou's other flight-test vexation, its behaviour at the stall, was resisting any cure. Neal was in the process of compiling a list of two dozen items that needed attention, including a stick-shaker device to warn pilots of the Caribou's impending stall. He considered the airplane's power-off stalls borderline, and the power-on stall controllable with the rudder and within certification standards of the time. But it was a concern. The issue resolved itself into a difference of opinion about what constituted an acceptable stall between DHC and the American Federal Aviation Administration.

The prototype CC-108 Caribou in RCAF markings, fitted with turboprop engines, thus becoming the flying test bed for the engines that powered the DHC-5 Buffalo, or CC-115 in RCAF service. But it was not the Buffalo prototype. DHC 13917

That summer of 1959 Bob Fowler was named chief experimental test pilot by Russ Bannock, who was still running that department in addition to his sales duties. Fowler was told to pick someone to help him solve the Caribou's stall problem, and he chose Ted Johnson to assist him in the right seat. (Neal was fully occupied testing four different types of airplanes as they came off the line.) Using both Caribou prototypes, Fowler and Johnson often undertook two sorties a day from June, when they undertook further dives to prove the flutter problem was solved, into September, when they were trying various aerodynamic fixes intended to make the Caribou's stall acceptable for scheduled passenger service, or, more literally, the American Transport Category Airworthiness Requirement, CAR 46.

Specifically, Johnson noted, "An aircraft to be certified under the transport category of the airworthiness rules had to have innocuous traits at the stall"—the point at which an aircraft is moving forward so slowly it literally falls out of the sky—"and explicitly was required not to roll more than 20 degrees before being brought under control." Johnson noted that when provoked, instead of having its stall gently approached, the Caribou would sometimes roll over almost onto its back.[11]

Eventually that summer others were drafted into the Caribou flight-test program, including Gordon Johnston, the aerodynamic mind behind Otter 3682's amazing STOL demonstrations. A package of wing refinements was adopted; it included stall bars (to initiate turbulence at a preselected point along the wing leading edge earlier in the stall process), along with wing fences just outboard of the engines and drooped outer wing leading edges (which together would delay the onset of a stall and limit the resulting roll), and, finally, the stick-shaker device that was required by CAR 46 on any aircraft that exhibited less than 7 per cent natural stall warning (buffet), which made it a necessity on the Caribou.

The first Caribou deliveries to the U.S. Army were made in September 1959. Seeing the first three YAC-1s being turned over on the rainy DHC apron, serials 57-3079 to 57-3081, with helmeted and fully kitted American infantrymen in ponchos and carrying their M-16s, ready to board, seemed like the realization of a small miracle.

That is the story of how the U.S. Army acquired the Caribou tactical STOL transports that resupplied the beleaguered mountaintop Marine garrison Khe Sanh, and worked closer to the shooting at Dak To and the Ia Drang Valley than any noncombat aircraft in Vietnam. Known to their various owners as the DHC-4, AC-1 (U.S. Army) and C-7 (so named by the U.S. Air Force when it took over all large fixed-wing aviation on the first day of 1967), the Caribou and its turboprop successor, the Buffalo, were prevented only by interservice rivalry from cloaking themselves in even greater glory.[12]

By 1959, it seems, DHC had become too successful for its own good. A cash crunch brought on by the delay in certifying the Caribou—with production fully underway—resulted in a missed payroll. The Caribou was the third airplane on DHC's production lines, and by far the most costly in materials and labour. Hatfield came to the rescue, guaranteeing a loan from Barclay's Bank, on whose behalf none other than the former RAF chief of air staff Lord Portal (who had flown in an Otter in 1954) approved the loan. But it was the United Nations, of all customers, who saved the Caribou program. UN peacekeepers in the Belgian Congo needed a STOL supply plane, and a quick order for four placed for the UN by the RCAF made a difference all out of proportion to the number of units involved.[13]

If the Caribou was a milestone design, its turbine-engined successor, the DHC-5 Buffalo, was a quiet, almost unnoticed breakthrough. General Electric had been working on a new-technology turboprop engine, the T-64, since 1957 for the U.S. Navy, and was looking for a testbed to evaluate it. The RCAF made the DHC-4 prototype, Caribou 5303, available to be re-engined. Bob Fowler flew the resulting airplane for the first time September 22, 1961, "and continued," Fred Hotson tells us, "with 220 hours of very interesting flying." Fowler had to fly the T-64 Caribou, as DHC was envisioning the new combination, with a light hand on the throttle. With the new engines giving twice the installed horsepower of the piston Caribou, the reborn prototype could exceed its original design maximum level flight speed on one engine and surpass its design dive speed in level flight on two.

The rest of the story is no different from accounts of the competitions won by the Beaver, Otter (in Exercise Skydrop II) and Caribou. STOL was simply not a priority with American aircraft manufacturers. There was a competition during May 1962 for a STOL transport that could handle a five-ton payload (matching the payload of the Boeing Chinook twin-engine, twin-rotor helicopter, a direct descendant of the H-21). This requirement was written around the performance specifications of the Caribou II, or, as it soon became known, the Buffalo. Twenty-five companies competed.[14]

In seven and a half months from the first flight of the re-engined T-64 Caribou, on April 9, 1962, the Buffalo flew for the first time in the hands of Bob Fowler, assisted by Mick Saunders and Bob Dingle. By the time the aircraft was certified in April 1965, under the same FAA CAR 4b regulation that had caused such a struggle with the Caribou, four Buffaloes were flying and the RCAF had ordered 15, making production feasible. The main recognition feature of the Buffalo compared with the Caribou, aside from the more streamlined turbine engines, is the T-tail, with its tailplane set at the top of the vertical tail to keep it in undisturbed air on takeoff, during stalls and during approach to landing. Like later Caribous, it has a nose-mounted, thimble-shaped weather radar. Four service test units were delivered to the United States, where their performance was so exemplary it was decided to test them under actual combat conditions. By mid-November 1965 two of the Buffaloes were in Vietnam. One week after its arrival, the first of these hauled 17,400 pounds of cargo and 112 passengers in five hours in the air during its first day as a front-line hauler.

The DHC engineering department heads at the Buffalo rollout. *Left to right:* Bill Heaslip, N. E. Rowe, Dick Hiscocks, Bill Burlison, Fred Buller, Bill Bozanin and Tom Higgins. The Buffalo first flew in April 1964. DHC 17362

"The test aircraft were an inspiration to all," Fred Hotson sums up, "for they carried greater loads and did everything with a little more flair than the hard-working Caribou.... Loads of 10,000 pounds were routine. Air drops included ¾-ton army trucks, and on one single paradrop mission the Buffalo dropped 64 Vietnamese paratroops.... Even the maintenance turned out to be quite reasonable for a new aircraft type so far from home with only 10 to 15 per cent of the available spare parts used. Needless to say, the operational commanders were pleased with the results."[15]

Later that year the Army requested procurement of 120 Buffaloes. Meanwhile, the combined efforts of the American aircraft manufacturers and the U.S. Air Force resulted in the Army being limited to helicopters in the airmobile role and the USAF taking over the fixed-wing tactical transport role. That December Secretary of Defense Robert McNamara ruled out Army purchases of the Buffalo beyond the four test aircraft. Thus ended a relationship between DHC and the U.S. Army that had been fulfilling for both.

But DHC and the Army could not resist staging another of those cheeky demonstrations. In September 1966 a Buffalo delivered a field hospital unit to three baseball diamonds on Governor's Island, a mile south of Manhattan, landing after a nose-down approach over four hundred-foot smokestacks, and then leaving. This, DHC was saying, is something the U.S. Army will henceforth not be able to do as quickly. Not in Gotham, nor anywhere else.[16]

Ten of the 15 Buffaloes ordered by the RCAF, at the hand-over in late 1967. Aside from the turbine engines, the Buffalo differed from the Caribou in having straight wings and a T-tail. DHC 28856

An almost-forgotten footnote to the Caribou-Buffalo story is that a final version of the Buffalo restarted the production line, which had been mothballed in 1972 after 15 had been assembled for the RCAF and 59 more for foreign air arms, in addition to the four U.S. Army/USAF service test units. More powerful T-64 engines made a new DHC-5D possible, and the line was reopened in 1974. For once, though, the additional power was used, not to enhance STOL performance but to add payload to transports that were now expected to operate from long, paved, air force runways, far from the front.[17]

For some, the step back from the glory days of STOL was regrettable. In Dick Hiscocks's words, "an outstanding opportunity was lost." Beavers and Otters, designed to thrive in the unforgiving bush-flying environment, had with minimal changes redefined fixed-wing army aviation. The Caribou/Buffalo series of battlefield transports could nearly duplicate those smaller airplanes' short-field exploits while hefting three- to five-ton payloads and extracting them on the fly on mountaintops. But the Buffalo was undermined by political decisions and the resentment of American manufacturers who saw military STOL as not worth pursuing—and not allowing anyone else to pursue either.

Nobody at DHC could see the future in 1963. But that year was a high point in the company's history. By then, with Avro Canada's assets and contracts absorbed, and Beaver, Otter and Caribou production humming along; the ultimate STOL Otter 3682 research program redefining the limits of fixed-wing short-field performance; and DHC heavily involved with such sidelines as hydrofoil design and manufacturing wings for the Douglas DC-9 airliner, the company was once again attractive to engineering talent from overseas.

One of the newcomers was John Thompson, another of those able Scottish engineers with backgrounds simply not available in Canada, who gravitated to DHC during the 1950s as the British aviation industry began to consolidate. Born near Kendall, in the north of England's Lake District, Thompson moved to Scotland at the age of seven. In 1945 he simultaneously became an apprentice at Scottish Aviation, Prestwick, and a student at the University of Glasgow, which offered a program in mechanical engineering that required exactly the kind of practical experience he was getting at Prestwick.

Thompson joined the Royal Air Force in 1950 as a technical officer posted to the RAF's fighter bases in Germany (Gutersloh and Wunsdorf), where he worked on Vampires and Meteors. He joined A.V. Roe at Manchester in 1952, where he married Mary Copeland and quickly became stress section leader on the Vulcan wing (which was most of the airplane). Still in the RAF as a reservist, Thompson was engineering officer of 617 Squadron, the celebrated Dam Busters. By the early 1950s that outfit had traded the Lancaster bombers with which it breached the Mohne and Eder dams during the war for Canberra jets.

By 1957 Thompson was finding Manchester an "unappealing" place to live. He saw an advertisement for aero engineers to work on the DHC-4 Caribou at Downsview.

Detail design was well underway at that point, and Thompson worked on the big Caribou wing, moving up to become wing group leader responsible for wing stress analysis. He was promoted to chief stress engineer in 1961.

"From then on," says the future Vice-President, Engineering, "I was involved in every project DHC ever did—including the hydrofoil and the DC-9 wing [inherited in the amalgamation with Avro Canada]." Including, of course, the DHC airplane most thoroughly tested before it ever flew, and the design that marked DHC's return to the civil market: the DHC-6 Twin Otter.[18]

John Thompson, at his desk at DHC February 24, 1970, a few minutes before he departed to investigate the ditching of a Pilgrim Airlines Twin Otter in Long Island Sound.
VIA JOHN THOMPSON

Facing page: PT6 turbine engines are installed in CF-DHC-X, the DHC-6 Twin Otter prototype, April 1965. The second of five prototypes, CF-SJB-X, has its fuselage nearly complete. The clever hinged lower nacelle allows easy access. DHC 20722

CHAPTER THIRTEEN

A Tough Act to Follow

By the early 1960s de Havilland of Canada and the U.S. Army were so closely in tune that it sometimes seemed as if Downsview knew the Army's needs before the Army did. Neither the Beaver nor the Otter was designed for military use, but pilots under fire are all the more appreciative of the same takeoff (and landing) characteristics that appeal to bush pilots.[1]

During the spring of 1963, Russ Bannock appreciated those qualities as he found himself being ferried between de Havilland maintenance bases in Vietnam—among them a repair depot at Vung Tau—in Otters. "For," Bannock smiles, "the Otter was the only way we could get around easily."

There were six army aviation companies flying Otters in Vietnam, each with 22 of them. The transport companies all told Bannock the same thing: the Otter was a fine airplane, but it would be better with twin-engine reliability and a tricycle (or nosewheel) landing gear for better control while operating in crosswinds. One general presented Bannock with what amounted to a set of specifications. Bannock wrote up these conversations during his long return flight and presented the notes to that week's management committee meeting at Downsview.

By then, DHC's engineering staff was headed by a triumvirate: Dick Hiscocks, Fred Buller and N. E. Rowe.[2] All three agreed with Bannock's assessment that there was a market for an Otter replacement, and not only for the Army.

"We had constantly been badgered by Max Ward to develop a twin-engine version of the single Otter," Bannock recalls. Ward was losing the freight-capacity advantage he had enjoyed for most of the previous 10 years and felt the only way to regain it was with a twin.

"The Ontario Provincial Air Service was interested, but theirs was not a strong interest. We knew there was growing interest in commuter aircraft in the U.S., but we did not bank on this interest. As it turned out, that interest came on much faster than we could have hoped for."

Peter S. Martin, who in April 1963 was finishing work on the proposal for the PT6 installation on the Turbo Beaver, began preliminary design "immediately."[3]

Managing director Phil Garratt asked Buller and Doug Hunter to come up with cost figures "by Friday," based on installing two engines on the Otter airframe. As Bannock remembers the subsequent meeting, the estimate for design, development and prototype construction was $6 million—an absurdly low figure by today's standards but nearly spot on, as events would prove.

The key meeting took place July 22, 1963. Present were the aforementioned individuals, along with sales personnel. The meeting discussed starting a completely new design but resolved not to do so. "This was ruled out," Hotson writes, "because time was short." Retractable landing gear were also ruled out because the speed gain was deemed marginal on short-haul operations.

"We sold the idea to management and the board of directors on the basis that there was a very good chance we could sell the same numbers we had sold of single Otters," Bannock recalls.[4]

Management not only bought the concept, it authorized a preproduction series of five aircraft to cut the normal certification time. The project was considered so conservative the company was willing to risk having to make any necessary changes on the production line.

There are arguments to this day over whether it was a mistake for DHC even to bother with a twin-engine Otter replacement. The company's new owners, the British Hawker Siddeley Group, which had taken over DHC's parent at Hatfield (and thus became a somewhat reluctant stepfather to Downsview), were against it. That meant things had to proceed piecemeal, on the sly, with materials and labour stolen from other projects. "It was a very low-key project," Bannock deadpans.[5]

Concept model for the Twin Otter. Wing-strut outer junction meets the wing outside of the engine nacelle, as on Otter 3682. It was redesigned to meet aft end of nacelle for better aerodynamics. The tail is also different from the production aircraft, and wingspan was increased. DHC 16747

As Wally Gibson remembers it, the Twin Otter began at the engineering level as a bare-bones $2.5-million project—enough to fund two fuselages and one wing. He felt that N. E. Rowe had stuck his neck out with his Hawker Siddeley superiors and paid the price, being replaced at the end of 1966 as VP, Engineering, by Bill Heaslip. After the first flight, the Experimental Shop was permitted to build two wingsets, Gibson recalls. The second wingset found a home on a fuselage that was authorized only after it was proven that the Twin Otter could fly. Changes were introduced only on the third airplane.[6]

Were Hawker Siddeley right? The primary market for which the Twin Otter was intended, the U.S. Army, bought only a handful. From the company's overall strategic point of view, the timing was all wrong: in 1963–64 Downsview was still badly overextended, its energy and cash resources drained off in several directions, from the building and testing of HMCS *Bras d'Or*, a naval hydrofoil, to missile development, to building DC-9 wings on a cost-sharing subcontract to Douglas Aircraft that was another factor in the near-bankruptcy of the company.[7]

Twin Otter cockpit and nose mockup, as of July 1964. Various black boxes representing avionics equipment have been placed in the nose, which, engineless, was now available for radios and navigation aids. DHC 18821

Another Fred Buller idea: easily maintained "nut-cracker" landing gear with urethane-block shock absorbers, reminiscent of the Beaver. Note the wing-strut inner pickup at the same point on the fuselage, near mid-range centre of gravity. DHC 20990

If Downsview's management had been overly optimistic in leaping into the unknown on the Caribou, the Buffalo and the Turbo Beaver, they were positively naive about what it would take to produce a twin-engine Otter. "Phil Garratt said, 'Take the Otter and put two engines on it,'" is how Mike Davy paraphrases the go-ahead.

Gordon Johnston, who oversaw the experimental Otter 3682 program that eventually yielded an airplane that had a few things in common with the Twin Otter—other than its jet engine, that is—nevertheless believes building the Twin Otter was a mistake. He lists feature after feature of the airplane that was compromised by the belief that hanging two turboprop engines on the Otter airframe and giving it a nosewheel would do the trick. It would have been better, Johnston believes, to have started with a clean sheet of paper.[8]

"The fuselage shape," Davy agrees, "is an abomination. It should've been squared-off somewhat." Another carryover from the single-engine Otter, fuel cells located under the floor, made retractable landing gear an impossibility.[9]

And yet Downsview built and sold 844 copies of an airplane that, in many ways, almost designed itself. For all its shortcomings—many of them visible only to those who worked on it—the DHC-6 Twin Otter became the most widely used propeller-driven airplane in the world on scheduled air services.[10]

Russ Bannock summarizes the design development of the Twin Otter as simply as the process itself evolved: "We took the Otter fuselage, added a six-foot plug, used the same wing box section and new leading edges. The flaps and ailerons are fairly much the same. We put on a new empennage [tail section], and then put on a tricycle undercarriage.

"The fuselage was a problem—eventually in the first hundred or so we had to reinforce it at the main undercarriage. And the wing stiffeners were a problem."

The reinforcement at the main undercarriage was as much of a setback as occurred in the Twin Otter program. It might never have become an issue except for the exhaustive static testing the Twin Otter's main assemblies underwent. It is almost axiomatic that an aircraft manufacturer's latest design is also its most extensively tested one. If the Caribou set new standards of flight-test rigour, the Twin Otter was the most rigorously static-tested. That is, its components, such as the wing and fuselage, were subjected to loading with weights and hydraulic rams inside special frames to simulate the strain they might encounter in flight. Static testing was not required, but DHC was curious about the fatigue lives of the main components.

John Thompson remembers being visited in the static test area at the old Avro facility at Malton by Bill Boggs on the new DHC president's first day at work. It was November 25, 1965. The five prototype Twin Otters were assembled, and the next 10

Preproduction milestone: Prototype Twin Otter fuselage being removed from its assembly jig during January 1965. DHC 20161

were on the line over at Downsview. Thompson explained to Boggs that they were testing for the one-wheel landing case: where one mainwheel touched down hard. "My explanation satisfied him. I had no reason to think it was as serious as it was."

Soon afterward, as the strain in the test rig mounted, the fuselage buckled at each frame along its length—at only 50 per cent of design load. The strut-braced wing aggravated the situation. Not only did the load affect the fuselage where the landing gear struts were mounted, but the load path continued, by way of the wing struts (anchored by their inner fittings to a pin near the landing gear attachment points) to the wings, pushing the near-side wing upward (a compression load) and the offside wing down (in tension).

The main landing gear of the Twin Otter consists of two parallel steel tubes that act against urethane blocks to absorb landing and rebound loads. "A beautiful bit of engineering, really," Davy calls it. "Fred's, totally." It was a refinement of the Beaver's nutcracker main gear. But it focussed the loads more tightly than the Otter's tripod gear struts.

The net effect was permanent buckling, "and," says Thompson, that rare Scot with a sense of humour, "you're not allowed to have that. We concluded we had a serious crisis on our hands.

"Fred Buller looked at this. Fred was famous for looking at a problem and coming up with a solution nobody else would dare suggest.

"Buller said, 'What we're going to have to do is cut all these airplanes in half and put in a heavier frame.'"

And, instead of bent sheet-metal frames, that particular frame member, which took loads from the wings, their struts and the landing gear, would have to be machined from slabs of aluminum, a labour-intensive and therefore expensive fix. Not to mention the cost of chopping and reuniting at least 15 severed airframes.[11]

That aside, "it was an easy design," Davy says. "The Twin Otter grew quite easily, technically."

The Twin Otter's wing was the best of a long line of outstanding wings from the hand of Dick Hiscocks—wings that had made DHC aircraft tidy STOL performers mostly on the strength of their aerodynamic lift. But this one was cleaner. The Otter needed its corrugated upper-wing-surface underpinnings, six butt-jointed panels and 7,000 rivets—many of which left dimples in the wing skins—to hold it together. It was 58 feet in span.

The Twin Otter's six-foot fuselage plug made seven more feet of wingspan necessary, but by 1963 the process of chemically milling large billets of aluminum stock into single-piece wing skins with integral stiffeners to micrometre tolerances, pioneered for supersonic fighters, was well advanced. The milling was done in California, then more than today the centre of aerospace technology. The wings were shipped from the U.S. West Coast to Toronto. "Mind you," Davy says, "it wasn't cheap."

Inside the wing, although the box spar was similar to that of the single Otter, it was roll-formed, resulting in a stronger, nearly one-piece unit. Fred Buller's famous wing-strut attachment, along with much of the flap-aileron actuation mechanism, did carry over from one airplane to the next. Double-slotted flaps and ailerons were no longer an issue. Each half of the wing was attached to the fuselage structure by two bolts.[12]

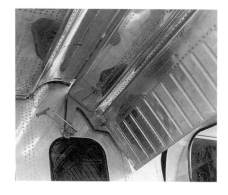

Above: This close-up of the inner flap section of DHC-X shows the double slots at the wing trailing edge and within the flap itself, and part of the flap/aileron actuation gear. DHC 20968

Facing page: Notes on hand-building an experimental prototype: DHC-X's tail complete in April 1965, but with dozens of details still to be checked and inspected. DHC 20877

The strut itself was "a nice piece of engineering," Davy thinks; a single machining with something close to an I-section with lugs on each end. "It was pretty. But at a time when it was fashionable *not* to make single pieces—one failure and the whole thing goes, of course."

And, indeed, the strut gave problems at the inner end, where a stainless-steel bushing had to be introduced to prevent fretting of the strut lug and its fuselage fitting. The tolerances were too precise. All it needed was to be loosened up a bit.

There was constant pressure at DHC, Davy remembers, to keep things simple. An example is the Twin Otter's hydraulic system. While other manufacturers were finding more and more tasks for hydraulics to take care of, DHC limited their use on the Twin Otter to the steerable nosewheel, brakes and operation of the flaps. Accordingly, while the industry as a whole was installing 3,000 psi systems, DHC installed one with half that pressure in the Twin Otter. It was one more way to make the airplane simpler and more reliable.[13]

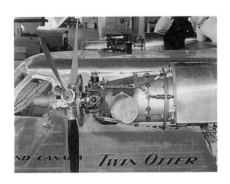

Above: Closeup of the port PT6 engine installation in the DHC-X prototype, May 1965. DHC 20981

Facing page: The DHC Experimental Shop, April 1965: DHC-X almost complete. Ahead of it, the DHC-5 Buffalo prototype; behind, the second prototype Twin Otter, SJB-X, without wingtips. DHC 20881

The Twin Otter embodies a number of other technical advances for DHC. The Pratt & Whitney Canada PT6A turboprop engines were new, of course. New engines make new and better aircraft possible, and that was especially the case with the PT6A and the Twin Otter. DHC knew almost as much about the PT6 as its makers did— Bob Fowler was knowledgeable about how they performed from flight-testing them. So, for once, there was no engine question. "If you can get good engines on an airplane," Mike Davy says, "you're halfway there."

It was more than just the dividend of 50 per cent more power for 35 per cent less weight with the PT6 compared with the single Otter's radial engine. By the time of the Buffalo and Twin Otter projects, Bob Klein had become DHC's chief of airworthiness, a title that required him to second-guess most decisions the company made. But the PT6 made it possible for the Twin Otter not just to continue flying on one engine but to climb.[14]

From a pilot's point of view, controlling the twin PT6s is easier than controlling the single piston engine on the Otter. Where the single Otter's engine is controlled with three levers (mixture, throttle and propeller pitch), the Twin Otter's power is governed by a power control set in the mid-cockpit roof that consists of paired levers, one for each engine, moveable with one hand from either seat, that automatically adjusted both engines' output and propeller pitch settings. (Two propeller pitch levers govern rpm and the manually feathered prop, and two fuel levers switch fuel flow on and off.) The beauty of the paired roof-mounted levers is that, with a twist of the hand, a floatplane Twin Otter can be turned within its own length on water.

Better yet, one common source of pilot-error accidents in the Beaver and the Otter—mismanaging fuel flow among the three (or five, with wet wingtips) tanks, was pretty much eliminated. The Twin Otter has four tanks grouped in pairs, each pair feeding one engine but able to be switched or crossfed.

Russ Bannock remembers the impression the Twin Otter made with its smooth turbine power when he flew it with George Neal or Bob Fowler:

"I was tremendously impressed with the performance. I was impressed with how simple the turboprop engines were to operate. In the development of the Twin Otter and the Turbo Beaver—and probably on that Beech Expeditor"—the trimotor Beech that Bob Fowler flew with one of the first PT6s in the nose—"DH really developed the beta system for control of the PT6. As you adjust the power, you also adjust the propeller pitch. The throttle and beta system are linked. On approach you can quickly lose height by retarding the throttle, which coarsens the pitch. On the ground, you can put the props in reverse with the throttle."

Above: CF-DHC-X on its first flight, May 20, 1965. Main landing gear strut fairings are missing. Note flight-test multi-instrument boom on the starboard wingtip. DHC 21040 / RON NUNNEY

The prototype Twin Otter, CF-DHC-X, flew for the first time May 20, 1965, in the hands of Bob Fowler and Mick Saunders. This time the registration took into account the contributions of a large, sophisticated organization in which individual contributions, though important, didn't stand out as they had on previous projects.

Flight-testing was more of a team game as well. Generally, with the exception of a wing drop at the stall—"a typical initial non-problem," Fowler says—the flying regime went smoothly, aided by the introduction of additional prototypes into the program.

Dick Batch, by then director of design development, remembers a painstaking process of carefully refining such trouble spots as the wing root leading edge and the outer wing-strut junction by building up surface contours with automotive putty, photographing them, flying them with wool tufts to show airflow, and then recontouring them to get the optimum aerodynamic shapes.

Fowler happened to mention to Dick Hiscocks how odd it was flying and looking at all of these tufts flapping merrily away outside. "Well," Hiscocks replied, "you have to remember, heh-heh, that the Otter is a fur-bearing animal."

Facing page: Bob Fowler has one hand on the ceiling-mounted throttles and the other exerting backward pressure on the control wheel as the float-equipped DHC-X nears takeoff speed near Toronto Island Airport, late August 1966. DHC VIA BOB FOWLER

With so much of fundamental value left over from the Otter, and so much that was new, the Two Otter, as many dubbed it when it appeared, was the critical transitional design that carried DHC into the airliner business. It carried on its strong wing the hopes of Dick Hiscocks and the company to be instrumental in a commercial aviation revolution, the coming intercity downtown-to-downtown STOL future.

The Twin Otter did show how such a future could work. It still does.

CHAPTER FOURTEEN

The Universal Airplane

There was something adventuresome about flying in a DHC-6 Twin Otter 30 years ago, when they began to appear in the Boston-to-Washington northeast corridor. By the late 1960s the second generation of medium-range jet airliners were in service: DC-9s, 727s. While these airliners were not intercontinental in range, nor were they as economical as short-haul city-to-city commuter aircraft. Early turbojet engines were thirsty, and jet airliners were more at home at high altitudes that reduced short-haul flights to takeoffs and landing approaches than with the extended cruise legs that could make money. The Twin Otter exploited this short-haul gap. It can be said to have created an industry: the third-tier air carriers.

For a passenger on Boston's Pilgrim Airlines, for example, a trip to New York was a return to the romance of aviation's golden era. You climbed aboard from good old terra firma instead of being funnelled into a numbered and alphabetized climatic tube. Until Pilgrim's Joe Fugere, a former U.S. Navy pilot, figured out a way to get a third row of seats into the DHC-6 (and often afterward, because they were seldom all occupied), almost every seat was a window seat.[1]

Which was a blessing. There was plenty to see at 2,000 feet. You could even watch the pilots at work during the flight. You watched the flaps operate a few feet away, you saw the airplane nose down and aim for the runway, and, for many people, this sensation of a flying machine that got back to basics was reassuring.

The northeast corridor of the United States is a long way from the bush. Most early-production Twin Otters worked for their first owners—commuter airlines such as Pilgrim, Commuter Air (which bought the second Twin Otter prototype), Newair (New Haven), Wings Airways (Washington) and Allegheny Commuter—in a densely populated, interurban context. Not only in the Northeast, but in other highly urbanized regions, such as California (for Westair, formed as Stol Air, in northern California, and Trans World Express, linking Los Angeles and Palm Springs), the Twin Otter became a city slicker. In Britain as well, Loganair, Brymon and Manx operated Twin Otters in airline feeder systems far from anything anyone at Downsview had ever imagined.

Not that the DHC-6 had gone completely uptown. From the beginning, it was a fixture in the Caribbean (Air Guadaloupe, Coral Air); South America (Aeropostale of Venezuela, Aces of Colombia); and, of course, Alaska (Wein Alaska Airways, Seair, Alaska Aeronautical Industries, Cape Smythe Air Service—who operated four—and ERA Aviation, among others). The Chilean and Peruvian air forces were practically launch customers, with Chile taking Numbers 7, 10, 11, 16 and 20 of the first two dozen built.

In providing intercity shuttle and taxi services, the Twin Otter was updating an enterprise that had fallen, by default, to war-surplus DC-3s, Twin Beeches and other piston-engine survivors from the 1930s. The popularity of those services, which led directly to today's hub-and-spoke system of feeder airlines, saved the Twin Otter program from crashing when the airplane's anticipated original customer, the U.S. Army, was unable to buy it.

But to many of the engineers who designed it, operating the Twin Otter from mile-and-a-half runways was a waste of the ruggedness that was built into each DHC-6. Nevertheless, the time for the Twin Otter to return to its intended origins was coming.[2]

There is at least one airway system in a remote part of the world that was built around the Twin Otter. Eventually Norway's Wideroes Flyveselskap A/S operated 18 of them from specially prepared 2,600-foot STOLports built at small coastal villages whose sole resort in emergencies hitherto had been Royal Norwegian Air Force mercy flights.

Norway has a shoreline so convoluted that the term "fjord" was appropriated into English to describe it. Like that of the Pacific Coast of British Columbia and

Aces Colombia long-nose Twin Otter Series 300s at Medellin. KARL KRAMER VIA PETER M. BOWERS

Back-to-basics commercial aviation: Skymark Airlines commuter Twin Otters N950SM and N951SM. Passengers actually walk to and from the airplanes. DHC 28725

Alaska, Norway's jumble of inlets and islands is hostile to any form of transportation other than boats or seaplanes. A string of hamlets runs north from Trondheim, halfway between Oslo and the Arctic Circle, and Tromso, well above it. The government committed itself during the 1960s to improving access to these isolated communities, and the Royal Norwegian Air Force was a longstanding Otter floatplane customer partly for that reason.[3]

Wideroes was founded in 1934 by Viggo and Arild Wideroe to pioneer services to those communities. Service began with a Waco floatplane, which operated out of Wideroes' base at Bodo, just north of the Arctic Circle. By 1967, the Wideroes Otter fleet consisted of six aircraft, including two of those surplussed by the RNOAF.[4]

The air force's procurement policies continued to influence Wideroes' choices of equipment. The arrival of the first four RNOAF Twin Otters in July and October 1967 renewed this interest at a time when the government was studying the matter. Mick Saunders, Bob Fowler's copilot on the Twin Otter's first flight, arrived in Norway with engineer Bob Irving at about the same time to demonstrate the aircraft. Runway lengths were determined on the basis of the Twin Otter's takeoff performance, and the system was called Norway's "short field services." Crews arrived for training and to take delivery of their first Twin Otter at Downsview June 1, 1968.[5] During 1969, the first year of operation exclusively south of Bodo, that first

Wideroes Twin Otter, LN-LMN, was in the air 12 hours a day, six days a week. This pace involved 120 landings a week and was delayed for technical reasons, Fred Hotson tells us, for exactly one hour. In 1971 Wideroes ordered four Series 300 DHC-6s to extend the service north. In time, the service comprised 35 airports, 20 of them north of the Circle. By 1980 Wideroes was operating 18 Twin Otters on its north-south coastline routes in a model demonstration of how aviation can enhance everyday life in remote areas.[6]

There is no particular point in trying to come up with an exact number of countries in which Twin Otters operate (or have operated) at any given time. Commercial flying is seasonal in some places, such as Antarctica. In others, such as Iraq, scheduled operations must respond to politics: a Twin Otter chartered by the United Nations was the last airplane to leave the cradle of civilization before the Gulf War broke out in 1990.

De Havilland Canada's official estimate is that Twin Otters were sold to 80 countries before production was terminated in 1988. That number alone justifies

Nearly 30 years of aviation progress poses for the camera in June 1965. DHC-X with the aircraft some of its production models will replace in service with Empire State airlines: a Twin Beech D-18, a type first flown in 1937. DHC 21718

calling the Twin Otter the universal airplane—if only because it could go to places within all of those countries DC-3s could not. But that number has risen because of the devolution of the Soviet Union into Russia and a dozen-odd new republics whose numbers continue to rise. Twin Otters have operated in many of those new states as, with the breakup of Aeroflot, the former Soviet airline, they find themselves without air services. So the official estimate of 80 countries is like the number of hours in some pilots' logbooks: once you get past 10,000 hours, what's the point of an hour and a half here or there?[7]

The list of places where Twin Otters have maintained scheduled services is full of surprises. The French Alps, perhaps needless to say, have no runways—at least, no level runways. There, Twin Otters operated by Air-Alpes make a virtue of necessity by taking off downhill and landing uphill—an arrangement that might logically be built into inner-city STOLports. Within Nepal, home of the highest mountain peaks in the world, a visitor has a choice of Twin Otters in which to fly: Canadian- or Chinese-built ones.

The Maldives are a group of 3,000 or so coral reefs in the Indian Ocean; not a runway anywhere in the whole kit and kaboodle. Not even a road. But there are 14 float-equipped Twin Otters there.

Fred Hotson, then a DHC test and delivery pilot, delivered the first Twin Otter, YA-GAS, into Chachcharan, Afghanistan, in late 1967 for Bakhtar Afghan Airlines. This was before tribesmen began shooting down Soviet warplanes with shoulder-mounted Stinger missiles. Twin Otter YA-GAS was a curiosity, which, upon landing, was surrounded by dozens of turbanned Afghans, clearly mesmerized by this First World newcomer.[8]

Airwest Twin Otter CF-AWF sets out from the sea plane dock in British Columbia's Victoria harbour. Twin Otters connect Victoria with Seattle and Vancouver, cities that otherwise require an ocean voyage to get to. PETER M. BOWERS

There are more frontiers on earth at any given time than we might think, and Twin Otters have a way of finding them. We could call it the Twin Otter Rule: the less friendly the environment for commercial aviation, the more likely it is to be serviced by Twin Otters.

It is much easier to estimate the number of Twin Otters still airworthy, if only because there are sources to ask. A total of 844 were built—not bad for an airplane put into production on the basis of an understood 100-plane order that shrank to six.[9]

"It's just a guess," Steve Penikett emphasizes. "But I think there are 750 still out there. I'd bet I'm right by 10 or so one way or the other." Penikett should know: he manages the world's largest fleet of Twin Otters.

Kenn Borek Air, Penikett's outfit, operates 32 of them. The Calgary, Alberta–based lease-charter outfit flies Twin Otters worldwide: in alphabetical order, from the Antarctic, where they have operated each southern-hemisphere summer for 15 years; to the Vancouver-Victoria harbour-to-harbour shuttle in southwestern British

Always a buyer: British Antarctic Survey Twin
Otter (152) VP-FAO, registered in the Falk-
lands, delivered November 11, 1968, was sold
to Air Paris August 20, 1971. DHC 30473

Columbia, which Borek Air flies with Twin Otters on behalf of Harbour Air, a
noted coastal floatplane operator of Beavers and turbine single Otters in which
Borek has a half-interest.[10]

The company started as an off-shoot of Borek's heavy-construction company,
which was active in oil exploration in Canada's far north. Kenn Borek Air was organized as a separate company in 1969 and bought its first Twin Otter the following
year. The airplane made such an immediate impact that Borek began buying one a
year, many of them factory-fresh. By 1980, the year Steve Penikett became general
manager, the fleet consisted of about 10 DC-3s, 10 Twin Otters and a mix of Beech
types, including King Air twins—mostly supporting the company's oil industry
activities. A Canadian government energy policy that raised taxes on fossil fuels following the oil crisis of the early 1970s had shut down much of the private-sector
exploration activities in the country, and Kenn Borek Air began looking for other

markets. It settled on a specialty-leasing business that now has a global reach. The go-anywhere Twin Otter became Borek's standard type.

"It is the best floatplane ever built," Penikett says. "The serviceability is good. Mechanically it's pretty straightforward. It has the best engine ever built. The Twin Otter is similar to the DC-3; every piece on the Twin Otter can be replaced."

Over the years, as Borek Air has evolved into a worldwide operation, the Twin Otter has re-evolved into the bush plane it was designed to be. The hundreds of Twin Otters that operated from major metropolitan airports on commuter and feeder routes—their STOL performance wasted on runways that were often 10 times as long as the Twin Otter needs—gave way to larger aircraft, many of them Dash-8s. So the Twin Otters went where they have always belonged: the Third World, the mountains, the jungle, the poles and the water that covers most of the planet.

"I'm in the business of providing air service in out-of-the-way places that require STOL airplanes," Penikett explains, in a tone of voice that says, *What other airplane* would *I use?*[11]

I could ask the same question. Late one morning in October 1995, my wife and I sat among a dozen or so travellers in the tiny waiting room of the airport at Pokara, Nepal. Pokara is a lakeside resort town in the centre of the country, near the foothills of the Himalayas. We had journeyed there by bus, scrambling with our luggage over the house-sized boulders of a rock slide that blocked the only road across the country, and reloading ourselves aboard even older buses at the other side of the slide.

So we had decided to treat ourselves to a flight back to Kathmandu. Far from being able to examine our aircraft at our leisure as the usual late-twentieth-century security checks and boarding routine unfolded, we wondered until the very last minute what we might be flying to the capital. As the group began to stir, concluding something had gone wrong, a small twin-engined aircraft alighted on the grass strip and taxied to a patch of bare dirt in front of the building.

"Okay, Mr. Airplane Expert," my wife gibed, "what is that?"

Well. To be honest, I didn't know. We had a view from the aircraft's seven o'clock, and although the plane had the general layout of a Twin Otter, the vertical tail did not have the Twin Otter's characteristic swept leading and trailing edges, and its corners were rounded off. It looked like the tail of a DC-4. And the landing gear looked like something from a MiG fighter: all three gears were suspended from knuckle-type oleo struts that appeared suitable for taking off from staircases.

The interior was finished, to be charitable, to military standards. The seats were basket-weave webbing, though not uncomfortable for the 40-minute trip we took. Bare metal was crimped around the window installations; plastic inserts had been forgone. The flight was spectacular, with orange-tinted morning light reflecting off

Series 200 N1375T is a universal airplane by itself. In Air New England commuter colours here in 1971, it has served in Florida, Germany, northern Canada, Japan and Australia. DHC 37812

the snowfields of the Himalayas well above our flightpath. Aside from a few mountain downdrafts, the flight was smooth, and the touchdown, onto a concrete runway, almost imperceptible.

Back on the ground in Kathmandu, I approached the pilot. He was a handsome kid, not a hair out of place, accessorized with, believe it or not, a white silk scarf tucked into his nicely aged dark leather bomber jacket. He spoke good English, the language of aviation.

"It's a Twin Otter," he said, with not a little pride.

"Not like any Twin Otter I've ever seen," I retorted.

"Well," he conceded, "it was built in Harbin, China."

That was my first look at a Harbin Aircraft Manufacturing Company Y-12, the Chinese copy of the DHC-6 Twin Otter.

When the People's Republic of China ordered their first three Twin Otters, the deal allowed 20 Chinese "inspectors" to view the assembly process in order to enforce that country's standards of quality control. They were housed in their own office at Downsview and spent much time making detailed drawings of the tooling, jigs and structural parts. They certainly learned, down to the millimetre, how to build a Twin Otter. "We knew exactly what they were doing," Russ Bannock chuckles.[12]

Soon thereafter, the Chinese government bought a couple dozen PT6A-27s from Pratt & Whitney Canada. And something called the Y-12 began appearing in those little-known corners of the world that remained aligned with the People's Republic—places like Mongolia, whose national airline operates five. They are ideal for those bleak, mountainous landscapes for the same reasons real Twin Otters are. Most, if not all, of Nepal's Twin Otters were supplied under various foreign aid programs, so when DHC production ceased, the Harbin near-copy must have been an attractive alternative.

For most of its production run, the Harbin version has remained uncertified in the West. More recently, though, the Harbin factory has contracted with the Lockheed-Martin company to revamp its production techniques and achieve certification. The latest Y-12 IV version was certificated under the U.S. Federal Aviation Agency FAR Part 23 rules March 26, 1995.[13]

Joe Fugere of Pilgrim Airlines *(left)* takes delivery of his first Twin Otter, N121PM, the fourteenth built, during October 1966. Fugere, a former U.S. Navy pilot, added a third row of seats to the DHC-6, making it a profitable commuter airliner. He is pictured here with DHC's Phil Halsey. DHC 39860

So, while original Downsview-built Twin Otters are flying at nearly 30 years of age in the far corners of the world, new Harbin-built near-copies may be in service on North American commuter routes by the end of the century. They are being offered to First-World commuter and feeder lines at prices DHC probably could not build them for today.

In fact, in a scarcely believable twist of fate, assembled but unfinished Harbin Y-12s are being shipped from China to North Bay, Ontario, to be fitted out with

The answer to the question, how do you operate fixed-wing air service in the Alps? Air Alpes Twin Otter F-BOOH (72), the company's first such aircraft. Tip: take off downhill, land uphill. DHC 31589

western avionics, interiors, wheels and brakes by the Canadian Aerospace Group before being delivered to customers. The first Chinese aircraft for completion at North Bay arrived there in July 1997 and was to be delivered to its owner by the end of the year. The Y-12s are marketed under the name Twin Panda.[14]

To have their airplane copied in a foreign nation and marketed again—as the Twin Panda, no less—after having manufactured nearly 900 of them themselves is a huge compliment to the engineers of de Havilland Canada. The only drawback is that, as president of DHC when the Canadian government owned the company during the late 1970s, and as an originator of a manufacturing program that would last another decade and bring in a half-million dollars or more per article, Russ Bannock could not go to his board of directors and convince them there was a worldwide market for the Twin Otter into the next century. It was only mildly ironic that it was the Boeing Airplane Company, as DHC owners from 1986 to 1991, who terminated production of the Twin Otter.

Maybe the Chinese knew better.

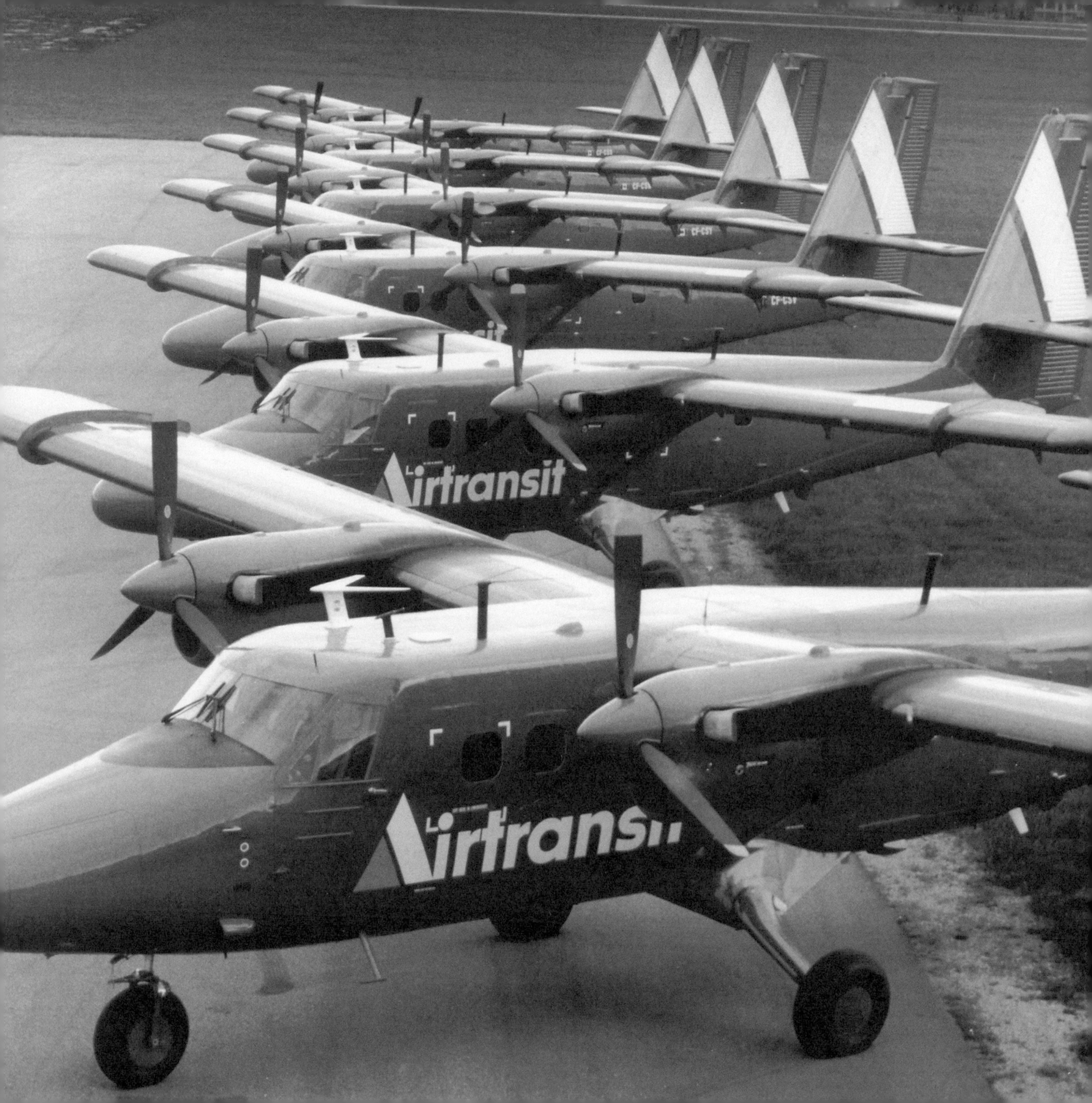
Airtransit

CHAPTER FIFTEEN

The Airtransit Experiment

The early 1970s were exciting and profitable years for de Havilland.[1] A number of intriguing experimental projects were being explored, including a high-performance twin-turbine pusher business airplane called the DHP 48. The company was poised to take advantage of a couple of environmental trends: the aversion to building sprawling exurban megaterminals to service the Boeing 747 jumbo jets then coming into service worldwide, and the fears of effects in the atmosphere and on the ground that led to the cancellation of the American supersonic transport projects.

The Twin Otter was everything the big jets were not. DHC was selling a small but growable, fairly quiet, turbine-powered Short Takeoff and Landing airplane that had proven it could operate from docks on the Hudson River. DHC had something even better on the drawing boards.

"Those were the years," writes one-time Dash-7 project manager Tom Higgins, "of the Northeast Corridor study of the Boston-Washington strip, and the 'no more big airports' syndrome. Pan American Airways, American Airlines, and Eastern Airlines were all deeply involved in studies of different approaches to metropolitan and downtown air services."[2]

Among the possibilities Higgins lists in his almost wistful reflections on those imaginative days were STOLports on office buildings or docked aircraft carriers along the Hudson River; rooftop STOLports on railroad stations in Houston; some Boeing promotions of hub-and-spoke and quiet short-haul concepts; and a McDonnell Aircraft presentation, in conjunction with Eastern, of a French Breguet four-engine STOL design, the four big propellers of which "bathed the wing in slipstream and were cross-shafted for power and lift symmetry."

So it appeared that everything DHC had stood for since the Beaver was about to be vindicated, in a fundamental redesign of the First World's aviation infrastructure that would put the company at the forefront of a more environmentally sound commercial aviation system. And DHC was hard at work—had been since 1969—designing the kingpin of this revolutionary future.

"Thus," Higgins continues, "in the very early days of the new aircraft designated DHC-7, a 40-passenger, four-engine, fixed gear vehicle with exemplary [if not, strictly speaking, STOL] performance . . . the company was involved in selling the need and defining the 'system.'"[3]

Small may be beautiful, but, as we now know, the future Higgins was working on has in only sporadic ways come to pass. The Northeast Corridor Study was closed down in early April of 1973, "due mainly to strong community opposition to air operations outside the major airports," Fred Hotson writes. "Locations outside major airports were one of the Civil Aeronautics Board's main objectives in eliminating traffic congestion. It was a major blow."[4]

By then discussions between DHC and the Canadian federal government aimed at demonstrating Canadian expertise in city-to-city STOL had been ongoing for more than two years. In May 1971 the federal government had instructed its Ministry of Transport "to plan, develop and evaluate a STOL commuter air system which could be economically viable and marketable internationally."[5]

Once the Americans lost their zest for decongesting the crowded Boston-Washington flyway, it fell to Canada and DHC to show how such a high-density interurban shuttle could work. Airtransit, the company that would operate the service, was incorporated June 19, 1973, as a wholly owned subsidiary of Air Canada. DHC provided the flying equipment. Four agencies of Transport Canada were involved, along with the ministry of Industry, Trade and Commerce, which hoped to market the system elsewhere.

Canada may not be the most obvious country in the world to demonstrate a high-density air shuttle between major cities, but it was the nation with the most to gain from whatever worldwide acceptance the demonstration might beget.

There was a youthful, dynamic idealism still abroad in Canada at the time, left over from the success of Expo 67, which celebrated the country's one-hundredth birthday. Canada felt it had much to offer the world, from United Nations peace-keeping to STOL technology. It was only a matter of showcasing the better mousetrap.

Furthermore, the Airtransit shuttle between Ottawa and Montreal was reminis-cent of the spirit of wide co-operation that had led to the Defence Research Board–DHC Otter 3682 program and the DHC-Boeing-NASA Augmentor Wing research program. But there was nothing exotic about Airtransit except the Twin Otters, which were perhaps the best-equipped of their type, and the intention that the shuttle would operate within "a total STOL environment." For passengers, the hourly flights between cities were designed to be as routine as possible, given that takeoff and landings would be, as the special brochure handed out to passengers warned, "at relatively steep angles."

These steep—six- to nine-degree—takeoffs and glideslopes were not intended to look impressive. They were to minimize sound pollution. Airtransit claimed their tests indicated that the noise associated with a Twin Otter taking off or landing, mea-sured at 500 feet, was about the same as a city bus at 30 mph, heard from 100 feet.

Six Twin Otters were prepared for the service, becoming known as the DHC-6 Series 300s model. The Ministry of Transport, perhaps understandably, labelled the Twin Otters DHC-6-300 [MOT]s. Whatever the "s" in 300s stood for, the airplanes were special—"the most sophisticated Twin Otters ever to leave the production line at Downsview," Hotson says.[6]

Included in their specification was equipment designed to allow steeper approaches: some of it, such as wing spoilers, pioneered by Otter 3682; some, such as higher-capacity non-skid and emergency brakes and hydraulic and electrical equipment improvements, simply logical additions to help the aircraft cope with the increased strain.

Cruising altitudes ranged from 3,000 to 8,000 feet, offering the 11 passengers (most Twin Otters seat 20) in their wider-than-standard seats a view of the rocky eastern Ontario countryside. A toilet, cabin air conditioning and a coat rack—a *coat* rack!—were added. The ultimate bushplane was going cosmopolitan.

Airtransit's "total STOL environment" included a Co-Scan glideslope and direc-tional microwave landing system on the ground and in the airplane, giving the pilot a visual indication of whether he was on the correct flight path to touchdown "in all but the worst of weather conditions." An RNAV (Area Navigation) system from Lit-ton Industries was installed to keep the Twin Otters out of the most congested airways by giving the pilot information needed to fly a variety of multi-leg routes between the Ottawa and Montreal STOLports. The airplane's navigation computer was programmed to a specific route simply by having the pilot insert a preprinted card in a slot just to the right of the instrument panel centreline. In the event that ground signals became faint or disappeared, the computer would choose an alternate route. Other new electronics included an autopilot, upgraded very high frequency receivers, navaids, and barometric and radio altimeters to give altitudes above sea level and over land.

At each end of the route was a STOLport with a 2,000-foot runway. This was the generous definition of STOL used by Airtransit and agreed to in DHC negotiations with the U.S. FAA. At the Ottawa end, historic Rockcliffe airport, 12 minutes from Parliament Hill, had a World War II–era runway of that length. The Montreal STOLport was located in the Expo 67 parking lot on an island in the St. Lawrence River. Neither facility occupied more than 44.5 acres.

For such an impressive system—this was the peak of the systems approach—some surprisingly low-tech glitches interfered with Airtransit's launch: "Everything," Hotson tells us, "from strikes to shortages of steel." To start off with, the company's hangar doors weren't tall enough to admit the Twin Otter's tail.

Nevertheless, on July 24, 1974, a one-and-a-half-hour service, downtown-to-downtown, between Canada's capital and its second-largest city cut one hour from the Ottawa-Montreal drive (which is less than 100 miles) and a half-hour from the regular airline time, all for a $20 fare. The shuttle started with 16 flights daily and was soon nearly doubled to 30. Load factors for the first year were close to 60 per cent, and a total of 160,000 passengers took advantage of the service. The overall Airtransit program was budgeted at $25.5 million.

From DHC's point of view, the program was a priceless opportunity to fine-tune its next big program. The aircraft and their avionics, the STOL environment, the pilot training—every aspect of the operation, in fact—was seen as a dry run to design and test the vehicle DHC saw as the universal, higher-capacity STOL vehicle: its upcoming DHC-7.

The experience of Harold Kalman illustrates the human side of flying the Airtransit shuttle, which Kalman did regularly during the early days of the experiment before moving to Vancouver. Then an Ottawa-based architectural historian and building conservation consultant who calls himself "a pilot manqué," Kalman would sit in the right-hand front seat so he could watch the pilot work.

He enjoys the steep ascents. "I've always loved taking off in Twin Otters. I've never been in a plane that could get off the ground so quickly." He found the abrupt descents less exhilarating; he claims to have dropped into Victoria harbour through a

Facing page: Airtransit Instrument Landing System (ILS) avionics. DHC saw the Airtransit Otters as a transition to fully IFR-capable commuter airliners, such as the Dash-7. DHC 38807

hole in the clouds at very close to a 45-degree angle in an Air West Twin Otter. He has flown in a Twin Otter from Vancouver to Victoria skimming the waves at 50 feet, rising higher only to clear Mayne Island. And he flew almost weekly on Airtransit.

"I really liked watching the navigation system," he recalls. "At a certain checkpoint it would beep, flash numbers on a screen, and I think the airplane changed course by itself, and the pilot would basically agree that yes, it would do that.

"I had the impression that the pilots were a little in awe of the navigation system and the electronics in general. One day we were probably halfway from Ottawa to

Montreal on a very clear Saturday afternoon. And a red light started flashing on the instrument panel. A vacuum in the starboard engine or something like that. Anyway, the crew ignored it. The light continued to flash. They ignored it, hoping, I guess, that it would go away. It continued to flash and, eventually, a buzzer sounded.

"So the copilot pulls out a very thick three-ring binder, which must have been the pilot's manual. He began thumbing through it. The light became more insistent. He turned the pages faster. Suddenly, the binder snapped open and the cockpit was filled with a blizzard of white pages. And, right then, the light stopped flashing."

Kalman thinks it was a mistake to reduce the number of seats on the Airtransit Twin Otters. The fact that Airtransit did not make money was the chief criticism, he says. It would never have occurred to the organizers of the experiment, Kalman believes, to show potential Twin Otter operators similar if less sophisticated 19-seat airplanes on the West Coast "making money hand over fist."[7]

There is a measure of defiance in Fred Hotson's words as he sums up Airtransit in 1983:

"The experiment was providing a wealth of data for what was becoming a new Canadian concept of transportation. All eyes were on the project—probably the least concerned was the regular passenger who was getting the kind of service he wanted and let it go at that. The planners held to their vision of a complete STOL package and did their advanced thinking in terms of a 48-passenger DHC-7. The critics looked mostly at the cost figures and scoffed at the limited number of passenger seats. The newspapers had a heyday reporting both sides. When the project ended April 30, 1976, it had completed all of its objectives and had proven that STOL could operate in the same sky as the major carriers in a complex area like Montreal and do it on a round-the-clock basis...."

"With the growing public interest in STOL, the company position of leadership in the technology and the success of the Twin Otter," Dick Hiscocks wrote in his essay "Whither STOL?", "it appeared that the market would be receptive to a larger and more advanced version of the airplane."[8]

"The Ottawa-Montreal Airtransit experiment was intended to sell the concept and encourage exploitation of a new opportunity in aviation and the ancillary infrastructure," Tom Higgins concludes in the above-cited article. "Airtransit was never intended to be anything more than an experiment and demonstration.

"It was not viable and it terminated naturally. It succeeded in performing its experimental task, but failed [in] the demonstration role, since nobody copied it."

Higgins's point is neither to bury Airtransit nor to praise it. It is rather to explain objectively the change in conditions that mandated a change in concept for the DHC-7 project from a fixed-gear, four-engine STOL extrapolation of the Twin Otter to what the Dash-7 became. As Higgins describes it: "48 passengers, with retractible landing gear, increased speed, 2,000-foot runway STOL performance and special emphasis on the environment. The airplane was to be very quiet and to conserve fuel. . . .

"The [Dash-7] airplane eventually went into production and was sold as a good piece of air transportation at its time in spite of carrying a penalty for a STOL capability that was never fully utilized. Nevertheless, despite the lack of a fully orchestrated STOL system, many operators, including Greenlandair, Wideroes (Norway), Ransome (USA), [and] Brymon (London City Airport), continue to this day to use the aircraft's steep descent, obstacle clearance and runway performance capabilities to significant advantage."[9]

Wideroes LN-BNX (353), one of no fewer than 30 Twin Otters that were used in Norway, helped equip another highly automated fixed-wing STOL service that linked coastal communities above the Arctic Circle.
JOHN WEGG VIA PETER M. BOWERS

While the Dash-7 was never the sales success DHC hoped it would be—it sold 100 copies—it did amount to a proof-of-concept vehicle for its successor, the most successful turboprop airliner in the world, the Dash-8. The differences between the two are significant less for aerodynamic reasons than for the Dash-8's success in the market.

No pretense has ever been made that the Dash-8 is in any way a STOL aircraft, and in being powered by two rather than four engines it has excelled in ways that turned out to be more important than STOL performance: it is quieter and even more fuel-efficient.

At the time of writing, 500 Dash-8s had been sold (with orders in hand for at least another 60), and a new model, the 8Q Series 400, is being flight-tested. It is a stretched 70-seat airliner that can fly 100 knots faster, at 350 knots, than the Dash-8 300 series. DHC has now produced an airliner as big as any commuter that can fly almost as fast as a jet. The 8Q Series 400 will be in service by mid-1999, presenting us with a preview of a new aviation millenium different in detail rather than the utter conceptual change DHC foresaw with the Twin Otter. Whether this is a disappointment is a philosophical question. The business question has been answered: DHC still exists—an impressive achievement in itself—and is making money by building what the market is asking for.

Meanwhile, to give Higgins, who along with Dick Hiscocks and the DHC team envisaged a better world with a more efficient short-haul aviation future, the last word: "The great STOL infrastructure did not develop as predicted and we still await it"—in 1993, his time of writing—"20 years later."

We continue to await it.

CHAPTER SIXTEEN

Flying the Otter and Twin Otter

Randy Mattocks spent most of his time at the controls of piston Otters supporting United Nations peacekeeping forces in the Middle East.[1] A major at the time, he became commanding officer of 56 Canadian Transport Company, Royal Canadian Army Service Corps, part of the United Nations Emergency Force (UNEF) I, the UN organization in the Gaza Strip, from June 1965 to June 1966.

Experienced Otter drivers know—especially when carrying heavy loads—to keep the nose of an Otter down on takeoff to build up airspeed before trying to climb. And, of course, the Otter was one of the first STOL aircraft to adopt a nose-down attitude on final approach. But the eventual Lt.-Col. Mattocks thought of the Otter as a nose-down flyer almost all the time:

"Yes, it had a nose-down attitude, but a nose-down attitude which leads to a sight-picture or thought: it's as if somebody's standing on a cloud, pulling you up. It's as if there's a rope attached to the centre of gravity"—not far from the flap hinge lines, that is—"pulling up. You don't get the impression that it's driving up.

It just looks like it's being lifted up by something, but you can't see the rope. That's always been my feel with respect to Otters."[2]

This is consistent with James Hay Stevens's *Flight* magazine impression of the nose below the horizon at 6,000 feet and "a view like that from a balcony." Mattocks is happy to concede that he seldom, if ever, flew Otters at anything like their gross weight, and that when he flew passengers, they were usually single soldiers rotating in and out of detachments or observation posts. He never flew Otters on floats, either in the southern United States or over Egypt. Moreover, the Otters he flew usually developed the full advertised power. "You know the military," he says. "They over-maintain."[3]

For a pilot who cut his teeth on Taylorcraft Austers as artillery observation post aircraft and flew Beavers as an exchange pilot at the home of U.S. Army aviation, Fort Rucker, the Otter came as, well, a change.

"With bigger machines [such as the Otter], it was more a case of setting it up the way you wanted, setting it up so you've got the proper sight-picture in front of you, and having made sure that everything is prepared for whatever you're gonna do, do it, and sit outside of it a little bit if you can, and watch to see what happened so that you can give corrective inputs to it. I learned that when I was instructing. That is very challenging work, because you have to know what the aircraft is doing, what the aircraft *should* be doing, and you have to know what you're gonna do about it if it doesn't do what it's supposed to do."

To fly the Otter, in other words, you had to fly by more than the seat of your pants.[4]

Lt.-Col. K. R. Mattocks: "You have to know what you're gonna do about it if the Otter doesn't do what it's supposed to do."
VIA K. R. MATTOCKS

As for flying the standard piston Otter from water, C. Marin Faure, author of *Flying a Floatplane*, writes that "It takes real skill. . . . [5]

"Not that the plane is hard to handle. Quite the contrary. Like the Beaver, the Otter combines stability with an impressive degree of maneuvrability. It's also one of the few airplanes that retains full aileron control throughout the stall. Hauling any airplane off the water at too low an airspeed is risky, but at least in an Otter you won't have to worry about dropping a wing, because you'll always have aileron control. You will, however, have to worry about the engine.

"This is where the skill comes in. Full power operation is limited to a maximum of one minute. Keeping the power in for more than a minute is a real gamble. If there's a loud bang and a big cloud of blue smoke, you'll know you lost. Sometime before reaching that magic 60 seconds, you'll have to throttle back to maximum continuous power. This will leave you with less than 400 hp and your climb rate will drop from mediocre to downright lousy. In fact, you'll be doing well to get 100 feet per minute out of the thing if it's fully loaded.

"Flying an Otter is to get off the water almost immediately only to wonder if you'll be able to clear the trees at the end of the lake. Throttling back will save the engine, in the process."

Bill Whitney and Gerry Bruder are high-time pilots with Seattle's Kenmore Air Harbor, which operates charter operations upcoast along the inside shores of Vancouver Island to 20 destinations north to Port McNeill, and scheduled services to the San Juan Islands and Victoria. Kenmore operates piston and turbine Beavers (it has the first and last Turbo Beavers built at DHC), Otters and Cessnas, all on floats. Whitney is Kenmore's chief pilot. Bruder is a former *Flying* magazine staff writer with several books on aviation to his credit.

Seattle itself consists of sizeable hills, often connected by high-span examples of iron-age bridge engineering that cross a dozen-odd bodies of water. One such body of water that borders on the city's downtown business district is Lake Union. Getting in and out of Lake Union is an important priority for Kenmore, and one of the main reasons why its five meticulously rebuilt (three of them ex-Indian Air Force) Otters have the Vazar Dash-3 conversion.[6]

Kenmore Air Harbor chief pilot Bill Whitney: "You have to plan ahead—especially on approach. You have to leave yourself room to be comfortable." KENMORE AIR HARBOUR

"We could not operate piston Otters out of there," Whitney says matter-of-factly. "You can tell they worked hard to compensate for that piston engine. That airframe is just super light. The thing just oughtta weigh more than it does, as big as it is."

Whitney, for one, does not necessarily believe the piston Otter is a blown cylinder waiting to happen. It does require finesse when operated on floats, though. An owner-pilot would soon develop the necessary touch, he feels, but, as a chief pilot, he has to keep in mind the varying preferences of his staff. Bruder insists that being assigned to fly Kenmore's Otters is not considered a reward or a promotion. Certain pilots just take to the Otter for their own reasons:

"The Otter has several characteristics that you should keep in mind when you fly it," Whitney says. "Its flap speed is lower than a Beaver's, so you have to plan ahead—especially on approach. Just being a bigger airplane, you have to leave yourself room to be comfortable. You leave yourself more room in confined situations, whether it's the terrain, or boats, or congestion. You just leave yourself more room, do a wider pattern, that sort of thing.

"How it behaves on the water depends on the floats. We use Edo floats, amphibs without the landing gear, 7200s modified to 7490. The other choice in Edos is the 7170.

"As far as lifting off [on floats] is concerned, the way it reacts to gusty conditions is less pleasant. It's all over the place. And, of course, with a bigger airplane, the controls are heavier, mushier.

"Taking the whole takeoff run into consideration, a Beaver gets off the water a little quicker than an Otter, with both of them at gross weight. Getting off the step, though, the Otter's really off the water faster. As a floatplane, it's considerably better. Once it gets off and is climbing, it leaves the Beaver behind.

"Does it fly nose-down? It kinda does with flaps. The climbout, until you get the flaps up, is nose-down. Of course, that's good procedure with floats [and their increased weight and drag], to keep the nose down. It flies with a very nose-down attitude on approach."

Bruder likes the challenge. "First of all, I have the feeling the guys who tell you they prefer to fly the Beaver over the Otter are talking about piston Otters. I flew a piston Otter for a season—I liked that, too. By that time—I'd been flying Beavers and Cessnas—it was a welcome change of pace.

"The turbine Otter is a totally different airplane. The conversion makes that much difference.

"It could also be that people who say they prefer flying the Beaver to the Otter aren't familiar enough with floatplanes to feel comfortable with the Otter. There is a perception—especially among passengers—that the more senior pilots fly the bigger planes. Not long ago I docked a Beaver and the customer said, 'So, you've been demoted.' It's true that, generally speaking, the more experienced pilots will fly the longer airplane.

"One of the major challenges I had with the turbine Otter was learning to keep the nose down on approach to landing. We've all been indoctrinated to keep the nose up on approach. It took me a long time to trust the airplane not to dig in the floats. The approach results in popping down rather than a smooth touchdown."

"I do like the Otter," Bruder continues. "I like having the ability to climb very quickly [with the turbine engine]. The decibels are a lot lower. And with less vibration from the engine and propeller, there's a lot less fatigue.

"There are other things I like about the Otter. I like the extra elbow room in the cockpit. I like the extra semi-privacy up front. And the power, of course.

"The downside is that it can be hard to handle in the wind. It's scary sometimes coming into a tight docking situation. With that long wingspan, that long nose, and you're very aware of that big tail behind you. So there is that stress level."

And, oh yes, there is one other disadvantage. Kenmore's turbine Otters are cleared to fly at 8,370 pounds or so, about 400 pounds more than standard Otters. Especially on the outbound leg, that extra weight often comes in the form of "box after box after box to unload: canned goods, cases of beer."

The Twin Otter was designed to update the Otter. It does so most completely on floats, as Kenn Borek Air pilot Michael Thompson demonstrated on the

Kenmore's Gerry Bruder:"One of the major challenges I had with the turbine Otter was learning to keep the nose down on approach."

VIA GERRY BRUDER

kind of round-trip flight the airplane is best at: half an hour or so each way, Vancouver-Victoria, harbour-to-harbour and back over stunning scenery, at the controls of C-GKBX.[7]

As new as KBX is by DHC standards at only 20 years old, this Twin Otter has a longer record than most career criminals. KBX has been around: Great Britain, the South Pacific and almost everywhere in the world Kenn Borek Air flies, which is to say, "Both poles and most places in-between." KBX is a Series 300, the 571st Twin Otter built and the first of its kind off the line in 1978, flying for the first time January 9. It was delivered to Brymon Airways in England as G-BFGP, on February 21, and was bought by Aurigny Air Services, which operates in the Channel Islands, in May 1980. It bounced around, doing two tours with an outfit called Spacegrand Aviation Services, Brymon again and National Airways, before being bought by BAC Leasing in mid-1989 and working for the rest of the year for Aerolift Philippines Corp. as RP-C1217.

Kenn Borek bought the aircraft in March 1990, leased it back to BAC and then took permanent possession in 1991, as close as Borek chief engineer Greg (Bones) Hudson can recall, at Jersey in the Channel Islands. He can't be positive. "We were buying a lot of airplanes then. It's all just a blur in my mind.

N3125S (407), Kenmore Air Harbor's first Otter, was RCAF 9424 and a U.N. New Guinea veteran. Kenmore acquired it in 1988 and leased it in Juneau for a year with the original engine. But it was unpopular with pilots until converted to PT6A power in 1992. Here it takes off from Seattle's Elliott Bay.
KENMORE AIR HARBOR VIA GERRY BRUDER

"We just pretty things up a bit and add knick-knacks here and there, little odds and ends," is how Hudson sums up the overhaul KBX underwent that year at Borek's base in Calgary. "We call it Borek-izing them."

Then it was back to the grind: two years in Burma; a summer's action at Resolute Bay, Northwest Territories; then off to Thailand in 1994. The aircraft was repainted in something Hudson calls "a funny rainbow scheme" for service in the British Virgin Islands the following year, and then returned to Borek's trademark colours: orange-red tail and upper fuselage, white underside and floats, and black upper wing and cheat line. KBX is an anomaly among Twin Otters, one of the very few long-nose models on floats. To compensate for additional mass up front, it is shod with long Wipline 13000 floats. Thus beautified and decked out, KBX made for the British Columbia coast, where Borek operates ten Twin Otters under its joint ownership of Harbour Air Seaplanes, in 1996.

The trip between Vancouver and Victoria otherwise requires a near two-hour ocean voyage connecting ferry terminals far from either city's centre. It also happens to offer one of the more spectacular vistas available in the northern hemisphere. We fly southwest over the Gulf of Georgia, in which the American San Juan Islands are alive with their mid-May beach-perimeter borders of bright yellow broom. River deltas and inlets add to the riot of geological forms below, where the North American continent begins to wrinkle up, producing waves of long, parallel islands and ridges before it plunges beneath the Pacific Plate under the ocean far off Vancouver Island's battered outer coast. Our horizons on three sides consist of mountain peaks that are all the more impressive from two- to three-thousand feet, where the turbine-powered Twin Otter is most at home, flying above most of the land-to-water updrafts.

Thompson, with 2,000 hours on Twin Otters, lost no time in demonstrating why this is the ultimate floatplane. Holding both roof-mounted throttles easily in his raised right hand, he backed away from the dock, steering with differential power from the twin engines with their reversed props simply by twisting his wrist slightly, turning his palm in the direction he wanted to go. At first I thought he was just showing off.

There was no noticeable engine noise or vibration, just the beating sound and tangible throb of the propeller blades moving air. As Thompson deftly manoeuvred backward, then switched to positive thrust and taxied into the harbour flightline, the woman behind me said to her companion, "I feel very safe in floatplanes."

We awaited the touchdown of a Baxter Air Beaver and watched a West Coast Air Series 100 Twin Otter, G-GOKN, take off ahead of us. With the nose up for

Kenn Borek Air Twin Otters in formation over the Pacific Northwest: C-FPAT (closer aircraft) and C-FOEQ. PAT, now retired, is the second DHC-6 built and spent 18 months in arduous flight-testing as CF-SJB-X. OEQ was an Ontario Provincial Air Service yellow bird from 1967 to 1979. KENN BOREK AIR

takeoff, a Twin Otter, with its float tips so close below, looks more like a marine organism than something planing over the surface. At a glance, it could be a breaching killer whale with the top half of its tail proud of the water and spray emanating from its blowhole. A floatplane Twin Otter looks as if it belongs in the marine environment. An overcast sky and loose patches of fog accentuated the effect.

Thompson applies full right rudder on takeoff, his right leg straight and rigid. We take off due north, across the harbour. The feeling is of smoothness rather than brute power. Instead of surging forward we simply keep going faster. We are on the step in 10 seconds—not particularly quick, but not bad for a crosswind takeoff from fairly choppy water. We are at 50 feet as we pass over the lighthouse that marks Brockton Point, which thrusts from forested Stanley Park on our left into Vancouver's harbour and forms the cove we have just taken off from.

Thompson and KBX execute a sweeping left-hand climbing turn over the park's vast expanse of evergreens. Suddenly everyone aboard sees the city's Big Picture: the harbour, open year-round, dotted with Asian grain ships anchored and waiting to load; further out, tugboats haul barges of sawdust to and fro. This is a functional view of the city unavailable from airliners.

As we approach the Strait of Georgia, we see the West Coast Twin Otter that preceded us into the air. The Twin Otter is a designed object. Whether you find it attractive or not depends on a number of factors, but seeing another airplane of the same type perhaps 300 yards from the one we are flying in, at our 10 o'clock, in a live air-to-air portrait lit by the diffuse light filtering through the overcast, makes me think we are flying in one gorgeous airplane. As we draw closer to it, the other Twin Otter begins to descend, flitting across our flightpath below and to the right.

Suddenly, after a strobe effect and heavenly light-shafts from the edge of a weather front, we are into brilliant sunshine. The rain shadow of the Olympic Mountains puts the Georgia Strait, lower Vancouver Island and the islands we are flying over in their own, drier microclimate. As we fly out from under the clouds, we encounter turbulence. In piston aircraft, turbulence amounts to additional vibration on a longer wavelength. It seems less of a threat in the Twin Otter. It would be worse down where various Beavers have passed below us.

Thompson sets the right-hand throttle slightly ahead of the other one. We begin a long, sweeping turn into a southerly course that will take us to Victoria. We align ourselves with the highway that leads south into British Columbia's capital, flying over downtown Victoria, throttle back over a seaside links, pass a fuel tank farm and execute a nose-down approach and flare that results in a gentle touchdown. Suddenly there is water on the windows of KBX. We're back on aqua firma. Too soon, I think.

Michael Thompson learned to fly Beavers with his father, Don, in the High Arctic, doing his own navigation by the sun. He is photographed here with Kenn Borek's Maldivian Air Taxi operation. VIA MICHAEL THOMPSON

Appendix

DHC-3 OTTER
466 built

LANDPLANE

ENGINE
One 600hp Pratt & Whitney R-1430 S1H1-G or S3H1-G Wasp

PROPELLER
Hamilton Standard hydromatic 3-bladed · Diameter 10 ft 10 in (3.3 m)

DIMENSIONS
Wing span: 58 feet (17.7 m) · Length: 41 ft 10 in (12.8 m)
Wing area: 375 sq ft (34.83 sq m)

OVERALL HEIGHT
Wheels: 12 ft 7 in (3.83 m) · Skis: 13 ft (3.96 m)

WEIGHTS
Basic weight: 4,431 lb (2,010 kg) · Disposable load: 3,569 lb (1,619 kg)
Gross weight: 8,000 lb (3,629 kg)

PERFORMANCE
Takeoff run, full load, zero wind: 630 ft (192 m)
Takeoff run, 20 mph wind: 395 ft (120 m)
Landing roll, zero wind: 440 ft (134 m)
Maximum speed: 160 mph (257 km/hr) @ 5,000 ft (1,524 m)
Cruise: 138 mph (222 km/hr) @ 5,000 ft (1,524 m)
Stalling speed, power off, full flap: 52 mph (83.6 km/hr)
Initial rate of climb: 1,000 ft/min (305 m/min)
Service ceiling: 18,800 ft (5,730 m) with S1H1 or 17,400 ft (5,304 m) with S3H1 engine
Range/payload (no allowances or reserves): 200 miles (322 km): 3,045 lb (1,380 kg)
   500 miles (804 km): 2,680 lb (1,216 kg) · 875 miles (1,408 km) [max cruise range]:
   2,100 lb (953 kg)

SEAPLANE/AMPHIBIAN
Standard Otter float: Bristol 7170
Standard Otter amphib: Bristol (Edo-designed) Model 324-7200

DIMENSIONS
Wing span, wing area same as for landplane
Height: 15 ft 6 in (7.72 m) / 20 ft 1 in (6.12 m)

WEIGHTS
Basic weight: 4,892 lb (2,219 kg) / 5,412 lb (2,455 kg)
Disposable load: 3,075 (1,395 kg) / 2,588 lb (1,174 kg)
Gross weight: 7,967 lb (3,614 kg) / 8,000 lb (3,629 kg)

PERFORMANCE
Takeoff water run, full load, zero wind: 1,020 ft (311 m)
Takeoff water run, 20 mph wind: 650 ft (198 m)
Alight to stop, zero wind: 730 ft (223 m)
Maximum speed at 5,000 ft (1,525 m):

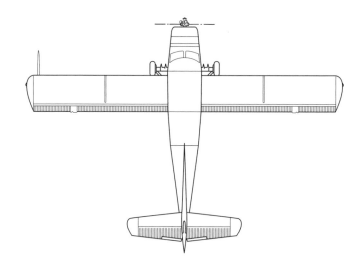

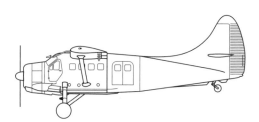

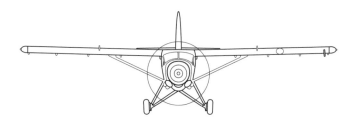

153 mph (246 km/h) / 146 mph (235 km/h)
Cruise: 129 mph (208 km/h) / 125 mph (201 km/h)
Initial rate of climb: 650 fpm (201.3 m/min) / same for amphib
Service ceiling, S1H1: 17,900 ft (5,456 m) / 7,900 ft (5,456 m)
Range/payload: 200 miles (322 km): 2,525 lb (1,145 kg) / 2,030 lb (921 kg)
   500 miles (804 km): 2,130 lb (966 kg) / 1,620 lb (735 kg) · 810 miles (1,303 km) / 780
   (1,255 km) [max cruise range]: 1,605 lb (728 kg) / 1,120 lb (508 kg)

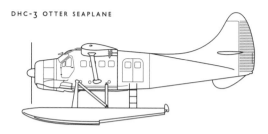

DHC-3 OTTER SEAPLANE

AIRTECH CANADA DHC-3/1000
(Specifications for seaplane)

ENGINE
One 1,000hp ASZ-621R-M18 9-cylinder radial

PROPELLER
AW-2-30 4-bladed propeller

DIMENSIONS
Wing span, wing area and height: same as standard Otter · Length: 42 ft (12.8 m)

WEIGHTS
Conversion adds 400 lb (181 kg) to empty weight of the aircraft
Maximum gross weight, as with all single-engine unmodified Otters: 8,000 lb (3,629 kg)
Empty weight: 5,650 lb (2,562.8 kg)

PERFORMANCE (IAS = INDICATED AIR SPEED)
Takeoff water run at s/L: 478 ft (145.6 m)
s/L landing dist over 50 ft: 1,500 ft (457 m)
Maximum speed: 168 mph (270 km/h) IAS
Cruise: 134 mph (215 km/h) IAS
Initial rate of climb: 1,570 ft/min (478 km/m)
Service ceiling: 17,500 ft (5,334 m)
Range/payload, cruise 5,000 ft (1,525 m) @ 126 mph (202.7 km/h) with 45 mins reserve:
   100 miles (160 km): 2,349 lb (1,065 kg) · 625 miles (1,006 km): 1,448 lb (657 kg)

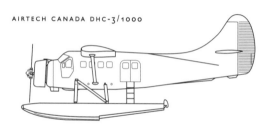

AIRTECH CANADA DHC-3/1000

VAZAR DASH-3 TURBINE OTTER
(Specifications for amphibious floatplane with Edo 7200 floats)

ENGINE
One Pratt & Whitney Canada 750shp PT6A-135 turboprop

PROPELLER
Reversing 3-blade Hartzell propeller

DIMENSIONS
Wing span and wing area same as for wheel Otters
Length: 46 ft (14 m) · Height: 16 ft (4.8 m)

WEIGHTS
Empty weight: 4,670 lb (2,118 kg) · Disposable load: 3,330 lb (1,510 kg)
Gross weight: 8,000 lb (3,628 kg)

PERFORMANCE (TAS = TRUE AIR SPEED)
Takeoff water run: 900 ft (374 m)
Takeoff water run over 50 ft: 1,725 ft (525 m)
Alight to stop, zero wind: 400 ft (122 m)
Cruise (10,000 ft): 156 mph (251 km/h) TAS
Initial rate of climb: 1,200 ft/min (365 m/min)
Normal range: 625 miles (1,006 km)

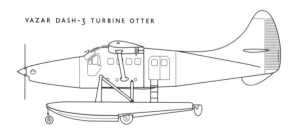

VAZAR DASH-3 TURBINE OTTER

DHC-6 TWIN OTTER

844 built; specifications for Series 300

LANDPLANE

ENGINES
Two Pratt & Whitney Canada 620shp PT6A-27 turboprops

PROPELLERS
Two full-feathering, reversible 3-bladed Hartzell

DIMENSIONS
Wing span: 65 ft (19.81 m)
Wing area: 420 sq ft (39 sq m)
Length: 51.9 ft (15.77 m)
Height over tail, landplane: 18.6 ft (5.66 m)

WEIGHTS
Maximum takeoff: 12,500 lb (5,670 kg)
Basic (20-pass commuter): 6,750 lb (3,060 kg)
Disposable load: 5,940 lb (2,694 kg)

PERFORMANCE (AT MAXIMUM WEIGHT)
Takeoff run: 860 ft (262 m)
Landing run: 950 ft (290 m)
Maximum speed s/L: 192 mph (309 km/h)
Max cruise, 10,000 ft (3,048 m): 210 mph (338 km/h)
Stalling speed, flaps down: 65 mph (104.6 km/h)
Initial rate of climb, 2 engines: 1,600 ft/min (487.6 m/min)
Service ceiling, 2 engines: 26,700 ft (8,140 m)
Range/maximum payload: 806 mi (1,297 km)

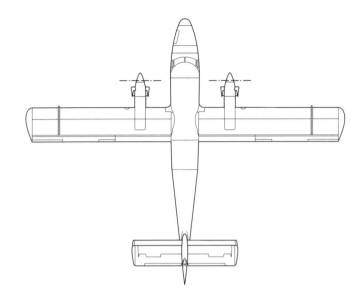

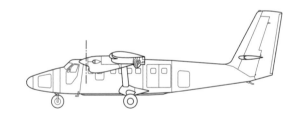

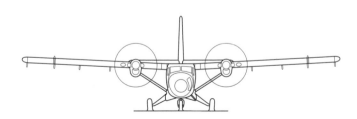

SEAPLANE

Standard Twin Otter float: Canadian Aircraft Products
 (Kenn Borek-built) 12000
Amphib: Wipline 13000

DIMENSIONS

Wing span, length, wing area as for landplane

WEIGHTS

Basic weight: 7,800 lb (3,538 kg)
Disposable load: 4,000 lb (1,814.4 kg)
Maximum takeoff: 12,500 lb (5,670 kg)

PERFORMANCE

Takeoff water run: 1,800 ft (548.6 m)
Alight to stop: 2,000 ft (609.6 m)
Maximum speed: 172.6 mph (277.7 km/h)
Cruise: 161-172.6 mph (259-277.6 km/h)
Stalling speed: 63.3 mph (101.8 km/h)
Initial rate of climb: 1,190 ft/min (362.7 m/min)
Service ceiling: 25,000 ft (7,620 m)
Range/payload: 200 miles (322 km): 3,400 lb (1,542 kg)
 with 2 crew and equipment
 500 miles (804 km): 2,300 lb (1,043 kg)
 conditions as above

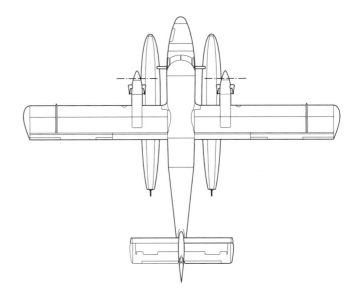

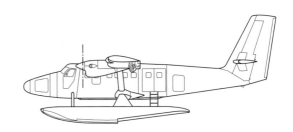

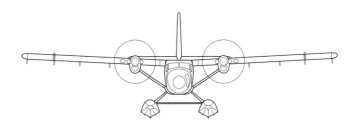

Endnotes

Preface

1. This impressive, if academic, claim is based upon the DHC-5 Buffalo's ability, demonstrated during flight-testing, to take off within 1,225 feet at a gross weight of 41,000 pounds, over a 50-foot obstacle. The football fields would be Canadian Football League dimensions, 110 yards (or 330 feet) long, with somewhat deeper end zones than American ones.

   It is arguable that the Buffalo could have done the same from water. Although the Buffalo that recorded the above feat was equipped with conventional landing gear, a Buffalo was tested with an air cushion attached to the fuselage and flying boat outriggers and floats for operations from land or sea. While there is no record of the Buffalo thus equipped taking off at the maximum gross weight specified above, it is also conceivable that, on water, the fully loaded test Buffalo could have indulged itself in however long a takeoff run was necessary to become airborne.

2. Essay by R. D. Hiscocks, "Whither STOL?" in Bert Ellis, Ed. *de Havilland, You STOL My Heart Away* (Toronto: Human Resources Dept., de Havilland Inc., 1993), pp. 269–277.

   The argument for DHC's emphasis on STOL was the company's success during a period when many aircraft manufacturers, including DHC's English parent, ceased to exist as independent entities. DHC sold 844 Twin Otters over 23 years—an impressive argument in itself.

   "For many years," Hiscocks wrote in his essay, the Twin Otter "represented 10 to 20 per cent of all scheduled aircraft in service."

Chapter 1: The X-Otter: 3682

1. It must have surprised Fowler that N. E. Rowe was interested in a ride in a fairly hairy, purely experimental airplane. Rowe was easily the most buttoned-up fellow in a company of shirtsleeve types. DHC photos of rollouts of new aircraft, such as the Twin Otter, show a formal-looking gentleman, usually the only one wearing a waistcoat under his jacket.

   Rowe's genteel formality extended to authorizing the test pilot to use his nickname. "If you want to call me Nero," Rowe said in his refined English accent, "please feel free to do that. When the time to call me Mr. Rowe comes along, I'm sure you will know."

2. "Investigations of the Steep-Gradient Landing Manoeuvre Employing Modulated Reverse Jet Thrust" is the title of a paper presented by Robert Fowler to the Test Pilots Symposium, Ottawa, November 26, 1964, and reprinted in the *Canadian Aeronautics and Space Journal*, February 1965, pp. 39–41.

   Given the universality of fixed-wing landing techniques, any improvements that could be realized without changing those long-established habits might have profound impacts on aviation worldwide, Fowler thought.

   Fowler divided the landing phase into two parts: the airborne portion, from 50 feet to the ground, and the ground roll, until the aircraft came to a stop. The ground roll had been "reduced mightily in recent years," Fowler wrote, "by the availability of prodigious amounts of wheel braking energy and reverse thrust.

   "As a result, it is the approach and airborne part of the fixed-wing landing which offers the most challenge from the performance-enhancement standpoint.

   "The two most direct ways to contract the horizontal distance required to bring the fixed-wing aircraft from the 50-foot point to the ground are:

   "(1) steepen the angle of approach to the point at which round-out or flare is initiated, and

   "(2) lower the airspeed on the approach to the point at which flare is initiated."

In other words, Fowler was prescribing steeper approaches to landing. By the time these brave thoughts were published, Fowler had been demonstrating such approaches for close to four years in Otter 3682.

3. Author interview with John L. Orr, August 30, 1997.

4. Karl Hayes, *De Havilland Canada DHC-3 Otter* (Dublin: Irish Air Letter, 1982), brief account p. 10. This test program lasted from June 1967 to May 1969, Hayes reports. Otter 3694 was not modified but used to compare its performance with the Model 47 helicopter, "which was fitted out with an Otter cockpit!

   "Direct comparisons were made by the pilots through alternate flights in the simulator and the Otter. They concluded that a very convincing simulation could be affected, particularly with respect to lateral directional chacteristics."

5. Otter 3682 was in impressive company. Another candidate for the same honour was flying at more or less the same time in Canada. The Canadair CL-84 Vertical/Short Takeoff and Landing (V/STOL) tilt-wing prototype first accomplished hovering flight at Cartierville, Quebec, on May 7, 1965, with W. S. Longhurst at the controls. The CL-84 program was also funded by the DRB through John Orr.

   The CL-84 was one of the world's first successful tilt-wing aircraft. It could take off with its wings tilted to a vertical position and its twin engines' oversized propellers acting like rotors, lift off the ground, then pivot its wings into the horizontal plane for the transition to normal flight. The CL-84 was extensively tested by all the flying arms of the U.S. armed forces, including a long stint at the U.S. naval air test facility at Patuxent River, MD, and many aircraft-carrier takeoffs and recoveries in both VTOL and STOL operations from the small escort carrier U.S.S. *Guam*. More developed versions of the CL-84 were being demonstrated to the U.S. Navy as late as February 1972.

   After only a 250-foot STOL takeoff run, the CL-84 could fly 2,100 nautical miles at 235 knots, using additional internal and external tanks, according to Mike Rogers's *VTOL Military Research Aircraft* (N. Yeovil: Haynes & Co, 1989), p. 156. "This is just sufficient for a Gander/Shannon Atlantic crossing," Rogers notes, "with nominal reserves."

   Although the CL-84 never achieved production—four were built—it proved the basic concept that led to the Bell-Boeing V-22 Osprey, which is currently in limited production for the United States armed forces. (The Osprey is not a true tilt-wing; its wingtip-mounted rotors tilt, rather than the entire wing.)

6. Fred Hotson, *The de Havilland Canada Story* (Toronto: CANAV Books, 1983) pp. 139–141.

Bob Fowler would amend the quote to say the Otter 3682 program was intended to assess the aerodynamic performance, stability and control problems of STOL aircraft, *along with the human factors relating to the piloting task*, with the object of finding new refinements in the art.

7. Gordon Johnston does not remember the exact height at which 682 was set on this stand. He imagines it must have been somewhere between 20 feet, which he thinks of as a useful minimum for such a study, and 25 feet, which would be half the distance to the 50-foot barrier the airplane would have to overfly before touching down in demonstrating STOL landing characteristics, and thus possibly supply data that could be extrapolated to the 50-foot height. Interview with author, May 27, 1997.

Chapter 2: The Otter Jet

1. One example of the many lift-jet experimental aircraft under development at the time in Europe was the French Balzac V 001 (V for Vertical), a Mirage III fighter equipped with no fewer than eight lift engines arranged in two rows of four in the fuselage above the aircraft's delta wing roots, in addition to its much bigger propulsion engine. The lift engines were Rolls-Royce RB.108s, and the Balzac went from its first tethered vertical takeoff on October 12, 1962, to a full transitional vertical-horizontal-vertical flight on March 29, 1963. The impressive feature of the RB.108 is that it developed a level of thrust measured at nearly 10 times its weight: 2,340 pounds for its weight of 270 pounds.

   Source: Mike Rogers, *VTOL Military Research Aircraft*, op. cit., and Bill Gunston, *World Encyclopedia of Aero Engines* (N. Yeovil: Patrick Stephens Ltd., 3rd ed., 1995), p. 152.

2. A jet engine's afterburner—called reheat in Britain—sprays raw fuel into the hot exhaust stream. The fuel ignites, giving a useful increase in thrust for a very short period of time. The thirst of the jet engines of the period and the limited tankage of the fighters of the 1950s made even a minute's use of afterburner a severely mission-limiting exercise.

   Information about the origins of the J-85 and its adoption for the Canadair CL-41 Tutor and Northrop T-38/F-5 series comes from several sources, including Gunston's *World Encyclopedia of Aero Engines*, p. 69, and Ron Pickler and Larry Milberry's *Canadair: The First Fifty Years* (Toronto: CANAV Books, 1995), chapters 5 and 6 (pp. 190–194). The story about Ed Woll and Bill Ballhaus is from "Northrop & the Light-Heavyweight Legend" by Steve Pace in *Wings*, August 1989, p. 12.

3. A couple of lightweight British engines, including the RB.108, were considered as powerplants for the study that became the Tutor,

although the prototype first flew January 13, 1960, with a Pratt & Whitney Canada JT-12. But the more than 200 Tutors that came off Canadair's line were powered by Canadian-built General Electric J-85s, and J-85s were used in nearly 3,000 Northrop F-5 series fighters (including 115 CF-5s and 105 Dutch NF-5s built by Canadair), many of which are still flying all around the world, as well as in 170 similar T-38 trainers, many of which are still in service with the U.S. Air Force. The F-5s and T-38s each use two J-85s. More than 13,500 J-85s have been delivered, plus more than 3,000 commercial derivatives. Sources: As cited in previous note, especially Gunston.

4. Details of the J-85 installation: A circular air intake hole was cut into 3682's top dorsal fuselage between the wing trailing edges, and a short duct fed the air to the J-85's turbine face. The engine was installed as close as possible to 682's centre of gravity, which placed it not far behind the flight deck. The jet engine was almost unbearably noisy, and emitted significant heat in the aircraft. Johnston notes dryly that the J-85, small as it was, drastically reduced the Otter's payload.

The difficult part was designing fully modulated diverters to direct the jet exhaust fore and aft from each side of the fuselage, and some kind of system to control the exhaust diverters. The solution was a T-shaped tailpipe leading to a pair of cylindrical nozzles protruding from the lower halves of the fuselage sides that could direct the jet's exhaust forward to create drag, or backward to produce forward thrust (and thus improve takeoff performance), or that could divide the available thrust equally backward and forward for a (self-cancelling) zero-thrust net result that allowed the pilot to keep it lit while extracting no thrust from the system.

These fore and aft nozzles operated only through movement of the lower half of the modulator valves that changed the fore and aft area ratio. Their upper halves were stationary. The nozzles were actuated by a hydraulic actuator from the retractable nose-wheel mechanism of a Caribou and connected by a torque-tube that moved both left- and right-hand modulator valves at the same time.

Heat from the jet efflux kept cracking the nozzle rings; today they would likely be made of titanium. These nozzles were 682's most frequent maintenance problem. Often, after flying in the immediate postdawn calm, 682 was grounded for the rest of the day for small welding repairs to the jet exhausts—most often the rings within which the modulators turned.

5. The first flight dates for Otter 3682 are taken from Bob Fowler's flight logs. They differ from dates published elsewhere, including this particular first J-85 date, given as September 1961 on page 115 of my book *The Immortal Beaver* (Vancouver: Douglas & McIntyre,

1996). The information is taken from the excellent and concise account in Kenneth H. Sullivan and Larry Millberry's *Power: The Pratt & Whitney Canada Story* (Toronto: CANAV Books, 1989).

This and other apparent discrepancies may be explained by Fowler's careful use of very specific qualifiers for his dates. In this case, 682 may well have flown *with* the J-85 in September, but Fowler's flight date of December 18 was made in 682 "with the J-85 running." Source: Robert H. Fowler letter to the author dated July 2, 1997.

6. Bob Fowler joined DHC in March 1952, after maintaining his proficiency in high-performance aircraft after the war by flying modified P-38s for Spartan Air Services, doing mining surveys with magnetometers over Yukon territory. Fowler came with a built-in link to one of DHC's best clients, the Ontario Provincial Air Service, launch customer for both the Beaver and the Otter: his wife, Margaret, is the daughter of George Phillips, longtime OPAS pilot.

In his initial capacity as a sales demonstration pilot, Fowler was hired by director of flight operations Russ Bannock, after being recommended by his friend from Spartan, Bill Ferderber, to impress likely buyers of DHC aircraft with the same imaginative, seemingly daring style Bannock specialized in. By 1953–54 Fowler was showing off Beavers in the Middle East. "You had to be a salesman first," Fowler recalls.

A year later, as chief production test pilot, Fowler flew the phenomenal variety of aircraft DHC was overhauling, along with the growing range of production types. These included new Chipmunks and Beavers, as well as Lancaster Anti-Submarine Warfare conversions, overhauled Canadair North Stars, Norsemans, de Havilland Doves, and Herons and Vampire jet fighters assembled from kits built in Hatfield for the RCAF, among other types and conversions.

Three years later, in 1958, Fowler was DHC's chief engineering test pilot. It was in this role, flying Otter 3682, that he became a contributor to the flying techniques of V/STOL, especially the use of jet power. He eventually became one of three prime pilots of the National Air and Space Administration (NASA) Boeing–de Havilland Augmentor Wing Jet STOL Research Aircraft, based on a DHC-5 Buffalo (a turboprop development of the Caribou) and extensively modified by Boeing with a new wing that carried twin 9,000-pound-thrust Rolls-Royce Spey turbofan engines under the wing and with spanwise augmentor nozzles and other lift-enhancing devices, including blown surfaces fed by bypass air from the Speys. It first flew May 1, 1972, and was still being used at NASA's Ames facility in 1986, according to Mike Rogers's *VTOL Military Research Aircraft*, p. 221.

Chapter 3: Otter 3682 Points the Way

1. It was Dick Batch, who spent much of his career in the direct line of authority from Hiscocks to Jack Uffen (whom he succeeded as director of development engineering), who insisted to the author that the Twin Otter's origins lead back to the same twin-engine studies of around 1954 that eventually yielded the Caribou design. The DHC-4 Caribou was quickly roughed out in early 1957 after one of Russ Bannock's Pentagon visits in response to a clearly articulated requirement—"This is what we want next"—for a three-ton tactical transport with rear loading. Sources: Author interview with Jack Uffen and Dick Batch, February 7, 1997. See also Hotson, *op. cit.*, p. 146.

   Hotson, whose studies of DHC history are the authoritative accounts, states on p. 141 of *The de Havilland Canada Story* that the Otter 3682 program terminated in 1963, the year the twin PT6s were fitted. Fowler's logbook notes the final flight of 682 as mid-July 1965. Source: Robert H. Fowler letter to the author, *op. cit.*

2. Ian Gilchrist was instrumental in resolving the unanticipated complications, including the fuselage extension and tail redesign, that made the Turbo Beaver project more a case of major surgery than the simple makeover that Dick Hiscocks told the author DHC management thought it would be. While the late Beaver Mk.III project engineer Peter S. Martin was honoured with the registration of the prototype of the 60 factory Turbo Beavers built, CF-PSM, Gilchrist deserves special credit for having designed many of the modifications and installations that are still being used to convert piston Beavers to PT6 gas turbine power. They happen to be quite similar to parallel developments on Otter 3682 and the Twin Otter, suggesting something like joint authorship.

   Gilchrist, born in Scotland, is a graduate of the highly regarded de Havilland technical school who worked in the stress office at Hatfield for a year before showing up in 1949 at DHC, where he remembers chief engineer Doug Hunter hiring him by saying, "I don't know what the hell you're going to do." He worked in Fred Buller's Otter project stress group with Bob Klein, a future DHC airworthiness chief, and, later, with Dick Batch. Source: Author interview with Ian Gilchrist, August 22, 1997.

   In addressing other questions with me, both Gordon Johnston and the late Dick Hiscocks have given Ian Gilchrist ample credit for such diverse contributions to each of these projects as the design of landing gear, tail group components and powerplant installations.

3. Another, possibly explainable, date conflict. Sullivan and Milberry, in *Power*, *op. cit.,* say the first flight for the J-85/PT6 682 was May 7, 1963. Fowler recorded March 7, same year, after doing runway skips only March 1 to 5. In his previously cited letter to the author, Fowler abbreviated March to Mar, rendering the date 07MAR63, raising the possibility of a one-letter typo accounting for the difference. It seems logical that Fowler would want to get into the air as soon as possible after his runway hops of March 1 to 5 with the J-85 as dead weight.

4. As Fowler well knew, the jet engine in 682 imposed much greater loads on its tailplane than it would encounter in normal forward flight. The jet nozzles changing the direction of thrust from forward to backward thrust or vice versa would impose some strains, although Fowler feels that high-frequency sonic and vibrational fatigue did the damage.

   Fowler, lifetime student of engineering that he is, found himself visualizing the path that such loads would travel from the horn balances outboard of the elevator tips, along the tailplane hinge lines, and into the structure inside the fin that Gilchrist had calculated was more than sufficient to withstand the anticipated loads and would do so with a healthy margin of safety.

   And, as it turned out, that margin was still adequate for some unknown period: from the time of the previous inspection until the components that took the loads had begun to fret.

Chapter 4: de Havilland Canada at 20

1. Bruce West. *The Firebirds* (Toronto: Ontario Ministry of Natural Resources, 1974), p. 126.

2. Fred Hotson, *op. cit.*, p. 11.

3. Bill Gunston, *op. cit.*, p. 42.

4. A. J. Jackson, *de Havilland Aircraft since 1915* (London: Putnam, 1962), pp. 192–205.

5. This short list of DH.60 achievements appears in West, *op. cit.*, and in more detailed form in Jackson, *op. cit.*, pp. 192–205.

6. There is contradictory evidence as to how quickly the Moths ordered for use in Canada were delivered.

   "Early Days," a 34-page booklet published by the Ontario Department of Lands and Forests outlining the history of OPAS until 1961, says on p. 9 that "16 [DH Moths] were purchased in 1927 and then others followed. They remained in service until 1942."

   West says that OPAS took delivery of its first four Moths in July 1927. They were G-CAOU, G-CAOV, G-CAOW and G-COUX. G-CAOW had the fabric burned from its wings July 20 at Mattagami in a refuelling accident.

   Perhaps not all 16 were delivered in 1927 if it is true that the peak number of Moths operated by OPAS, as West reports, was 14.

   Hotson, *op. cit.*, agrees (pp. 12–13) that four arrived in July 1927, flying "700 hours during their first four months of operation to the satisfaction of all concerned. Another six were ordered for delivery in 1928." He further notes that "By the end of 1927 the total number of Moths registered in Canada had grown to eight."

7. Hotson, *op. cit.*, p. 15.

8. Hotson's accounts of the early activities of the Canadian de Havilland branch are detailed and enjoyable to read. This paragraph is condensed from material on pp. 10–19 of Hotson's book, *op. cit.*

   The 70 acres apparently were acquired piecemeal, a 20-acre frontage on Dufferin Street first and then an adjoining 20 acres fronting on Sheppard Avenue, purchase of which was announced in the December 20, 1928, Toronto *Evening Telegram*. This second parcel cost $21,000. Others followed. Source: "de Havilland—Our Heritage," with preface by Fred Hotson, 1991 (brochure).

9. My account of the brief career of G-CAHK is taken from Hotson, *op. cit.*, p. 12, and Jackson, *op. cit.*, p. 198.

10. West, *op. cit.*, pp. 126–7.

11. April 28, 1916, is the date of issue of P. C. Garratt's Aviator's Certificate. The date given in a profile of him in a 1936 issue of *Canadian Aviation* for "winning his wings" with the Royal Flying Corps is May 21, 1916.

12. "I thought my father-in-law was the first to do that," says retired DHC test pilot Bob Fowler, who is married to the daughter of the late OPAS chief pilot George Phillips.

    Any other claimants?

13. This biographical material on Phil Garratt is from a limited edition book, "PCG 50," prepared by personal friends to commemorate the DHC managing director's fiftieth anniversary as a pilot and kindly loaned to the author by Garratt's son John. Many of the dates are from Garratt's pilot's logbooks, selected pages of which are reproduced in the limited edition book.

14. Karl Hayes, *op. cit.*, pp. 5–7. In his succinct summary of the 60 years of DHC to his time of writing, July 1, 1982, the Otter's foremost historian calls 1937 "the company's coming of age." That year the company built 25 DH.82A Tiger Moth trainers—the first aircraft built by DHC—for the Royal Canadian Air Force. This was an important step beyond assembling kits of parts from Hatfield. Manufacturing the Tiger Moths, which incorporated a number of changes from the British ones, certainly was an important early milestone.

15. Asked by the author whether his father might not have won his McKee Trophies for the Otter and the Caribou, which were greeted by the aviation world as much more impressive achievements than the Beaver at the time, John Garratt disagreed. Since that time, of course, the Beaver has been elevated to the status of a cult.

16. The struggle to get Canadian Mosquito production going involved a five-fold increase in the size of DHC and, after the cancellation of wartime contracts and subsequent layoffs, left a lean, versatile and highly skilled company that was in a better position to innovate than many aircraft manufacturers at the time. More detailed portraits of most of these DHC personalities can be found in the early chapters of the author's *The Immortal Beaver* (Vancouver: Douglas & McIntyre, 1996).

17. "Whither STOL?" by R. H. (Dick) Hiscocks, in *de Havilland, You STOL My Heart Away*, op. cit., pp. 269–276.

Chapter 5: Birth of the King Beaver

1. Writer unnamed, "Bush Pilot's Workhorse," *Time*, February 11, 1952. Kindly made available by Betty Buller.

2. Kenneth Molson, *Canada's National Aviation Museum: Its History and Collections* (Ottawa: National Aviation Museum, 1988), p. 137. Molson writes that the design that became the Otter was "ordered into production" in November 1950, but Fred Hotson, *op. cit.*, p. 119, explains that "on November 29 a factory instruction was issued for a design start with the understanding that a single prototype would be built."

   Hotson ties the factory order for 15 preproduction Otters to the aura of optimism that accompanied the announcement of Beaver sales to the U.S. military, which became known November 13, 1951 (U.S. military sales, p. 114; coincidence of dates, p. 122). This was about a month before the Otter's first flight.

   One indication of how intense the effort was to get those first 16 Otters finished is the fact that proper drawings and tooling to manufacture the complicated cowlings that housed the Otter's engine and induction and exhaust systems were not yet ready, as Mike Davy, who joined DHC in October 1950, remembered it in an interview with the author, May 1997. "Those first 20 Otters had hand-built engine cowlings. We hadn't drawn anything yet—just a few templates."

   Those handmade cowlings reflect more than the all-out effort that put the Otter prototype in the air at the end of 1951. They were made possible by the level of sheet-metalworking craftsmanship available in DHC's Experimental Shop under Bill Burlison, personified by the arrival, in 1952—in time to work on the third prototype—of Karl Frisk, who had worked on every type of aircraft built by Saab, including the J-29 jet fighter.

3. West, *op. cit.*, pp. 215–34.

4. Hotson, *op. cit.*

5. The excitement generated by a design with the ambitious performance goals of the Beaver's successor aroused sufficiently widespread interest in an account of its origins for Dick Hiscocks and Fred Buller to have presented a paper entitled "Design of the de Havilland Otter" to the sixty-sixth annual general and professional meeting of the Engineering Institute of Canada at Vancouver, B.C., May 7, 8 and 9, 1952, and to have had their paper reprinted in the *Engineering Journal* the following July.

Assuming the text was unchanged between its delivery in Vancouver and its reprinting, the authors' assertion that "design work was initiated some fifteen months ago" places that date very early in 1950. May 1952, when the paper was delivered, was less than six months after the Otter's first flight on December 12, 1951.

A suggestion that the basic layout and principles of the King Beaver design were fixed some time before 1950 is suggested by Milberry and Sullivan's assertion on p. 73 of *Power, op cit.*, that the project "remained on the back burner until the OPAS expressed interest"—which could only have been after the first of their Beavers, CF-OBS, had been proven in service (it was delivered April 26, 1948)—"and the RCAF came forward with development funds."

It is widely believed that the RCAF underwrote development of at least the Otter's powerplant. Russ Bannock says that is not so. Bannock recalls about $3 million in funding for Otter development from the Department of Defence Production, forwarded as a forgiveable loan, repayable from sales income. If the RCAF *had* committed itself in any way to the Otter before production, it certainly took its time about ordering any of them. Bannock, DHC's military sales director, says he was in Ottawa many times between December 1951 and summer 1952 without making the sale. The RCAF was happy enough with its Norsemans, of which it still had more than 30. Source: Author interview with Russ Bannock, July 26, 1998.

6. The Avro Canada C-102 Jetliner may have been the first jet-powered transport built, but it was only the second to fly, on August 10, 1949. The de Havilland Comet prototype flew from Hatfield, England, two weeks before, on July 27.

7. "Bush Pilot's Workhorse," *op. cit.*

8. Hotson, *op. cit.*

9. This account of the development of the R-1340 is taken from *The Pratt & Whitney Aircraft Story*, published on the company's twenty-fifth anniversary, August 1950. No author credit is given for one of the best-written accounts of the history of pre-jet aero engine development in the United States. The quote is from Hershel Smith, *A History of Aircraft Piston Engines* (Sunflower University Press Ed., 1986), photo caption p. 106. Other material comes from Bill Gunston's excellent summary of the R-1340's development on pp. 119–20 of the *World Encyclopedia of Aero Engines, op. cit.*

10. Depending on whether Noorduyn licence-built 1,800 Harvards, as Bill Yenne's history of North American, *Rockwell: The Heritage of North American* (New York: Crescent Books, 1989), claims on p. 27, or the 2,800 listed by Ken Molson, *op. cit.*, p. 182, either 17,952 or 18,952 of the AT-6/Harvard family, also powered by R-1340s, were built. (Milberry and Sullivan, *op. cit.*, agree with the higher figure.) Either way, it's a lot of airplanes and a lot more engines, very few of

which were available to Dick Hiscocks when he was making the powerplant decision on the King Beaver.

11. In a report on Otter accidents involving Canadian civil operators from 1970 to 1981—a total of 99—the largest category comprised takeoff accidents, no fewer than 36, and a further 19 involved airframe or engine malfunctions. The problems came for the most part with the aircraft's use in short-hop bush operations, in which a couple of takeoff and landing cycles might typically be included in every hour of flight time.

Statistics from Hayes, *op. cit.*, pp. 138–142. "Although accident reports do sometimes make grim reading," Hayes writes, "they are a fascinating source of information as to what in fact occurs in the course of day-to-day operations and to the ever present dangers of operating in the challenging bush environment."

12. Data for the Wright R-1300 comes from Hershel Smith, *op. cit.*, p. 140. Smith dates the R-1300 as 1940; Bill Gunston's *World Encyclopedia of Aero Engines* calls it "the 1942-designed Cyclone 7, marketed from 1945 as the R-1300," and notes that it was licence-built by Kaiser-Frazer and later Lycoming.

Smith says that Wright's licence-builders (he refers specifically to Avco) felt they built better Wright engines than Wright did, but the likelihood that no licence-builder would offer the service P&WC had demonstrated with its R-985s in Beavers must have counted heavily in the decision to go with the P&W R-1340.

13. The question has been asked. In a conversation February 19, 1997, with the author, Marin C. Faure, author of *Flying a Floatplane* (New York: TAB Books, 1997, 3rd ed.) mentioned a rumour he has heard that the Otter was originally designed around another, more powerful engine. In an article Faure wrote for the 1990 *Water Flying* annual, he urges owners to undertake the Vazar Dash-3 turboprop Otter conversion as "the solution to the problem which has plagued Otter operators ever since the plane went into production in 1952: the unreliability of its 600-horsepower engine."

The comparisons between the P&W 1340 and the Wright R-1300, and the information that the Wright engine was considered for the King Beaver, come from Sullivan and Milberry's *Power, op. cit.*: "DHC chose the Wasp based on Pratt & Whitney Aircraft's reputation and Pratt & Whitney Canada's record on product support." Going with P&WC, which did open an overhaul and assembly line for geared R-1340s, may not have been the way to give the eventual Otter anything like the margin of power the Beaver enjoys, but it was the continuation of a close and rewarding business relationship between P&WC and DHC that went on to even more productive joint projects.

It may be that it was the availability of a geared Wasp, the R-1340-S3H1G—G for Geared—that made the difference in what would, either way, have been an arguable engineering decision. Sullivan and Milberry go on to reproduce an unfootnoted but revealing quote from Hiscocks on the same page: "It all goes back to basic propulsion theory," he [Hiscocks] said recently. [*Power* was published in 1989.] "It's better to move a large mass of air slowly than a small mass quickly. I wanted to use a larger three-blade propeller to obtain maximum static thrust for takeoff. A larger propeller gives higher thrust for a given horsepower."

The Sullivan-Milberry account is authoritative because Keith Sullivan is a former director of P&WC who worked on the King Beaver powerplant project.

He is quoted on p. 74: "To perfect its engine/propeller installation required many modifications and adjustments. We had a 600hp engine and had to determine how to modify the gearbox and what gear ratio and propeller to use. We narrowed the choice to two blade types. These varied in shape, twist, and whether the tips were square or rounded. . . . We did many tests with various engine-propeller combinations on a test stand. We finally settled on a fairly wide and heavy Hamilton-Standard DC-3 type of propeller, but with blade length reduced to improve efficiency."

For P&WC, the geared R-1340 program was an opportunity to begin overhauling engines with a fully proven design and to build the reduction gearing from scratch once the Swedish war surplus examples were used up on DHC's production line.

14. Hiscocks and Buller, *op. cit.* A careful reading of the *Engineering Journal* article suggests that Hiscocks, a prolific writer all his life, did much of the drafting of the piece. It is full of typical Hiscocks dry humour. In explaining the wing section selected for the Otter, Hiscocks says it was chosen to "have moderate drag by current standards, have docile stalling characteristics and remain insensitive to manufacturing irregularities, the bodies of insects and small ice accretions." He goes on to say: "It is not entirely surprising, perhaps, that the section selected after a rather involved study bears a strong resemblance to that adopted a long time ago in Nature for the soaring birds."

15. Hotson, *op. cit.*

16. It was a supreme irony for DHC old-timers to be building Beaver jigs out of wood. Jigs, frames that assure proper alignment when components are assembled in them, had been the subject of many trans-Atlantic arguments during the war. Hatfield built its jigs from wood, which was, for the most part, faster to fabricate and easily adaptable to changes, while DHC's North American engineers insisted upon steel or concrete for more durable tolerances. But once the big Beaver sales to the U.S. military had begun to energize the production lines at Downsview, the jigs were needed fast.

Source: Mike Davy interview with the author, May 27, 1997.

17. A word or two about flaps. Flaps are, generally speaking, hinged flight surfaces located along the trailing edges of wings. (Some flaps appear on the leading edges of wings, but by and large such devices are otherwise designated.)

A plain flap consists of a hinged trailing edge. The Beaver has plain flaps. A split flap is a section of lower-surface skin that deflects down into the airstream. Split and plain flaps, the first types of flaps devised for airplanes, have the disadvantage at greater deflection angles of producing high drag due to the breakup of airflow behind them.

Slotted flaps combine aerodynamic qualities of both the above types; they are fitted into the wing in such a way as to have the upper lifting surface of the wing extend back over the hinge line. As a slotted flap is deployed, it opens downward at its lower-surface hinge line, admitting fresh boundary-layer air—the air flowing along the wing's surface—which flows through the slot to the upper surface of the flap, "refreshing" the airflow there and alleviating the turbulence that causes parasite drag.

A double-slotted flap of the type fitted to the Otter is a two-piece flap, the upper flap directing air above and below to refresh the air over both itself and the rearmost flap, multiplying the lift-enhancement effects of the flap without necessarily paying an equivalent price in drag. To increase drag for landing, however, the lower or rearmost flap can, on the Otter, be set at an angle of as much as 60 degrees.

A readable recent treatment on the aerodymanics of wing flaps is "What's All the Flap About? STOL Explained" by Barnaby Wainfan, in the April 1988 issue of the American *Flight Journal*, pp. 72–79. It is to Wainfan I owe thanks for the word "refreshing" to characterize the downstream airflow effect of slotted flaps.

18. The material edited out here consists of the sentence, "The additions to tail surfaces and wings were almost negligible."

It hardly seems fair to allow Hiscocks and Buller to be contradicted by the future addition of substantial vertical tail area, added in part to compensate for the destabilizing effects of floats, when they were writing so soon after flight-testing began. Moreover, benefiting from their experience with the Beaver, the wing-to-fuselage aerodynamics and the handling of structural twisting loads at the wing roots imposed by the big flaps were faultless.

They made their stringent deadline: from design start 15 months before the article appeared in early May, 1952—that would make it December 1950 or January 1951—to first flight in December 1951: "Almost exactly one year later," they add proudly.

Quotes are from Hiscocks and Buller, *op. cit.*, p. 5.

19. James Hay Stevens, "DH Otter: Constructional Features and Air Impressions of the Dominion's Latest Aircraft," *Flight*, April 11, 1952, pp. 428–33.

Hotson, *op. cit.*, deals with the airworthiness question succinctly on p. 222 of his book.

Chapter 6: The Otter Flies

1. The rollout of a single-engine airplane that DHC regarded as a world-beater immediately raised the question of whether a small twin-engine bush plane might be capable of again increasing the payload of the Otter—just as it doubled that of the Beaver—while retaining the same short-field performance. Within a year formal studies of an airplane DHC referred to as "the small twin" were underway. Those studies bore fruit by 1957 in the unexpected form of a fairly big twin, the 26,000-pound gross weight DHC-4 Caribou, the heaviest fixed-wing aircraft the U.S. Army had ever ordered. Not until 1965 did the small twin appear, and only then because of the development of lighter, new-technology gas turbine engines. That was the DHC-6 Twin Otter.

DHC was not such a self-important organization in 1951 that it recorded the dates of rollouts for posterity. The December 10 date comes from George Neal's extensive and carefully kept logbooks.

2. Although CF-DYK-X was rolled out in OPAS colours, it never joined Ontario's fast-growing air force. Neither did any of the first dozen Otters.

DYK-X's identity from the first of November 1952 was RCAF Otter 3667—officially, given its status as a prototype, 3667-X—but it remained with DHC as a test aircraft until 1969, when it was sold to Lambair Ltd., The Pas, Manitoba. It crashed in 1970 as CF-SKX-X.

The second prototype, CF-GCV-X, was likewise used as a test aircraft until it was delivered to Eastern Provincial Airways, Gander, Newfoundland, December 18, 1953. A dozen years later it was sold to Pacific Western Airlines of Vancouver, a notable Beaver operator, and returned to Ontario in 1976.

The third Otter, CF-ODH, was delivered to Arthur Fecteau of Senneterre, Quebec, December 29, 1952, who at one time operated the largest fleet of Otters anywhere. The fourth, CF-GBX, was the first production article (Hotson, *op. cit.*, p. 122) and was delivered to Hudson Bay Air Transport Ltd., Flin Flon, Manitoba, November 11, 1952. The fifth is celebrated as the first multi-passenger aircraft of the eventual Wardair international charter airline, CF-GBY, delivered June 2, 1953.

In other words, the launch customer, the OPAS, did not receive the first of its order of Otters until the relatively late date of May 22, 1953: the thirteenth Otter built (including prototypes),

CF-ODK. OPAS also received the next two. In between Max Ward's Otter and ODK, the RCAF received six. OPAS was a very special, very understanding DHC customer.

The delivery dates tell us how committed DHC was to its Otter manufacturing program. The Otter was certified as airworthy November 5, 1952, at which time the three prototypes had been built and production articles Number Five (Hudson Bay) and Number Six (Imperial Oil, delivered December 19, 1952) must have been virtually complete. The six Otters were delivered to the RCAF within three days, from March 28 to April 1, 1953. Sources: Hayes, *op. cit.*, p. 34.

3. Looking up this information in the fifth of his 10 logbooks, Neal noted that, as of a week before the Otter's first flight, he was closing in on 15,000 hours of flying.

4. Hiscocks and Buller, "Design of the de Havilland 'Otter,'" *The Engineering Journal*, July 1952, p. 2.

5. No aerodynamic devices to channel airflow over the upper, or lifting, surface and prevent outward, or spanwise, airflow had been added to the prototype Otter's wing. Some wind-tunnel work had been done at the National Aeronautical Establishment's facility in Ottawa. That part of the work underwritten by the DDP had focussed upon the benefits of the powerplant's extractor exhaust and the big propeller's downstream effects in blowing air along the wing roots. But the flaps also benefited from the wind-tunnel work.

There were small changes to the flap hinge positions and the shapes of the slots between the inboard flap components that yielded, Buller and Hiscocks thought, "quite considerable gains in maximum lift and in the rolling power of the ailerons," and were incorporated on the advice of NAE staff people. In time, wing fences would be added to the upper surfaces chordwise (fore-and-aft) at the inner edges of the ailerons, for the announced purpose of improving lateral stability in stalls. They had the further merit of directing air straight back over the outer flaps, making them, as Buller and Hiscocks claimed, more effective when used as ailerons. They would help make the Otter turn better. Source: Fred Hotson, *op. cit.*, DHC-3 Otter cutaway, p. 120, item 43.

6. First flight recollections are from the author's interview with George Neal, May 28, 1997, and subsequent correspondence. George Neal was, at the time of writing, still a licenced pilot, anticipating the first flight of an aircraft he was building. At 76, he had passed his annual physical the day before our interview and was in great spirits. His only objection to talking about his days at DHC was that he would have preferred spending the time working on his project, a full-scale combat aircraft replica. Neal believes that having an obsession is the key to longevity.

Chapter 7: Reviews and Improvements

1. James Hornick, "To Sustained Applause: New Canadian Aircraft Takes Off in 90 Feet," *The Globe and Mail*, January 19, 1952. Kindly made available by Betty Buller.

2. "Bush Pilot's Workhorse," *op. cit.*

3. The newspaper clipping, headlined "Plane 'Stops' over City," is, unfortunately, undated. The *Toronto Telegram* is, unfortunately, defunct. But the accompanying photograph, which claims to be of the Otter "which worried citizens," is on floats, suggesting sometime after April 1952, and it has the eventual larger, more graceful vertical tail, which would place the incident sometime after June 13, 1952, the first flight of the second prototype, CF-GCV, on floats.

4. Stevens, *op. cit.*, Stevens's article, kindly made available by Dick Batch, a retired DHC director of development engineering, is a valuable insight into the early stages of Otter flight-testing. Assuming a six-week lead time for publication of his piece, Stevens would have accompanied George Neal on test flights sometime in February.

   At that stage final maximum settings for the double-slotted flaps (eventually 40 degrees for the forward section of the flap, 60 for the rear) had yet to be determined. (Takeoffs and initial climbs at that stage were done at flap settings of 30 and 50 degrees.) The tests underway when Stevens was there were measurements of glide angle on approach to landing at various speeds with full load. "The unfurnished cabin contained ballast, automatic observer [a camera rigged to photograph the instrument panel as a record of the flight], a multiple manometer for flap pressure-plotting and two flight-test observers."

   The takeoffs with Stevens aboard were from a windless, partly frozen runway—"not the best venue for demonstrating a slow-flying aircraft," Stevens writes—"but, even so, the Otter nipped very smartly into the air at about 55 mph [indicated]. Thereafter we climbed . . . at an angle so steep that a head-rest would have been an added comfort!"

   Cruising at 6,000 feet, the Otter prototype could do 145 mph (maximum was 163) at an engine setting of 33 inches supercharger boost and 2,200 rpm. "The nose was well below the horizon under these conditions and the view was like that from a balcony." With "a little flap," Neal could maintain that altitude using only 20-inch boost and 1,780 rpm at 50 mph indicated airspeed.

   Stevens is more specific about certain aspects of the Otter's design development and pricing than other sources. He reported, for example, that the Otter was built "to an RCAF specification" and that it "was designed by Mr. R. D. Hiscocks under the general direction of Mr. Douglas Hunter," leaving out the name of Fred Buller, the chief design engineer. Stevens also stated that the Otter would carry a basic price of $65,000, plus $7,500 for floats and $1,800 for skis, plus, in Canada, sales tax of 10 per cent. Those prices may have gone up by the time Max Ward bought the fifth Otter off the line for more than $90,000.

   In Ken Molson's *Canada's National Aviation Museum*, *op. cit.*, the late dean of Canadian aviation historians states on p. 137 that "Following the success of the Beaver, the Ontario Provincial Air Service decided they needed a larger machine with similar abilities and told de Havilland Canada that, if the company built an aircraft of about twice the Beaver's capacity and with similar performance, the OPAS would order 20."

5. At the same time, the newly arrived Swedish immigrant Karl Frisk was hard at work implementing various fixes for the flap-actuation trim problem on the third prototype, CF-ODH, which would go to Arthur Fecteau. Servo tabs were one solution Frisk remembers working on, as were various combinations of turns of the control cables on the trim drum that redirected the cables from the cockpit to the elevators. Different numbers of turns would produce more or less movement of the elevator leading edge for a given revolution of the trim wheel in the cockpit.

6. Author interview with Mike Davy, May 27, 1997.

7. The Fox Moth was an impressive achievement in the early 1930s, using major assemblies from soon-to-be plentiful Tiger Moths to create an inexpensive small transport that was cheap to operate. G-ABUO, the prototype, which flew January 29, 1932, was shipped to Canada and flew there for nearly 20 years as CF-API, retiring in 1950. The DH.83 was "unquestionably the first British Aeroplane, in the words of the late [editor of *The Aeroplane*] C. G. Grey, to support itself financially in the air." Quoted by A. J. Jackson in *de Havilland Aircraft since 1915* (London: Putnam's, 1962), p. 296.

   The Fox Moth could carry five adults, including the pilot, on short flights. With four people and additional fuel, it could theoretically fly 360 miles, although Max Ward would be much more conservative about its range flying out of Yellowknife than an English pilot would have been operating out of, say, London's Croydon Airport.

8. Ward's $100,000 Otter came with the floats it was delivered on at the Toronto Harbour waterfront, and presumably with skis and wheeled undercarriage components, not to mention the custom paint job, a snazzy blue with white and red trim.

   Not everyone paid that much. Hotson puts the price of an Otter at $80,000, and *Time* magazine, a couple of months after the first flight of CF-DYK-X, quoted the Otter's price at $65,000. The earlier a customer's commitment, the lower the price?

9. Max Ward, *The Max Ward Story: A Bush Pilot in the Bureaucratic Jungle* (Toronto: McClelland & Stewart, 1992), pp. 102–3. The subtitle of Ward's book refers to, among many other adventures, the delay in his acceptance of CF-GBY into the month of June because he had neither the $75,000 balance on the purchase price nor the licence to operate it.

"That's *Holly*wood!" exclaimed George Neal when I repeated the story of his Otter demonstration for Max Ward.

Almost anyone else would have used an eight-letter word that begins with "B" and implies exaggeration.

Okay, okay, okay: so they weren't 10 feet from the hangar. If they were 10 times that distance, the story is still memorable. One such Otter takeoff of Neal's was filmed and shown on the Flightpath series of aviation topics in 1997: the hangar doors were open—a dark, yawning abyss that you'd have sworn the Otter was about to fly into. By 1953 Neal had plenty of practice doing short takeoffs in Otters.

For what it may be worth, Max Ward has himself said that, despite tales of bush pilot derring-do, he never did anything that was not carefully planned and calculated. And neither did George Neal.

In fact, as Ward acknowledges in his memoir, he learned all too well the tricks of demonstrating the Otter to customers. He would point CF-GBY at a forested hill that seemed too close to clear, tell the passenger what he was going to do, wait for the gasp of incredulity and then do it.

Chapter 8: Military Otters: Triumph and Tragedy

1. "Selling Aircraft to the U.S. Armed Forces" by Russell Bannock, in *de Havilland, You STOL My Heart Away, op. cit.*, pp. 122–26.

    Information augmented by author interview with Russ Bannock, May 29, 1997.

2. "Speech to U.S. Army Otter and Caribou Association, Dallas, Texas, 17 August 1990," by Lt.-Gen. (ret'd) Robert R. Williams, reprinted in *de Havilland You STOL My Heart Away, op. cit.*, pp. 152–6. The 260-order figure Williams uses must include some cancelled units: the combined U.S. Army (190 Otters); U.S. Navy (14) and U.S. Air Force (4) orders that Hayes lists in *DHC-3 Otter, op. cit.*, do not add up to 260; although Hayes's totals apparently do not include Otters ordered by the U.S. military and diverted to other users.

    The U.S. Navy did operate four Otters that were additional to their 14-aircraft order. Three were RCAF Otters donated to their Antarctic squadron VX-6 in 1957 to replace aircraft delayed by the 1955 strike at Downsview; three Navy Otters crashed the first year on the ice and were replaced by the strike-delayed ones. And the Navy inherited the Royal Air Force's Trans Antarctic Otter, operating it briefly.

3. Hotson, *op. cit.*, p. 133, writes that it was the then-director of Army Aviation's idea to include the Otter in Exercise Skydrop II, and that the exercise took place in the late summer of 1954.

4. Givens was a big man, 260 pounds as Bob Fowler remembers him, who chewed a cigar "and could fly like a million bucks." He had flown Spitfires during the Second World War. Givens was smart enough to have a full colonel with him in the Otter the first time he approached the strip, bordered at both ends by bush, where the helicopters were to deliver their loads. Nobody was expecting an airplane, and the colonel ordered personnel on the ground to clear the strip for Givens.

5. Bob Fowler was understandably reluctant to talk about Ferderber's crash but happy to memorialize his late good friend and colleague. Author interview with Fowler June 10, 1997.

    A valuable outline of postwar aerial survey work in Canada appears in Larry Milberry's *Aviation in Canada* (Toronto: McGraw-Hill Ryerson, 1979), pp. 92–95, from which such details as the registration for Ferderber's Sea Hornet, pictured on p. 95, are taken. Milberry points out that the Canada Forestry Act of 1947 required a complete inventory of the nation's forests, which was possible only by air.

6. Hotson, *op. cit.*, p. 138.

7. Hotson, *ibid.*

8. In a tight, well-written retelling of the Otter accident saga that covers most of a page in his book (and is my main source), Hotson does not identify the Otter that went down at Goose Bay or date the accident. Hayes, *op. cit.*, says it was an RCAF Otter without otherwise naming it. Hayes's production list indicates that RCAF Otter 3666, the twelfth built, was written off at Goose Bay April 10, 1956.

    Dick Hiscocks told me a story about how difficult he found it to work with Buller on a project that fully engaged him, as this one did. Fred would go almost without sleep in a crisis. Hiscocks had a more normal constitution; that is, he needed sleep. Throughout the Otter accident investigation Dick felt he was at least a step behind Fred, who was relentless.

9. This account of the H-21's air-refuelled transcontinental flight is pieced together from several sources, including the author's interview with Russ Bannock cited above. Bannock supplied notes for the Dallas speech by Lt.-Gen. Williams quoted several times in this chapter. Bannock also disclosed that it was the British Flight Refuelling system that was used for the air refuelling. The Piasecki H-21 entry in Norman Polmar and Floyd D. Kennedy Jr.'s *Military Helicopters of the World* (Annapolis: Naval Institute Press, 1981), pp. 362–65, gives the mileage and elapsed-time figures. Hayes, *op. cit.*, identifies the air-refuelling Otter, p. 87.

10. The ellipsis in the quote from Lt.-Gen. Williams's speech at Dallas credits Stebbins with a 32-hour flight, rather than the 37-hour flight recorded for the H-21 in Polmar and Kennedy; a difference that could conceivably be accounted for by the time the H-21 took to use its initial and final fuel loads. (No range figures are given in Polmar and Kennedy for the H-21. Nor do they give a listing for a CH-21 model, as Williams first refers to the helicopter. However, they do list the H-21C, with a more powerful engine than previous models, which was redesignated CH-21C when U.S. armed forces aircraft designations were harmonized in 1962.)

Assuming the air-refuelling Otter carried a single tank of fuel for the H-21 (with its own fuel in its three subfloor tanks), Stebbins's most difficult task might have been to fly the Otter, fully loaded at its aftmost centre of gravity, slow enough to match speeds with the H-21 and keep the hose looped below the helicopter's forward rotor. The faster the H-21 flew, the lower its nose and front rotor would pitch, blanketing the probe with downwash and threatening the drogue hose connecting the two aircraft.

11. This account of training for the Huey record flights will ring a bell with some readers. With a single important difference, the same story appears in the author's *The Immortal Beaver: The World's Greatest Bush Plane, op. cit.*, pp. 103–4.

The difference is that, in fact, then-Lt. Mattocks was flying an Otter, not a Beaver. A number of details, such as almost counting the propeller revolutions and the seven-hour-duration flights, make more sense with an Otter. Source: Author interview with Col. K. R. Mattocks (ret'd), May 25, 1997.

Chapter 9: The Trans Antarctic Otter

1. My account of Operation Deepfreeze—the first of 10 expeditions so named by the U.S. Navy—comes from three sources. Hayes, *op. cit.*, devotes more than three pages to U.S. Naval use of Otters, most of it in Antarctica. Because the Otter was so vital to Antarctic exploration for so long, Hayes's retelling of the various Operation Deepfreezes from the airplane's point of view is quite complete.

Basil Clarke's *Polar Flight* (London: Ian Allan, 1964) is the best treatment of that subject I have read. Chapter 19, "The International Geophysical Year," adds much detail to Hayes's Otter-based framework.

My references to "one account" are to Al Muenchen's *Flying the Midnight Sun: The Exploration of Antarctica by Air* (New York: David McKay Co., 1972), the chatty style of which makes it a good introduction to the subject. Muenchen names people in incidents who in other accounts go nameless.

2. For more detail on Beaver NZ6001/6010, the Trans Antarctic Beaver and the two Beavers since painted in its orange-red scheme to memorialize it, see the author's *The Immortal Beaver, op. cit.*, pp. 107–9.

3. The incident is mentioned in Clarke, *op. cit.*, p. 116. Although Clarke does not give a weight for the building, he does mention that the Otter's maximum payload is "only" (no insult intended) a ton, implying that the building weighed more than that. Like most aircraft, though, the Otter can trade range for payload. The ground route from Shackleton to South Ice zig-zags, making it difficult to estimate the distance between the two points, but Hayes says they were 300 miles apart. Depending on its empty weight, a piston-engine Otter could carry more than 2,600 pounds for that distance. The Otter specifications in Hotson, *op. cit.*, p. 230, note that on a trip of only 200 miles, a piston Otter can carry nearly 3,000 pounds.

4. Clarke says that he flew with S/L Lewis some years later on his first flight to the North Pole, where the pilot did the same circumnavigation at 90 degrees north.

My account of the flight of Otter XL 710 is assembled from information in Hayes and Clarke, *op. cit.* Both wrote compelling descriptions of the flight, but they chose to include different material. Clarke, perhaps because of his extended acquaintance with Lewis, is more descriptive and includes such tidbits as XL 710's circling the South Pole, while Hayes's treatment is longer and more purely factual. Hayes also qualifies the record of XL 710 as the first single-engine aircraft to cross Antarctica by recalling that in 1935 Lincoln Ellsworth (for whom the U.S. Ellsworth base was named) flew his Northrop Gamma, a single-engined monoplane, across Antarctica, "but he apparently made four intermediate landings and ran out of fuel 16 miles short of his destination, being forced to walk home." We could call the exploit of XL 710 and its RAF crew the first nonstop single-engine flight across Antarctica.

5. In one of the few factual differences between the Hayes and Clarke retellings of the Trans Antarctic Otter's historic flight, Clarke says it was greeted at Scott Base "by almost every aircraft from the New Zealand (Scott) base and from the American field at McMurdo Sound."

This variation is footnoted only because, with naval versions of the four-engine C-54 Skymaster and other multi-engine airplanes at the big flight facility at McMurdo, the scene at tiny Scott base on XL 710's arrival, in the Clarke scenario, would have been an air traffic control nightmare. Which is not to say it didn't happen, given Clarke's access to S/L Lewis's personal recollections of the epic flight.

6. With that much history behind it, Otter Number 126 was still far

from finished. Hayes devotes two large-size pages to that single aircraft (pp. 135–37), Hotson most of another (pp. 134–37).

"By 1970," Hayes continues, "the Otter had been purchased by La Ronge Aviation Services, and based at La Ronge, Saskatchewan. Sadly on the 14th May 1976 at 12:25 local time, while taking off from the airfield at Lynn Lake, Manitoba, the aircraft pitched up due to improper loading, stalled, and crashed into the runway. Only minor injuries were suffered by the pilot and eight passengers, but CF-PNV was badly damaged, and never flew again for La Ronge."

But Number 126's amazing career was still not over. We will return to PNV in Chapter 11 of this book, "Altered Otters," and take up its career under yet another identity as the prospective second Cox Turbo Otter. Hayes's account of 126's career is lavish with fascinating details; his separate account of its career, entitled "Tale of an Otter," is a highlight of a book filled with them.

7. Clarke, *op. cit.,* p. 118.

Chapter 10: Civil Otters:
Firebirds, Peacekeepers and Wardair

1. Except, of course, for those times established by the Concorde and Tupolev Tu-144 supersonic transports. The de Havilland Comet, and subsequently the Boeing 707, established today's air-travel expectations. The 707 cruised at nearly twice the speed of, for example, a Lockheed Super Constellation.

2. The comparison between DC-3s and their variants and the Otter is, as Hayes, *op. cit.*, notes on p. 101, "apples and oranges—the aircraft are not designed for the same task." But for an operator such as Max Ward, the business opportunity was to deliver goods to places the DC-3 couldn't service and exploit the Otter's cost advantage in markets both aircraft could get in and out of.

3. Jack (Rowdy) Rutherford, was, despite a nickname that might suggest otherwise, a very capable former RCAF pilot, hired by Ward to fly the Fairchild Husky he leased from a mining company. The Husky "wasn't nearly as useful an aircraft as the Otter, of course, but it didn't cost nearly as much, either." Rutherford deserved credit for operating an airplane roughly the Otter's size with the same power as a Beaver, and when Rowdy knocked the tail ski off the Husky, Ward returned it to its owners and bought his first Beaver.

4. Hayes, *op. cit.*, provides a concise and accurate summary of Wardair's operations on pp. 130–31, just as he outlines the history of practically every Otter user at the time of publication in 1982. Ward's autobiography, *op. cit.*, is entertaining and informative, if understandably preoccupied with his struggles to build an airline

in a country where the transportation policy has been geared to support only one airline—the one the government owned. Ward's animal passenger, piano and gold brick stories appear on pp. 123–30.

The former Constable Mattocks is the younger brother of the K. Randall Mattocks who flew Otters both as an exchange test pilot at Fort Rucker during the early 1960s and in Egypt with the United Nations later that decade. Having been impressed when Max Ward flew into Aklavik in the latest word in bush planes, Don Mattocks never made any secret of his preference for Wardair's sumptuous in-flight service once the airline began flying charters to Europe—especially after he left Aklavik and had a choice in the matter.

5. Author interview with Karl Frisk, March 23, 1998.

GBY was flown to Downsview, where DHC made Ward a bid to rebuild his first Otter. Frisk offered to do the job for $2,000 less in Vancouver, and while the low bid got him the work and he achieved his aim of being his own boss, he still can't say whether he made any money on the job. It's a great story, though. McCartney is working on his memoir of a career spent repairing aircraft in the bush, to be entitled *Picking up the Pieces*.

6. Bruce West, *op. cit.*, pp. 215–34.

In Chapter 16, entitled "Deluge from the Sky," West describes Carl Crossley's totally successful demonstration of equipment and techniques that would later become universal, and adds ruefully:

"Yet, for some reason, this water-dropping method wasn't fully utilized until some time after these first successful experiments had been completed. Interest . . . seemed to stray from the float-tank system and move for a while toward another method, which seemed much more simple and less expensive—except that it didn't work very well. This involved the dropping of actual water bombs upon the fires. These bombs consisted of special wet-proof paper bags containing about three-and-a-half gallons of water."

The 27-inch-diameter hole in the aft ventral fuselage of the Beaver that gave designer Dick Hiscocks such concern was there at the request of the Ontario Provincial Air Service, specifically for dropping those paper bags full of water on forest fires. Having already discovered the best possible method for using floatplanes to combat forest fires, OPAS reverted to a technique reminiscent of the high jinks of college sophomores loose in highrise hotels. Meanwhile, the Otter float, adapted from those installed on Norsemans, has from the beginning been a little short—perhaps to alleviate the Otter's reluctant takeoff from water with piston power—when it was in OPAS' interest to have Otter floats be as long as possible (consistent with centre of gravity considerations), in order to carry as much water as possible to fire sites.

Consequently, it was only during the spring of 1997 that Harbour Air of Vancouver had Canada's Department of Transport test pilot, Leo Galvin, test longer floats developed by the charter carrier's chief engineer, Bob Bator, for its pair of turbine-powered Otters, which are longer (if lighter) ahead of the cockpit than piston-powered ones. The single-engine Otter had to evolve into a turbine-powered weightlifter before it became possible to address one of its historic flaws: rather short floats.

7. West, *op. cit.*, does not identify the first Otter converted for forest fire-fighting. The first three OPAS Otters were production Numbers 13 to 15, CF-ODK, -ODJ and -ODL. -ODJ was the first delivered, May 8, 1953. All three were delivered within the month of May to the Sault Ste. Marie base, where Tom Cooke figured out the rolling-tank system and oversaw the modifications.

8. West implies, but does not state, that Beauchene was flying a Turbo Beaver. The context suggests that the float installation of Field Aviation's equipment enabled Beauchene to attack four fires without having to make changes to a Turbo Beaver configured for normal flight operations.

9. Although West's book provides the basis for my account of the development of aerial fire-fighting as pioneered by the Ontario Provincial Air Service on behalf of Ontario's Department of Lands and Forests (later the Ministry of Natural Resources), I have used information from a couple of other sources.

Scale Aircraft Modelling, of all sources, provided a wide-ranging look at water-bombing in its December 1995 issue. Its survey of fire-fighting aircraft used worldwide overlooks the contributions made by DHC types (which SAM has documented in separate articles on the Beaver and Otter) but does include such specialist types as the Russian Beriev 12P amphibian and the giant Martin JRM Mars flying boats used in British Columbia.

Another worthwhile source is Colin J. Ashford's thorough two-part series "Canada's Flying Firemen," in *Aeroplane Monthly*, June/July 1976. The information on Turbo Beaver and Twin Otter capacities and loading times comes from this source, as does the "Dial-O-Matic" feature of the Field Aviation water-bombing installation on the Twin Otter.

Chapter 11: Altered Otters

1. Author interviews with Bob Bator at Harbour Air Seaplanes hangar, Vancouver South Airport, April 30 and May 6, 1997.

2. Hayes, *op. cit.*, pp. 81–92, lists 20 military users: the U.S. Army, Navy and Air Force; Argentina; Australia; Bangladesh; Cambodia (20, from U.S. Army stocks); Canada (69 ordered, 66 used); Chile; Ethiopia; Ghana (first nation to use all of the first four DHC types); India (36); Indonesia; New Zealand; Nicaragua; Norway; Panama; Paraguay; the Royal Air Force (XL 710, the Trans Antarctic Otter); and Tanzania.

3. U.S. Army U-1 55-3318 (184) was photographed in November 1958, somewhere in the continental United States, on what were called "hydro-skis." The idea was to start on land, apply full throttle and take off from water. Presumably takeoff performance was improved over that on floats. It survived these trials but crashed in 1970; it was repaired, then sold off, and has since flown for various owners as C-FQMN in Ontario and Quebec.

4. Even the encyclopedic Karl Hayes is unable to say much about possible Otter roles in combat (Hayes, *op. cit.*, p. 87), but he does note that Otters often appear in photographs festooned with aerials the exact purposes of which cannot be divined.

Aside from being used in the utility roles of supply and transport among army camps in Vietnam (Hayes says they equipped two companies; Bannock remembers six), for which their ability to climb helped evade snipers in the hostile areas between U.S. installations, Hayes reports that "a few Otters were modified for Radio Research. They were filled with specialist radio equipment and flew around for hours at altitude intercepting enemy broadcasts which were taped and subsequently analysed at base."

George Neal says a near-standard Otter could be made capable of a five-hour mission endurance. During the early 1960s Canadian exchange test pilot Lt. Randall Mattocks tested Otters (among other Army aircraft) at Fort Rucker with rubberized fuel bladders that could be strapped into the copilot's seat, avoiding centre-of-gravity problems. The worst part of these endurance tests—Mattocks flew one from Rucker, in Alabama, to the Bell Helicopter plant in Dallas–Fort Worth, a number of times—was the absence of relief tubes in Army aircraft, which were not supposed to be airborne that long.

5. Otter 55-3272 was delivered May 19, 1956, and had a relatively uneventful U.S. Army career before being honourably discharged in 1974. A DHC photo of it with its radar pods also shows perfect paint and a shiny fuselage, raising the possibility that the Radar Otter trial, conducted entirely at Downsview according to Neal, took place in 1956 rather than '57. Since 1974 it has been CF-BEP, based during that decade at Wawa, Ontario, not far from Sault Ste. Marie.

6. Information from an article by Brian Eggleston, formerly of the DHC Advanced Design Group, entitled "Drawing Board," in *Canadian Aviation*, June 1988, Special de Havilland Issue, pp. 56–63. Kindly loaned by John Thompson.

Eggleston reveals that a study for a single-engine Otter replacement, the DHP56 project, was launched upon the return of Russ

Bannock (who resigned over termination of Beaver and Otter production by Hawker Siddeley in 1967) as president of DHC in 1976. Soon after, Dick Hiscocks returned to DHC as VP, Engineering, after his second stint at the National Research Council. Turbine engines from Lycoming, Garrett and the P&WC PT6A-127 were considered as powerplants. (The higher the PT6A dash-number, the more shaft horsepower it delivers.) The DHP56 was a taildragger with a cantilever (unbraced) wing and a Dash 7–like T-tail.

Eggleston implies that a subsequent consultancy by Bannock and Hiscocks with Cessna led to that company's Caravan. "This is a fitting tribute to the ability of ex-DHC professionals to correctly identify a market niche. The inability of DHC to exploit the DHP56 in concert with the Dash-8 development is one of the sadder facts to be pondered." DHC was now out of the small aircraft market.

7. Hayes, *op. cit.*, pp. 10–11.

8. It is characteristic of turbines that they wind up to their rated power more slowly than piston engines, which react quickly to throttle inputs. Turbines are quieter, smoother and more efficient in cruise.

    Similar in size and capacity to the Otter, the An-2's gross weight is 12,125 pounds versus the Otter's 8,000 or so, and so despite its much greater power the An-2 is slower and has less range, in part because of its biplane configuration. The Otter, Hayes (*op. cit.*, p. 14) concludes in his brief comparison of the two airplanes, "comes out as an altogether more efficient machine."

9. These rash comments are made on a promotional videotape commissioned by Airtech consisting of interviews of engineers, pilots and owners of PZL-powered Otters. Pilots occasionally exaggerate, of course, but the testimonials are unquestionably sincere.

10. Author phone interview with James Mewett and Bernard LaFrance of Airtech Canada, April 29, 1998. Airtech is working on an Otter conversion using the new Orenda V/8 aero engine that promises to fill a piston power gap from 400 to 750hp, be more fuel-efficient than turbines, and be installed for the cost of a turbine overhaul. Orenda hopes this engine will revive general and private aviation, inspiring new small airplane designs. See *Design Engineering*, April 1997, "Orenda Aims V/8 Engine at Aviation Market" by Ed Belitsky.

11. C. Marin Faure, *op. cit.*

12. Olson quoted by Faure in the *Water Flying* 1990 Annual, "The Vazar Dash-3 Otter," pp. 4–13.

13. One hundred *feet*? I was at the show but did not see the opening. Vazar's marketing manager says yes, it was 100 feet. Landing *and* takeoff: 100 feet. Wow.

14. Testing for the Vazar Dash-3 conversion revealed much about the inherent strength of the Otter. Torque testing of the fuselage to ascertain whether it could take the loads generated by 750shp showed that it would take more than 1,200 shp. Wilder discovered that Otters in Vietnam had flown with gross weights exceeding 12,000 pounds—one-third over the maximum all-up weight. Faure, *op. cit.*, p. 11.

15. Author interview with Dave Barron of AOG Air Support, May 1, 1998.

16. A float's buoyancy is measured by water displacement, i.e., a 7100 float displaces that many pounds of water. By regulation an airplane's floats must displace 180 per cent of its gross weight; which the two 7170 floats, displacing 14,340 pounds, almost do.

17. We might recall Fred Buller's single piece of advice to test pilot George Neal before the Otter's first flight. *Watch for flutter*, he said. Nobody was sure then where it might appear. Now we know.

18. Bator overhauls one of Harbour Air's pair of turbine Otters each winter at Sea Island, the site of Vancouver International Airport. One of them, C-GOPP (355), spent 16 years in the U.S. Army before donning the uniform of the Ontario Provincial Police. Maintained for most of its life by government organizations, OPP is an especially desirable Otter. It is insured for $CDN1.27 million.

    The Otter's rise in value has been slower than the Beaver's—the Beaver has become a collectible rich man's toy—but steadier, as its commercial possibilities are compared with those of, say, a Cessna Caravan. Suddenly a turbine conversion that costs $US200,000 (with tax) makes sense.

Chapter 12: DHC Survives the DHC-4

1. "He never talked to me," says Karl Frisk, the Swedish SAAB expatriate who rerigged the control cables on the third Otter prototype (Fecteau's first Otter) in the Experimental Shop as part of the effort to resolve the flap-trim problem during the test flight stage and also rebuilt CF-GBY, Max Ward's first Otter, after making it flyable following its misfortune on Baffin Island. Of course, Frisk was still learning English when he worked at Downsview (although the language of craftsmanship is universal).

2. Hotson, *op. cit.*, pp. 125–27.

3. Hotson, *op. cit.*, p. 146. Many sources, including two recent studies, date the appearance of the first Light Twin study in October 1954.

4. Dick Hiscocks concluded from the abortive attempts to improve on the Otter by designing a Light Twin that DHC was pursuing "a chimera called 'twin-engine safety.' Most twin-engined airplanes of that era, fully loaded, were unable to provide more than an extended glide when an engine failed. Nevertheless, they were by definition 'safe' whereas the Otter, with the ability to land almost anywhere, and one-half the probability of an engine failure, was not!" Source: "Whither STOL?" by R. D. Hiscocks, in *de Havilland, You STOL My Heart Away*, *op. cit.*, p. 270.

5. Hotson, *op. cit.*

6. Hotson, *ibid.* This is one of several great stories that came out of DHC's warm relationship with U.S. Army Aviation procurement officers. Lt.-Gen. Williams recalled that the Beaver, Otter and Caribou were developed by DHC "without being contaminated by U.S. military advice and control."

   His speech is reprinted in *de Havilland, You STOL My Heart Away, op. cit.*, pp. 152–56. Williams's speech used notes prepared by Russ Bannock, so both date the submission of the raw specifications that whetted the Army's appetite to September 1956. General-arrangement three-view drawings dated January 1957 show a DHC-4 with a very different tail from the eventual one: twin vertical tails set at right angles at the ends of sharply upturned tailplanes, the overall appearance being of twin end plate tails bent upward.

   Bannock's account of the sale, *op. cit.*, p. 125, notes that the aircraft were to have civil certification in the Normal Transport category. This turned out to be a more difficult requirement than DHC anticipated.

   Williams said the U.S. Army bought 165 Caribous. Close enough, and maybe right on. My count, based upon the numbers in Wayne Mutza's *C-7 Caribou in Action* (Carrolltown, Texas: Squadron/Signal Publications, 1993) includes 5 YAC-1 service test models, 56 AC-1s and 103 AC-1As (all Army designations as ordered), for a total of 164.

7. Hotson, *ibid.*

8. Hotson, *ibid.*, pp. 128–29. Not only were the Trackers a useful learning experience for DHC, the contract for their assembly was the largest postwar defence expenditure to that date in Canada: $100 million. The survivors continue to generate employment for Canada's aerospace industry; they are being converted to turbine-powered Firecat water-bombers at Abbotsford, British Columbia.

9. Johnson's account, in *de Havilland, You STOL My Heart Away, op. cit.*, pp. 94–98, is entitled "The Summer of a Thousand Stalls."

   My account of the troubles in certifying the Caribou is assembled from Hotson, *ibid.*, pp. 148–50, Johnson's narrative and Wayne Mutza's chapter on development of the YAC-1s in his *C-7 Caribou in Acton, op. cit.*, pp. 7–8.

   One way of summarizing the problem is to observe that proving the Caribou could lift itself into the air with three tons from a dirt strip—performance that was utterly unique in military aviation at the time and remains remarkable—was only the beginning. Once off the ground, it had to fly as well as a commercial transport in situations of marginal control. In engineering terms, these are difficult requirements to reconcile.

   Along with the Otter's flap actuation problems, the troubled

certification of the Caribou to civil standards led some DHC engineers (notably Mike Davy, Hiscocks's deputy Jack Uffen and head of airworthiness Bob Klein, among many others) to wonder whether the military sales attributable to the STOL performance of DHC products were worth the trouble. See note 16, this chapter.

10. Don Henly and Ken Ellis, authors of "Globetrotting Reindeer," in *Air Enthusiast* 74, March/April 1998, pp. 20–33, date the crash March 23, 1959, and Fowler's log records his search for the wreckage with Mick Saunders and finding it near Udora, Ontario, the following day.

11. Johnson, in *de Havilland, You STOL My Heart Away, op. cit.*, p. 96.

12. A total of 307 Caribous were built, with production terminating around 1973. In 1996 the Caribou was still in service with the air arms of seven countries, including Australia. Source: *Air International*, April 1996, "Military Transport Aircraft Directory," Pt. 2, by Dave Allport.

    A more recent history of the Caribou, "Globetrotting Reindeer," *op. cit.*, tracks Caribous through their service lives with the air arms of 20 nations (and the United Nations) and the subsequent civilian careers of the survivors.

    The statement about being denied further battle honours is based on the observation that, to the air forces of the United States and Canada in particular, front-line tactical transports like the Caribou have little use other than as search-and-rescue vehicles and for dropping paratroopers. Having won the franchise for fixed-wing aviation above certain gross weights, those air forces pretty much ignored the category.

    These are, of course, general comments. The specific dilemma posed by the Caribou's STOL capabilities, from the USAF's point of view, was that the first medium-sized transport it fielded in Vietnam, the Fairchild-Hiller C-123 Provider, could carry a payload (including fuel) almost three times the Caribou's. STOL was critical for Special Forces resupply from forward strips, but beside the point in a Low Level Extraction (LOLEX) resupply situation, where the transport did not actually touch down.

    The Caribou vs. Provider comparison is a classic case of deciding how important STOL is. Is it worth the difference in payload? According to Mutza, *op. cit.*, p. 45, when contemplating a post-Vietnam Caribou replacement, the USAF considered converted turboprop C-123s, more Caribous or Buffaloes, or C-130s modified for better short-field performance. In the end, the Caribou was not replaced. (In fact, 33 of them fell into North Vietnamese hands in 1975.)

    Regarding the RAAF's use of the Caribou in Vietnam and continuing to the time of writing: Australians are laudable exceptions to almost any rule of human behaviour one can postulate.

13. Author interview with John Thompson, May 26, 1997.

14. As Hotson, *op. cit.*, p. 163, points out, the tactical load for a Buffalo could include a Pershing medium-range ballistic missile, a 105-mm howitzer and a ¾-ton truck. Mutza, *op. cit.*, p. 44, says it was designed to carry 41 fully equipped troops or up to 25 litter patients. (The Caribou was designed, in practical terms, to carry two Jeeps and a fully equipped squad of infantry, or 34 soldiers.) The difference was in the new turbine engines, which developed 2,344 shaft horsepower (the standard turbine power measurement), augmented by 565 pounds of direct thrust.

15. Hotson, *ibid.*, pp. 163–67.

16. Information on the causes of the Army's loss of the fixed-wing tactical transport role, a more complicated saga than can be fully recounted here, come from both Hotson, p. 167, and Wayne Mutza, *op. cit.*, p. 44. Hotson blames McNamara. Mutza, an American, blames the U.S. airframe manufacturers: "Since the Canadian design had won out over entries from U.S. companies, pressure from those companies forced changes in U.S. military procurement policies designed to protect U.S. industry. This change in policy limited sales to the U.S. Army to the four CV-7A evaluation aircraft (63-13686 to 689), which were delivered in the spring of 1965."

The Buffalo did sell overseas, although in smaller numbers than the Caribou had.

The field hospital stunt is cited in Hiscocks's "Whither STOL?" in *de Havilland, You STOL My Heart Away, op. cit.*, p. 273.

17. The ultimate Buffalo, the DHC-5D, used more powerful GE T-64 engines, not for enhanced STOL performance but to carry larger payloads from paved runways. Rather than representing a change of heart within DHC's Engineering Department, the new priority is likely to have reflected the USAF's requirement for army airlift support in the post-Vietnam military climate as it assumed control of fixed-wing aviation.

Mutza, *op. cit.*, p. 45, informs us that a standard production 5D-model Buffalo was used to set six new time-to-height records on February 23, 1976. DHC test pilot Capt. Tom E. Appleton had noticed how quickly it climbed, checked the record (held by a Lockheed P-3 Orion ASW aircraft), and beat it with a crew consisting of copilot Bill Pullen and engineer Barry Hubbard, all of DHC.

Nearly 50 more aircraft were assembled after the Buffalo assembly line was reopened in 1974, but despite the five-ton hauler's impressive capabilities, the line was shut down for good in December 1986, with a total of 126 Buffaloes delivered.

The Buffalo was the basis of two noteworthy research aircraft, a common fate for aero engineering masterpieces that fail in the marketplace. The first was a standard RCAF CC-115 (as the RCAF designated the Buffalo), redesignated XC-8A and fitted with a rubberized Bell Air Cushion Landing System (ALCS), a skirt-type inflated under-fuselage hull, which, along with wing-mounted float/skid devices, enabled the XC-8A to land on almost any surface. Fowler did the initial testing. Hotson calls it "the Bell-Bottom Buffalo." It is this aircraft that demonstrated in 1975 how high DHC had raised the STOL bar: the company had designed and built airplanes that could lift payloads of up to nine tons from almost any relatively smooth surface three football fields long.

The other experimental Buffalo was the Boeing/de Havilland/NASA Augmentor Wing aircraft, one of the most exciting flight-test programs Bob Fowler ever undertook. After removal of nine feet of each outer wing panel, the Buffalo's engines and its wing trailing edge from the spar back were replaced with Rolls-Royce Spey turbofan jet engines with their hot gases exhausted through swivelling nozzles much like those on the Harrier jump-jet. All bypass air from the engines was ducted to the flaps, increasing their efficiency. It first flew May 1, 1972, and was tested until 1980, achieving 7½-degree approaches at from 55 to 60 knots, with takeoff ground rolls as short as 300 feet (450 feet to clear a 35-foot screen). Source: Hotson, *op. cit.*, pp. 209–11.

18. Author interview with John Thompson, *op. cit.*

Chapter 13: A Tough Act to Follow

1. The U.S. military bought 978 Beavers and 240—190 of them for the Army—Otters.

2. N. E. (Nero) Rowe, the chief engineer who was taken for a ride by Bob Fowler in Otter 3682 at the beginning of this narrative, made a contribution to DHC during this hectic period that is seldom remembered. He was, like the man he replaced, Doug Hunter, a diplomat at a time when the company's talented engineering department needed that kind of leadership.

Rowe had spent his war at Boscombe Down, the British flight-test centre, and supervised Blackburn's engineering group during its postwar flowering, during which types as varied as the Buccaneer strike aircraft and the bulbous Beverley transport were being developed. After Blackburn was absorbed by Hawker Siddeley in the first British aircraft company consolidations, Rowe was posted to DHC, where he presided over the engineers at Downsview after Hunter's death in 1961, from mid-1962 to the end of 1966.

As for the task of reconciling egos, "it was an arrogant office," Mike Davy says, meaning it was what it had to be. Six years at Avro Canada had convinced him that servility had no place in an aircraft engineering department. John Thompson, who should know, says Bob McIntyre was also a candidate for the top job in Engineering.

3. Hotson, *op. cit.*, p. 172. Peter S. Martin was honoured for his lead role in developing the Mk.III Turbo Beaver by having its prototype registered CF-PSM. There is much similarity of design between the Turbo Beaver and the Twin Otter, especially in their respective vertical tails. Martin, who died in 1997, was a very fast worker who moved from the Turbo Beaver to the Twin Otter project almost overnight. A critical hand in all of these near-concurrent projects involving P&WC PT6 turbine power was Ian Gilchrist, who worked on Otter 3682, the Turbo Beaver and the Twin Otter.

My account of Bannock's 1963 trip to Vietnam and its aftermath is pieced together from my conversation with him of May 29, 1997, and Fred Hotson's recounting of the weekly management meeting at Downsview at which Bannock presented his ideas and the engineers quickly agreed with him: "In fact Peter Martin began, immediately, preparing a set of preliminary drawings."

Bannock does not remember exactly when he was in Vietnam, so my estimate of when that trip took place is based almost solely upon Hotson's statement, coupled with Walter Henry's assertion in "The Twin Otter in Review," *Canadian Aviation Historical Society Journal*, Summer 1988, p. 41, that "Preliminary design work on the new DHC-6 began in April of 1963."

These dates are much earlier than those published elsewhere, and they emphasize the deliberate haste with which DHC sought to bring the DHC-6 to market.

4. Another production run of 466 airplanes, the number of single-engine Otters produced, would have been considered a tremendous success—especially at unit prices that rose during the production run from $250,000 to $450,000. DHC built almost twice that many Twin Otters, a total of 844.

Indicative of the Twin Otter project's smooth passage was its approval by the DHC board of directors. According to Hotson, Phil Garratt had almost nothing to say until all the engineering presentations were finished, at which point he asked, "Any objections?"

5. The hectic atmosphere within Engineering is summed up by John Thompson, VP, Engineering, from 1971 to 1979: "In the DHC of 1963–64 I would not have been 'assigned' to the DHC-6 project, but just expected to take it on along with all the other current projects, namely the DHCT2 Turbo Beaver, DHC-5 Buffalo, FHE400 Bras d'Or [hydrofoil] and DC-9 wing detail design. My stress, weights, liaison, structural test, etc. engineering staff were individually assigned to one or the other of the projects as fast as they could be hired from outside or moved over from a completed project."

Thompson points out that ex-Avro personnel allowed DHC to get going on the Buffalo and DC-9 after 1962, but it took new hires from the U.K. to fully staff those and the hydrofoil. The Turbo Beaver and Twin Otter were not considered sufficiently big projects to merit new staff.

"Well into 1964 I think there were only two stress engineers assigned to the DHC-6. Their job was to work directly with designers so that the structural sizing would be as correct as possible at that stage." Source: Letter to the author, July 3, 1997.

6. Wally Gibson was head of flight test during the mid-1960s. Source: Author conversation with Wally Gibson, May 28, 1997.

That somewhat illegitimate second Twin Otter became CF-SJB-X, which flew more than a year after DHC-X and was the first Twin Otter sold. After a brief period with Air Commuter until improved Series 200 models appeared, it went north to support oil and gas exploration as CF-PAT, eventually becoming the senior member of the biggest Twin Otter fleet in the world, that of Kenn Borek Air. It was retired last year but could fly again if a cheap wingset turned up.

7. DHC assigned Punch Dickins to sort out the DC-9 wing production problem at Avro's old plant at Malton, now Lester B. Pearson International Airport. The problem was that the DC-9 became a best-seller very quickly, causing Douglas to ask DHC to double and triple production when the company could barely finance all the projects it was already involved in. Dickins realistically projected six months for an expansion that needed to happen overnight. Eventually, Douglas took over the Malton facility, which it operated until early 1998, when Boeing's takeover of McDonnell Douglas led to the phaseout of the DC-9 and its many MD-prefixed derivatives.

To be sure, one man's bad timing is another man's shining moment of destiny. Fred Hotson, *op. cit.*, introduces his account of the birth of the Twin Otter on page 172 with a few words from *Julius Caesar*: "There is a time in the affairs of men," said Shakespeare, "which taken at the tide leads to fortune." In similar vein he went on, "We must take the current when it serves or lose our ventures." No words could more aptly describe the logic behind the Twin Otter.

Nor, even if taken at the flood, could words express the good fortune DHC enjoyed when, the U.S. Army having been denied aircraft larger than helicopters, the commuter airline industry exploded during the late 1960s. Russ Bannock perceived what was going on. The father of the Twin Otter left its nest at Downsview in 1968 to follow the airplane into the commuter airline business. He had seen one New York operator squeeze six more seats into his Twin Otters by doubling the number of seats to the left of the aisle. This became the standard cabin layout.

Bannock did not actually end up in the commuter airline business, although he did help set up Time Air, a western Canadian commuter success story, before he began buying and selling Twin Otters. Through his company, Bannock Aerospace—"for lack of any other name"—he recycled 110 of them (along with 200 Beavers, single-engine Otters and Caribous) in an ongoing process that had the net effect of returning DHC aircraft to North America from every corner of the world.

8. Gordon Johnston interview with the author, May 27, 1997.

Johnston's remarks about the Twin Otter were asides in a conversation that focussed mainly on the experimental STOL Otter 3682 program. He has been for many years based at the University of Toronto's Institute for Aerospace Studies.

9. Davy points out that the Otter fuselage, seen in cross-section, is squared off at the top and tapers down the sides to a rounded belly. For the optimum floor space, it should be the opposite.

10. Dick Hiscocks made this claim in an article he wrote on the DHC Engineering Department entitled "The Engineers," in the special "de Havilland at 60" issue of *Canadian Aviation*, April 1988. As noted earlier, Hiscocks has also written, in *de Havilland You STOL My Heart Away* (p. 273), that the Twin Otter "represented 10 to 20 per cent of all scheduled aircraft in service."

I have seen those claims made nowhere else, but Hiscocks supports them by referring to the explosive growth of feeder and commuter airlines, especially in the United States, for which the Twin Otter and its stretched derivatives, such as the 20-seat Series 300, were ideal equipment.

11. Author interview with John Thompson, May 26, 1997.

12. That problem aside, Fred Buller was proud all his life of the soundness of his Beaver flight-surface actuation mechanisms, some of them conceptualized overnight, the basic principles of which remained the same in each DHC airplane into the company's present Dash-8 regional airliners.

13. DHC installed 3,000-psi hydraulic systems on the bigger Caribou/ Buffalo series, which had more functions (retractable landing gear, for example) to be powered.

14. Klein, half of the two-man stress team on the Otter, feels he became "the conscientious objector" at DHC, especially for his opposition to STOL, which, he says, "is simply, by definition, illegal." He feels that it compromises safety, for which he was directly answerable at DHC.

That fact makes it all the more remarkable when he reports with pride that the FAA was "ecstatic" that the Twin Otter could climb on one engine. He quotes the head of the Federal Aviation Administration as having said to him, "You guys have designed an airplane so that whatever happens, nothing can go wrong."

When the owner of Pilgrim Airlines added a row of seats to his Twin Otters to accommodate 21 passengers, the airplanes "were flying 23 people," Klein says, "the same as a DC-3. And we were safer." Source: Author interview with Bob Klein, December 18, 1997.

Chapter 14: The Universal Airplane

1. "We never dreamed you could jam 19 people into it," says John Thompson, one of the Twin Otter's engineers. It was built for 14 to 15. "It turned out that, lo and behold, people *would* fly in them." Source: Letter to the author, July 3, 1997.

2. Many of these Twin Otter users have aircraft pictured in Paul R. Smith's *de Havilland Canada DHC-6, DHC-7, DHC-8* (London: Jane's Transport Press, 1987). Other early delivery data is from John Roach and Tony Eastwood's *Turbo Prop Airliner Production List* (London: The Aviation Hobby Shop, 1990), the most recent such list I could find.

3. Norway's air force operated a total of 10 single-engine Otters, six of them ordered in 1953 (Otters Number 18, 20, 21, 29, 30 and 31), two in 1960 (395 and 397) to replace two donated to the U.N. peacekeeping force in the Belgian Congo, and additional units ordered in 1961 (423) and 1964 (441). The order year and the DHC constructor's number became the RNOAF serial number, making the aircraft easy to track.

Shipped in crates, the Otters were assembled by Wideroes airline personnel and cared for in thorough Scandinavian fashion, suggesting they were highly prized. The only one to come to grief, 60395, ditched in the frigid waters off Tromso shod with wheel-skis; it was heavily damaged and corroded but rebuilt afterwards to flying status. The crew and their dog were rescued.

During 1967–68 the Otters were withdrawn from service, with four staying in civilian use in Norway, one being acquired by the British Antarctic Survey and the other three returning to Canada. They were replaced with Twin Otters. Source: Hayes, *op. cit.*, p. 86.

4. Hayes, *op. cit.*, p. 131–32.

5. Hotson, *op. cit.*, pp. 178–79. Hotson calls his account of the Norwegian short-field system "A STOL Showcase." I have relied on Hayes for Norwegian Otter use, and Hotson for Twin Otter operations there.

6. The number of Wideroes Twin Otters is from Walter Henry's article "The Twin Otter in Review" in the Canadian Aviation Historical Society *Journal*, Summer 1988, p. 49. That issue of the CAHS Journal celebrated DHC's first 60 years in business.

7. Walter Henry reached the same conclusion in his article, *op. cit.*: "There is little point in trying to guess the number of countries in which the Twin Otter has seen service because aircraft of this type change owners frequently from country to country, so, although company figures show 80, the actual international travels of the aeroplane would be complex indeed to figure out."

Henry, who acknowledges research help for his article from Fred Hotson, does list the following operators: Aeropostale (Venezuela); Greenlandair (for both passengers and ice patrol); Wideroes

Flyveselskap (who by 1980 operated 18 Twin Otters, including the seven hundredth-built); Tanzania (the seventieth country to order); Portugal (the eightieth); the People's Republic of China; Papua New Guinea; and Brymon, the first English user.

8. YA-GAS, the seventy-seventh Twin Otter built, returned to Canada in 1976 and flew as C-GDQY in Quebec and Labrador as recently as 1990, the date of the Roach/Eastwood production list, *op. cit.*, in which its latest entry (1978, Labrador Airways) appears.

9. DHC had every reason to believe the U.S. Army, whose senior aviation personnel had practically written its specifications, would buy the Twin Otter in numbers much larger than 100. The Army had bought every other DHC type in larger numbers than that except the Buffalo, which ran afoul of the new restrictions in the size of fixed-wing aircraft the Army could operate.

    In 1976 the Army did take delivery of two Twin Otters, writes Henry, *op. cit.* (p. 44), designating them UV-18As and assigning them to that frequent first home to DHC aircraft in the American military, Alaska. Two more, likewise with wheels, floats and skis, were added in 1982. Another pair, designated UV-18Bs, were purchased by the U.S. Air Force for parachute training.

10. At latest count, Harbour Air was operating 16 Beavers and a pair of turbine Otters out of its bases at Richmond, south of Vancouver, and Prince Rupert, B.C. Harbour's fleet of immaculate Beavers and Otters is expanding, and it is complemented by the nine or 10 orange-and-white Twin Otters Borek stations in Vancouver each summer and the pair that maintain the Vancouver-Victoria service through the off-season. Most summertime trips are fishing parties bound for upcoast B.C., often the salmon-rich Queen Charlotte Islands.

    Aside from the states and regions listed in the text, Borek Air also operates in Saudi Arabia, Brazil, Burma, Kurdistan, Panama, Thailand—and in the U.S. of A., dropping parachute smoke jumpers on fires for the U.S. Forest Service.

11. Source: Steve Penikett phone interview with the author, April 24, 1998.

12. Source: Russ Bannock phone interview with the author, July 25, 1997.

13. Aircraft & Industry update, *Air International*, July 1997, p. 6.

14. *Ibid.*

Chapter 15: The Airtransit Experiment

1. "My Presidency of de Havilland" by Bernhard B. Bundesmann, in *de Havilland You STOL My Heart Away*, *op. cit.*, pp. 162–5.

    Bundesmann opens his article by declaring that during his tenure as president of the Hawker Siddeley–owned DHC, from 1970 to 1976, "except for the first year, every year was highly profitable." Bundes-

mann had an extraordinary career as an aviation executive, parleying his early wartime experience with the U.S. construction giant Bechtel into key positions overseeing production of the milestone B-29 and B-47 bombers for subcontractors Bell Aircraft and Lockheed. He came to the Hawker Siddeley Group in 1963 to sell the DH.125 business jet in the U.S., Canada and Mexico. He had the good fortune to leave his post shortly before the unprecedented (in Canada) development costs of the Dash-7 program began to cripple DHC and drain whatever traces of enthusiasm Hawker Siddeley still had for its Canadian satellite, ultimately sending it into government ownership.

2. I have altered Higgins's quote, from his article on pp. 166–68 of *de Havilland, You STOL My Heart Away*, *op. cit.*, in the interests of brevity. In his text, Higgins refers to "the CAB/FAA/DOT Northeast Corridor study," thus indicating how important it was. Backed by the Civil Aeronautics Board, the Federal Aviation Administration and the U.S. Department of Transportation, the study could have resulted in a more rational allocation of resources within the most heavily travelled air corridor in the world than has resulted from airline deregulation during the 25 years since.

3. Higgins, *ibid.*

4. Hotson, *op. cit.*, p. 195.

5. Bilingual brochure prepared by Transport Canada for distribution to passengers embarking on Airtransit flights, entitled "Canada STOL Project." Brochure is undated and uncredited.

6. Hotson, *op. cit.* The six Twin Otters were: CF-CST 351, delivered July 19, 1973; CF-CSU 352, delivered October 11, 1973; CF-CSV 354, delivered July 19, 1973; CF-CSW 355, delivered October 11, 1973; CF-CSX 357, delivered November 6, 1973; CF-CSY 358, delivered November 2, 1973. Hotson is right about these six being the most sophisticated Twin Otters ever. Bob Klein says that the avionics (navigation and landing systems) on those aircraft cost more than the airplanes themselves. Source: Author interview with Bob Klein, December 18, 1997.

    All six became property of the Canadian Ministry of Transport as of June 1976. As of 1990, the publication date of the *Turbo Prop Airliner Production List*, *op. cit.*, five of the six were still active. CF-CSV crashed near Cambridge, Ontario, February 27, 1981.

7. Author interview with Harold Kalman, April 1998.

8. "Whither STOL?" by R. D. Hiscocks, *de Havilland, You STOL My Heart Away*, *op. cit.*, pp. 269–276. This essay is a kind of last will and testament by Dick Hiscocks, summing up the achievements of the technology he spent most of his working life perfecting.

9. Higgins, *op. cit.*

Chapter 16: Flying the Otter and Twin Otter

1. Exactly how much time Col. Mattocks spent flying Otters remains

unknown, even to him. His flight logs sank, along with much of his personal gear, as it followed him to Egypt, one of his many overseas postings. Like the Beaver, the Otter was taken from his menu by the RCAF, and he got to fly them only with the Americans or on United Nations duty. He is the first to say that, as an army service corps pilot, he was more accustomed to lighter, more responsive types, such as Bell H-13 helicopters, and artillery Air Observation Post (AOP) types such as the Taylorcraft Auster and Cessna L-19. That experience gave him a fresh perspective on the heavier Otter when he flew it. Source: Author interview with Col. K. R. Mattocks, May 25, 1997.

2. North American West Coast aviation old-timer Bob McCollum, an aero engineering graduate of both the Sperry Instrument and Boeing schools during the mid-1930s and a mechanic with Canadian Airways (which became the basis for Trans-Canada Air Lines), agrees with Mattocks. He calls the Otter "the only aircraft in the world that takes *off* nose-down." Source: Telephone conversation with the author, March 23, 1998.

3. To the oft-heard retort that the Otter flies like a truck, Mattocks agrees. At Rivers, Manitoba, a tri-service air base during the late 1950s, he flew Bell H-13 helicopters, and practised controlling the rotor's torque effect by touching down in the prairie snow and leaving parallel impressions with the landing skids, then turning exactly 90 degrees and touching down to create a balkan cross. Then, wind gusts and all, you would keep touching down without making any further impressions in the snow, dropping right into your own tracks.

With the H-13, "I always felt it was connected to me. Connected. Around my ass. It felt natural. With the Bell I always felt I had that kind of control."

Flying the Otter was simply a different proposition, as far as Mattocks was concerned; maybe not as much fun, and certainly less a physical sensation than a mental discipline. Source: Interview *op. cit.*

4. Mattocks has one more insight into early DHC designs, something he says he has thought about over the 30 some years since he flew Chipmunks, Beavers and Otters—"airplanes that had a lot of British engineering in them"—none of which, as an officer in the Canadian army, he was supposed ever to have flown.

An airplane designed and developed in the British fashion, he says, "is not the most comfortable piece of equipment. In fact, sometimes you feel they've forgotten the pilot. But is it ever durable, and is it ever practical. Everything is where it should be, from the standpoint of operating it."

He remembers the first time this feeling about British aircraft came over him. He was sitting in the cockpit of—believe it or not, for an army aviator—a Hawker Sea Fury carrier fighter. A friend's

mount, it was on the apron at the Canadian Joint Air Training Centre (CJATC), Rivers, Manitoba, during its annual rotation from the carrier HMCS *Magnificent*. Half the year the carrier embarked Anti-Submarine Warfare (ASW) aircraft, such as Grumman Avengers, while the fighter complement did gunnery and rocket-firing exercises at Rivers, a prairie base.

The overwhelming feeling he got sitting in the Sea Fury surprised him. Surprisingly, he felt it was "not all that far removed from a bloody Auster. It all looked the same. It's like there's a British way of . . . The way you might look at three paintings and decide they were all Van Gogh, rather than two Van Gogh and one by some other artist."

Now, on the face of it, this is a ridiculous assertion. An Auster is a light airplane, built for artillery observation, not much different from a Piper Cub. The Sea Fury was the ultimate development of the wartime Hawker Typhoon-Tempest series of heavy fighters; arguably, the ultimate piston-engine combat aircraft.

"It was different, but there was a sameness. The downside of this is that the pilot is never very comfortable. And so, you're sittin' there, being uncomfortable, thinking, 'Bloody British, and the way they built this thing.' But, when you think it through, the object of the exercise was carried out. You got a machine that did what it was supposed to do, that wasn't engineered for anything but the job. Nothing extra, perhaps just enough to do the job and do it well." Source: Interview *op. cit.*

5. "The Vazar Dash-3 Otter" by C. Marin Faure, *Water Flying* 1990 Annual, pp. 6–7.

6. Bill Whitney was introduced to the author as one member of Kenmore's highly qualified staff of float pilots who is as happy flying Otters as he is the company's fleet of Beavers and Turbo Beavers.

Gerry Bruder is the author of, among other books, *Heroes of the Horizon* (Seattle: Alaska Northwest Books, 1991), a collection of profiles of Alaska bush pilots. He had 15,000 hours on floats when he began flying Otters. "By that time," he says, "the Otter was a welcome change of pace." Source: Author telephone interview, March 31, 1998.

7. Thompson started out with his father, Don Thompson, flying with Alert Bay Air Services in the High Arctic in Beavers (OCQ, JFQ) and a Grumman Goose amphibian, dating himself by saying he learned to navigate over the North by taking his own sun shots. He has flown for Borek in the Maldives (where he acquired his springtime suntan), Pakistan, Burma and Peru. He has flown executive jets and Dash-8s, and calls the Twin Otter "the most fun you can have on floats." Source: Author interview and demonstration flight, May 12, 1998.

Bibliography

There are few books written on the DHC-3 Otter and DHC-6 Twin Otter. Information on these aircraft comes from a wide variety of sources, which I have grouped as follows, with books listed before articles:

On the de Havilland DHC-3 Otter:

Hayes, Karl E. *DHC-3 Otter*. (Dublin: Irish Air Letter, 1982). An Otter encyclopedia, including production list. Out of print.

"DH Canada Otter: Constructional Features and Air Impressions of the Dominion's Latest Aircraft," by James Hay Stevens, *Flight*, April 11, 1952, pp. 428–33. An account of flight-testing with the author's impressions of the aircraft.

"Design of the de Havilland Otter," by Fred Buller and Dick Hiscocks, a paper presented to the sixty-sixth annual general and professional meeting of the Engineering Institute of Canada at Vancouver, B.C., May 7, 8 and 9, 1952, reprinted in *The Engineering Journal*, July 1952. How the Otter was designed, by its chief engineers.

On the de Havilland Canada DHC-6 Twin Otter:

Blatherwick, John. *de Havilland Canada: Buffalo, DASH-7, Twin Otter, Saunders ST-27*. (Vancouver: FJB Publications, 1978). Production lists to that date for those DHC types.

Roach, John, and Eastwood, Tony. *Turbo Prop Airliner Production List* (Ruislip, Middlesex: The Aviation Hobby Shop, 1990). Includes DHC-6 production list to 1990.

Smith, Paul R. *de Havilland Canada DHC-6, DHC-7, DHC-8* (London: Jane's Publishing Co. Ltd., 1987). Colour pictures of DHC types in their airline livery.

"10 Years of STOL—The Twin Otter's First Decade," by Mike Davy and Peter S. Martin. Address to the Society of Automotive Engineers, Air Transportation Meeting, May 6–8, 1975.

"Air Test No. 89: DH Canada Twin Otter Series 300," by The Manager, *Air Pictorial*, October 1970, pp 363–67.

"The Twin Otter in Review," by Walter Henry, Canadian Aviation Historical Society *Journal*, Summer 1988, pp. 40–49. This issue of the CAHS *Journal* celebrated DHC's first 60 years in business.

On de Havilland of Canada in general:

Ellis, Bert, ed. *de Havilland, You STOL my Heart Away* (Toronto: Human Resources Department, DHC, 1993).

Hotson, Fred W. *The de Havilland Canada Story* (Toronto: CANAV Books, 1983). The definitive DHC history; new edition forthcoming.

Molson, K. M. *Canada's National Aviation Museum: Its History and Collections* (Ottawa: National Aviation Museum, 1988). Includes histories and specifications for the museum's Beaver prototype and ex-RCAF Otter My edition does not include the Twin Otter prototype, which is also enshrined in the museum.

Canadian Aviation, June 1988, Special de Havilland issue. Celebrates DHC's sixtieth anniversary.

On de Havilland Aircraft, England:

Jackson, A. J. *de Havilland Aircraft since 1915* (London: Putman, 1962 ed.) Especially valuable for its treatment of the various DH.60 Moth models, the aircraft with which DHC was founded.

On the Pratt & Whitney engines that power the Otter and Twin Otter:

Author unknown. *The Pratt & Whitney Aircraft Story* (Hartford, Conn.: Pratt & Whitney Aircraft Division of United Aircraft Corp., 1950). Published on the company's twenty-fifth anniversary.

Gunston, Bill. *World Encyclopedia of Aero Engines* (Yeovill: Patrick Stephens Ltd., 1995. 3rd ed.).

Smith, Hershel. *A History of Aircraft Piston Engines* (Sunflower University Press Ed., 1986).

Sullivan, Kenneth H., and Larry Milberry. *Power: The Pratt & Whitney Canada Story* (Toronto: CANAV Books, 1989).

"Dependable Power," by Duncan McLaren, in the Canadian Aviation Historical Society *Journal*, Fall 1988, pp. 93–97. Recollections of flying P&W radial-powered aircraft, with many rare photos.

"Pratt & Whitney Canada," by Neil McArthur, in the Canadian Aviation Historical Society *Journal*, Fall 1988, pp. 98–193. A history, with photos and a list of Canadian-built aircraft using P&W engines.

Index

Page references to photographs are in *italic type*